So you want to tread the boards...

So you want to tread the boards…

…the everything-you-need-to-know insider's guide to a career in the Performing Arts

JENNIFER REISCHEL

BOOKS

To Caroline, the bravest person I know

First published in Great Britain in 2007 by JR Books,
10 Greenland Street, London NW1 0ND
www.jrbooks.com

A catalogue record for this book is available from the British Library.

ISBN 978-1-906217-02-0

1 3 5 7 9 10 8 6 4 2

Printed by Creative Print and Design, Wales

All information expressed in this book was current at the time of
going to press. It is advised that readers check at time of use.

The opinions provided are the views of the author and are in no way
representative of the views of JR Books.

Always check with a doctor or expert before undertaking
any exercise – vocal, physical or otherwise.

Contents

Acknowledgements

This book would not have happened without the following people: Jeremy Robson, my publisher, who took a chance on my ideas, and Lesley Wilson and Jane Donovan, my editors, whose constructive feedback has been invaluable. Leslie Bricusse, who contributed an amazing foreword. PC, you have been my anchor. Sharry Clark who patiently read my endless flow of 'revised drafts' and has always believed in me. Simon Dunmore who 'nudged' me to write this book in the first place. My parents and family, from whom I inherited the writing bug. My sister Julia Reischel who encouraged me that my ramblings are actually entertaining. My friends in the industry (in no particular order): Helen McBriarty, Gay Soper, Eloise Irving, Maggie Grace, Nathan Dowling, Keith Hodiak, Simon Robinson, Kyle Bares, Mark Jacobs, Lee Ormsby, Jake Thornton and Liza Martin, who offered so many helpful tips and advice, all of which made this book what it is. My friends outside the industry (again, in no particular order): Jonathan Cobb, Caroline van Gorkom, Sue Godfrey, Rachael Andrews, Elaine Garofalo, Olivia Finton and Nili Leemon, who keep me grounded. And my friends and acquaintances aspiring or training to enter the profession – Alison Ward, Leighton Martin, Chris Tester, Chris Waplington, Anita Karam, Bethany Audley, Linda Patrickson, Ashley Nunn, Emily Mizen, Jessica Bastick-Vines and Olivia Wood, who took on the roles of guinea pigs for various chapters and tests!

Foreword

One of the first things I ever learned as a young writer, venturing for the first time into the awesome and unknown new world of theatre and cinema, was to appreciate and admire not just the talent, but the courage, tenacity and resilience of actors.

The first place where writers and actors usually cross paths is at auditions. I have never enjoyed the audition process, for while I appreciate that it is a necessary and democratic evil, giving anybody who wants it the opportunity to prove themselves the best, there is a built-in cruelty and heartlessness involved that is destined to hurt far more people than it helps. For every actor who gets that job, several hundred don't.

The quest for excellence, however well intentioned, always creates the dubious by-product of a massive amount of rejection. It is a long way from the thumbs-down at the Roman Colosseum to today's equivalent at the London Coliseum, 2000 years later, but the principle is the same.

Which explains why I truly despise the current glut of search-for-talent shows on national and international television – from *Pop Idol* and *American Idol* to the endless 12-week searches for Marias and Josephs and Dannys and Sandys using television to create theatrical hype for what would otherwise be just another revival. I find them hard to watch, even for a few minutes, because achieving the success of the one winner necessitates shattering the hopes and dreams of countless others. Mystifying as it all is, it helps to explain why success in the performing arts has always been so sought after, so glamorous and so elusive, and why so many will suffer anything to achieve it.

So, how should a young would-be actor prepare him- or herself to reach for the seemingly unreachable star? If it were a horserace, the odds would be unbearable. No-one would bet. Climbing Mount Everest backwards would be a breeze by comparison. The only chance would be unimaginable dedication, training and method.

Which brings us to the remarkable Ms Jennifer Reischel, who here appears out of the dark clouds, like an angel of mercy, to offer the wandering and aimless hordes of showbiz wannabes the ultimate theatrical 'How To' book.

You've heard of Method Acting? This is Method Training. How to stand up and take your first steps. How to walk. How to run. How to talk. Who to know and where to go. And so on. If theatrical success is Everest, this is how to climb every mountain, negotiate the foothills, head for the peaks and get to the top. Ms Reischel offers with mind-blowing detail, efficiency and organisation 'The Yellow Brick Road Guide to How to Succeed in Show Business'.

If you want to be an actor, this is your platinum American Express card. Don't leave home without it.

Leslie Bricusse
Saint-Paul de Vence
June 2007

Introduction

I was 16 years old when I started seriously researching information on how best to pursue a career in the performing arts. Since none of my family or friends is in any way connected to this field, I had no idea where to begin. I couldn't find any guides or books in the UK, I wasn't part of a youth theatre or stage school and I didn't know which teachers or part-time courses to trust, or why. Really, I had no idea what I was looking for. The Internet was still in its infancy with regard to finding chat rooms, forums or any sort of free information on acting, singing and dance – all of which is taken for granted these days. There were no reality TV contests to gain insight from, or even audition for. Most of my early realisations dawned on me while attending a musical theatre summer course at GSA (Guildford School of Acting, now also known as the Guildford Conservatoire). Thanks to a helpful acting tutor and my experiences at summer school, I ended up with a general idea of what to expect from drama school auditions. I was still totally unprepared, though, for what actually happens in this industry and what one really faces on a daily basis.

When I was encouraged to write this book, I kept in mind everything that I myself had always been desperate to know, including my experiences after leaving drama school, a time when a whole new set of questions usually arises. The result is a compendium of my own experiences and those of friends and acquaintances in the industry, covering everything I have ever been asked and everything that I myself have needed advice on. Time may have moved on and technology develops at a frantic pace but the basic questions posed about the industry and finding one's feet remain the same. Everyone worries about what really happens in the audition room, they're curious about daily life as an actor and keen to find themselves a good agent.

This book is not the Gospel; it's not a set of rules to follow for guaranteed success or a guide to becoming famous. It is, however, a truthful insider's account of what life as a professional actor can be like and the lessons I have learned in the past 10 years of trying to get my foot into various doors. I am not the only person who 'has the answers' – many industry professionals you encounter will have similar advice and experiences. I have simply summed it all up with the aim of making some sense of a very unpredictable, unfair, often bizarre and ever-changing business, where our primary goal is to make a living doing what we love. Rarely will the best or most talented person get the job, rather, it's the one who manages to get noticed and auditioned by those who make the casting decisions. And this is precisely the purpose of the pages that follow: a compendium of tips and advice on how to actually get seen for work opportunities from someone who has not only 'been there and done that' but, just like you, is out there now. I wish you a lot of luck, self-belief, supportive friends and family members, inspiration, a thick skin and the ability to stay patient as well as emotionally and financially afloat throughout your journey. In the words of Walter Matthau: 'Get out of show business! It's the best advice I was ever given, but I'm a stubborn man so I'm staying until the bitter end.'

From the Beginning

★

**'If you want to make your dreams come true,
the first thing you have to do is wake up.'**
– J.M. Power

Ten honest industry truths

The following list is not a tactic to try and put you off from entering the acting profession. I'm giving you an insight into facts and figures so you know you are not alone when it comes to dealing with rejection and lack of feedback. In a very overcrowded industry, on average you will be rejected many more times than offered work and this may have nothing to do with you and your talent. Consider the following:

1. Every time you go up for a part, on average there will be several hundred people in competition with you and these are just the people who have been sent in and suggested by agents and casting directors, or have applied through contacts in the industry. They're not the thousands of others who would like to apply but are often unable to do so because they don't know who to send their CV to, when productions are casting or maybe they don't have an agent. For girls the statistic is often much higher than for guys, as for every man in the industry there are at least two or three times the number of women. This is heightened by the fact that there are generally more male parts around.

2. Of all CVs and photos sent to agents and casting directors, most make it straight to the bin. If you don't send out a decently typed CV, a good covering letter and a very professional black-and-white photo, then your chances are next to nothing. A well-respected London agent receives about one large, black bin bag full of CVs and photos per day! At the same time a reputable agent receives about 40 invites to showcases and other performances each week. Usually they attend about one or two a month, but some agents only attend three or slightly more throughout the year.

3. Even if you arrive two hours early (recommended, to stand a chance), the average waiting time for a musical theatre open audition can be up to five hours, mostly sitting outside in the street – often it's still not certain whether you will be seen. The average number of applicants chosen for a recall at an open audition is maybe 10 out of around 500 applicants. Statistics for the new type of reality TV opens, such as ITV's *You're The One That I Want*, are even higher.

4. Up to 3,000 people apply to every NCDT (National Council of Drama Training) school each year, though figures vary between schools. As an average, each school usually takes around 100 new students on all courses (meaning the three-, two- and one-year courses) every year, so about 1,000 places are offered annually. Around 1,500 new drama school and related university course graduates enter the industry each year, too.

5. For every genuine agency there are many other bogus ones who try to con you by asking for upfront 'admin fees', stating you must only use their photographer and asking you to pay for online or paper directories sent out to casting directors and potential clients. They will put you on a general Internet database without any personal guidance or attention, they won't even see/hear you perform before they take you on and they may even ask you to pay for classes that are part of their agency. *See also* Agents, pages 67–76.

6. At the time of writing the estimated average spend on performing tools is as follows:

★ *Spotlight* (the UK's largest and best-known online and book casting directory of actors, presenters, etc.): Around £129 per year (if you join mid-year it's more expensive).

★ Equity (the actors' union): If you have earned less than £20,000 a year working in the industry it's about £125. Otherwise expect to pay more. More details are available on the Equity website; *see also* pages 203–205.

★ Photos: Anything from £100–£350 depending on your photographer. Unless you change dramatically, photos should be redone every five years or so, too.

★ Extra prints of photos: Probably £100 a year, if not more.

★ Dance/character shoes: About £150 a year if training regularly.

★ Dance and movement/other interview clothes: Around £100 a year.

★ Dance lessons: One lesson a week works out at about £300 yearly.

★ Singing lessons: If you are doing one hour a month, this can be about £400 a year.

★ Postage costs (sending out CVs and photos): On average you might send out 300 CVs a year, so allow about £300.

★ Buying plays and other publications: This varies greatly but probably around £100. Allow £20-plus if you want to buy *The Actor's Yearbook* or *Whose Where?* on a regular basis.

★ Stage make-up: Allow about £100 a year.

★ Contacts: £12 or so a year, if renewed annually.

★ PCR (Production Casting Report, *see also* page 203): £260 per annum if you receive a copy every week. Depending on where you register, any other casting service subscriptions such as Castweb or Castnet will cost you about £200 per annum.

★ Actor's Centre membership (networking and classes/workshops): Around £55 a year for membership plus the cost of any classes you choose to do.

★ Show reel: £300 or so.

★ Demo CD: £300 or so (20 copies will cost around £60 if you burn them yourself).

★ Backing tracks, sheet music, etc: Allow about £100.

★ Travelling expenses (auditions and castings): This very much depends on the individual.

So, just to start your career and keep it going, at the time of writing you need to allow just over £3,000 each year, some of which you will be able to offset against your tax bill (see pages 152–160). Of course, costs may vary and this is just an estimate.

7. The average percentage of professional performers living solely off acting-related work is about 10 per cent. All others are forced to work in different professions to survive, mainly by temping although some have their own businesses. There are approximately 30,000 entries in *Spotlight* (which also includes presenters) and about 39,000 Equity members.

8. The minimum wage for West End musicals and plays is £381.13 a week at the time of writing and as stated by Equity, minus taxes, National Insurance contributions and 10–15 per cent agent fees depending on your deal, which leaves slightly less than £300 a week. If you rent in a very cheap part of London and share with three or four other people, you will still pay about £300 a month, again at the time of writing, plus bills and other expenses (travel, food, mobile phone, clothes, etc.). If you are lucky your rent may include council tax. Work outside London, non-West End work and tour work is nearly always not so well paid.

9. If your audition is unsuccessful, in most cases you will never hear from the casting team of that particular production again. They won't even let you know you were unsuccessful. The possibility of any feedback depends entirely on the goodwill of the casting director (or whoever else was there), how much of an impact you made and who your agent is. Do they have a good relationship with the casting director that allows them to call, actually get through to the right person and ask for honest, helpful feedback? Many agents consider it bad form to contact casting directors after auditions. Mostly you will simply hear nothing – even if you got down to the final two candidates for a part.

10. Only a very small number (maybe 5–10 per cent) of all castings/auditions are announced in publications such as *The Stage*, *Castnet*, *Castweb*, *Castingcallpro*, *PCR*, etc., which anyone can read and apply for. All of the other auditions are handled directly through agents or cast internally, meaning the director, producer, etc. know who it is they want right from the beginning and they call the agent of that particular person to see if they are free.

The 'it' factor: finding your niche

'You're not a star until they can spell your name in Karachi.'
– *Humphrey Bogart*

Long before ITV's *The X-Factor* became a national phenomenon, phrases such as 'the it factor', 'that certain something' and 'star quality' were commonly used in industry related conversations. But what does 'it' actually mean? How do you know if you have it, and do you need it to succeed? There are lots of talented performers who work regularly all their lives but remain one of the crowd. These people can act well, perhaps they have a very good voice or are blessed with stunning looks. However, this is not what differentiates them from the next person auditioning or what makes them unique. In Great Britain alone, there may be fifty examples of 5ft 5in curly-haired blondes who can belt out a top E, who are all suitable for the part for which you, too, might be auditioning. Don't get discouraged if you are then rejected even though you know you're suitable and have all the necessary skills because that's not what it's all about; it's not necessarily what a panel and audiences want. They're looking for something a little bit different, someone different. That someone who does something unique with the material given to them or that they choose to perform in an audition.

So what makes someone stand out from the crowd? Why should the panel pick *you* and not the next person? What makes someone stand the test of time and become an indispensable part of the profession, such as Judi Dench, Daniel Day Lewis, Fred Astaire or Judy Garland? I believe it's something called 'personal style', also known as 'your own personal interpretation'. It's something only you exude, which makes you unique as a performer and makes it impossible for anyone else to be hired for the job, something special that only you can offer to the character or performance. And it's not the fact that you can hit a top F – it's the style in which you hit it that ultimately matters and pulls you out of the general group of possible candidates for any job. Style does not mean a special skill such as being able to juggle six balls at once or knowing how to do complicated dance twirls. You don't have to be the best singer or dancer or even the best-looking. It's much more than that – it's the way you draw in an audience and how you interpret material.

Style is something you're born with; however you can also learn and develop style through watching and listening to those who have mastered it, and finally practising what you've learned on audiences and panels to see how it is received. Other common expressions used are to 'sparkle' and 'I cannot take my eyes off them when they perform'. This relates to the energy you convey; you are performing in a way that's irresistible to those watching, which again, has to do with the particular personal style you exude while performing, or in some cases, also when being yourself off stage. The audience and panel have to want to see *you*, not the next person down the line. You and only you!

So how do you accomplish this? If you want to learn about and develop your personal style, look at and learn from those who have lasted throughout the years. If you are a singer, try this simple exercise: When listening to the radio, can you recognise the person singing immediately? If yes, then they have mastered their own personal style and have something to give to a song that is totally unique and theirs. Examples include Eva Cassidy, Billie Holiday, Frank Sinatra, Michael Jackson, Christina Aguillera, Ella Fitzgerald and many more. We associate certain songs with these artists, even if fifty different interpretations have been recorded after their original. Look especially to long-gone artists. Why are their albums still available and in such demand throughout the world years after their death? Billie Holiday had a tiny range and her voice was damaged from drugs and smoking too much. Still, her albums are available in every music store around the world. Why? Because her personal style appeals to people and/or she has a tone of voice they like; also no-one else can be substituted, hence the demand for her interpretation. All the artists mentioned above have style and their interpretation of any song touches people. It's as simple as that.

In terms of actors, the same applies. Why do we still watch Humphrey Bogart, Jack Nicholson and Maggie Smith? What made Audrey Hepburn such an amazing star? Again, each has or had a very unique and irreplaceable style. In addition to personal style, another factor is versatility. Very few actors can handle comedy and drama to an equally high standard. There's also humanity. An actor who makes you believe every word they say in that moment is true and invites you in to their character and their performance is a great actor. But you don't necessarily need to cry on command to be a good actor. Sometimes the best performances are of the 'less is more' variety. Good acting looks easy and natural. Spencer Tracy, for example, never looks as though he is working hard to make us believe in his character, nor does Cate Blanchett. Never mind the preparation that went into a performance, when actually giving a performance of any kind, don't show the work behind it. Just be.

In dance it's often said that once you have mastered the steps the work really begins. Being technical is important to start your performance but don't make it the be all and end all. Add your personal style. No-one wants to see you showing great technique: after the technique has been rehearsed and perfected as a basis, audiences are interested in your own interpretation. Don't try and copy anyone either. A bad copy of someone else won't make you unique. You want people to see you as *you*, only then will your personal style unfold.

So, do you need a special style to succeed and be a working performer? Not necessarily; not all of us can be irreplaceable and possess such a gift, not everyone is lucky enough to be born that way. There are hundreds of actors who get job after job and are just part of a working crowd. As a working performer what you do need is stage presence, though. This again is something you naturally have, although the right training, whether drama school or through other forms, can help you discover and release it as you learn to feel comfortable on a stage, learn to exit and enter, and learn how to project your character and his/her intentions. Finding stage presence is a reason to train.

Style is a personal thing and can be subjective. Some of the greatest artists were adored by some and disliked by others. You may not understand all the fuss about Celine Dion, while your friend might own every album she's ever made. Style does not always reach everyone but to make an impact it needs to touch the majority of those watching and listening. Panels and audiences do not necessarily need to like you, but they still need to be drawn to you as a performer and to feel they must watch and/or listen to you. They have to desire your personal style.

Drama School: The Myths and Truths about Formal Training

'Theatre is like a virus, once you get it you can't get rid of it.'
– *Robin Boisseau*

To train or not to train

The training debate seems to be one without a conclusive answer, as the past proves there are many ways to enter the acting industry. In a business where so much is based on luck and being in the right place at the right time, there is no one, certified route to success. After some research and discussions with other professionals, I personally have come to the conclusion that formal training of some shape or form is necessary for the aspiring performer, whether it be attending full-time drama school, part-time training, evening courses or workshops, to learn the basics. It must be said that it is equally important to gain performance experience in any way, shape or form on top of this training to practise your craft.

So, is it necessary to train to get professional performing work? Well, not necessarily. Is it recommended? Yes, many professional publications and organisations stress the importance of training in this overrun business. According to *Contacts* (2006): 'professional training will increase an actor's chance of success, and professionally trained artists are also more likely to be represented by agencies'. Simon Dunmore states in *An Actor's Guide to Getting Work*: 'nowadays getting started without formal training is virtually impossible for the school leaver', while according to Equity's website: 'Professional training on an accredited course is perceived as by far the best way to enter the acting profession'.

Of course there will always be people who achieve success and have long-lasting careers without ever seeking any formal training (drama school or other courses) in both musical theatre and acting. With regard to the current market of younger actors or those just starting out, however, I personally have found them to be largely in the minority. This may be due to the current massive popularity of a career in the performing arts, leading to multiplying numbers of aspirants entering the industry. It is fair to say that since the 1960s the acting business has easily expanded by ten times in sheer volume of performers striving to find regular work. Conversely, the latest reality TV trend actually decreases work opportunities for performers, as less and less professional actors are needed, instead being replaced by members of the general public. Competition has risen to such an extensive high that drama school can prove to be a very good way to get yourself noticed by agents, casting people, directors and other industry professionals responsible for giving out the work.

This leads on to another question: Do certain schools open doors? I would be lying if I said no. Yes, they can. The casting director of the RSC (Royal Shakespeare Company) is known to attend showcases of some schools. Certain agents favour particular annual showcases where they choose their new talent; some schools are better than others. Does this mean you *must* attend certain schools to succeed? This is not necessarily the case. No school offers guarantees, simply opportunities.

> **TIP!**
>
> The Theatre Royal Haymarket in London hosts an annual masterclass with Geoffrey Coleman (head of acting at Central School of Speech and Drama), where you can ask questions about drama school and training, even present your audition speeches for advice/helpful criticism from Geoffrey himself. *See also* page 275 for further details.

Other courses and their value

Drama school is not for everyone. Some would-be actors benefit more from part-time or other courses – every individual has different circumstances, strengths and weaknesses to work on. However, if you go this route then make sure you choose a reputable part-time/evening course with tutors who have sufficient professional experience and will provide plenty of performance practice. Several years ago it was possible to learn 'the rep' way. Briefly, this method involves learning on the job from your more experienced peers by joining a repertory company (a company of actors performing various shows/plays 'in rep', meaning a number of different shows a month or week, often on tour). You work behind the scenes and understudying as the famous 'spear carrier' or assistant stage manager (ASM) before being offered participation on the actual stage. Unfortunately, learning in rep is no longer possible as this system no longer exists and you could say that in some ways drama school has taken its place.

What about performance studies at university? There is no right or wrong answer here as there will always be university graduates who succeed in getting paid performing work. It is, however, important to keep in mind the differences between attending a university acting course or a drama school course when making a decision about where to train. The main difference is that most university courses are academic rather than practically orientated. As a performer what matters is that you are able to practise your craft in a practical way, not write essays about it. Although some drama schools may ask for the occasional essay or written form of work, university courses often make this form of learning the main element of the course and the standard of the practical side is generally lower than offered at drama school. Sometimes the ratio is 50:50. Drama schools offer about a 90:10 ratio (90 per cent practical, 10 per cent written). Some university courses specifically state that they are *not* looking for students who wish to become professional performers. Read the career opportunities link for your course on each university's website to check where the focus lies. An audition of some sort should be mandatory to be considered for a place.

There are university courses offering a higher amount of practical hours. The question you must ask, though, is how many practical hours do they really offer? Drama school students easily attend 40 practical hours a week, often more. This is a lot of hours and a lot of training and performance experience. Often university courses do not offer more than 20 or 25 hours a week and therefore less performance practice. This is why drama school is so expensive: generally you get a lot more hours and tuition. You pay for the experience and industry recognition of your tutors, as well as their time. Do universities offer a showcase and public productions? Usually the answer is no, although it varies from course to course.

TIP!

If you would like to consider university as an option, make sure you research: (a) the amount of *practical* hours offered, including performances; (b) the tutors and their background, and (c) do they offer the chance to be seen by industry professionals in a showcase setting or other public productions?

A popular option seems to be to attend a three-year university course and then complete a postgraduate year at drama school. Everyone is different and some may feel a university acting course is sufficient. Ask yourself: Will I feel prepared enough for this difficult industry by attending university and will this course give me the necessary exposure to be signed by an agent and/or be seen for professional work opportunities? For a list of all universities offering undergraduate drama degrees and postgraduate drama courses, visit www.scudd.org.uk and press the arrow to the right of the scroll down menu.

Can I learn on the job? The problem nowadays with this method of learning is lack of time. Producers, directors, and so on in professional productions simply don't have the time to wait for people to learn on the job. This is not just relevant for film and television where shooting schedules are usually extremely tight and time equals a lot of money. Some plays are put on after just ten days' rehearsal and when musicals are recast, you can be asked to learn a part, dance numbers, songs, and so on, sometimes within a few days, and be expected to give a convincing and professional performance at the end of it all. Of course a performer always keeps learning and with each job you take on you learn more about yourself, acting and new skills. But a professional job is not the place to learn the basics. In my opinion, this is where some form of training is essential.

Alternative training

Visit www.repcollege.co.uk, which offers an interesting course involving performance-related as well as backstage training. I have no personal experience of this course but I know that being versatile can increase working opportunities as many theatre companies like to employ actors to be understudies/assistant stage managers. Hiring one person for two jobs saves them money.

'You ask my advice about acting? Speak clearly, don't bump into the furniture and if you must have motivation, think of your pay packet on Friday.' – *Noel Coward*

Drama school: the fundamentals

For most people, getting a place at drama school seems to be the equivalent of a golden ticket to Willy Wonka's Chocolate Factory, especially with application numbers rising alarmingly each year and more and more hopefuls trying to follow their dreams. Let me tell you now, drama school won't solve all your problems and it's not a guaranteed route to paid work, success and fun. Instead, it's just the beginning of a long road. Drama school involves much more than learning how to act, sing and dance. Only after I left drama school and sometimes even now do I realise just what attending full-time training triggers in a performer and how, even years later, things affect me. The most important thing I learned was that drama school is not the Gospel. Not everything they tell you will be the best approach for your personal needs and problems. You cannot switch off your thinking cap and just go with the flow; no school will be all good or all bad either. There's no perfect drama school and you won't graduate as a flawless and perfectly trained performer. Training is just the start of a possible career and you need to put in your own work, your own thoughts and ideas to evolve and grow as an actor. Simply turning up to classes on time, learning and absorbing what you are taught without question and not doing any extra work yourself won't work. An artist needs to question and must have their own stance on things. That's what makes a great artist and what will make you an individual performer.

Drama schools make mistakes, too – for a start, they are run by human beings! Teachers can be careless, miss out important things pupils need to know and misjudge. Egos get in the way. Each school will have flaws and teachers you cannot relate to and classes you feel are pointless. If you are taught things you don't understand, allow a little while for them to settle into your system. Sometimes it takes time to register change. If you don't feel it working for you, ask questions. Talk to the tutors involved about your problems. Don't just sit back and think, well, they tell me it's so, that means it has to be true. Of course tutors have a certain amount of experience and you are paying for them to guide you, but if you feel uncomfortable then do something about it. Definitely give everything a go and be open to change but if it doesn't work for you, think about it and try to find a solution. Also, sometimes by working with individuals you find it hard to get along with, or doing a class you dislike or perhaps playing a character you don't feel connected to, you learn the most. Sometimes it's as important to discover what you don't feel comfortable with and don't enjoy as it is to practise the skills you already love.

'It is widely acknowledged to be the toughest job to get any two acting teachers to agree about anything.' – *Robert Lewis*

Most importantly, develop and keep your individual style! Be open to change, constructive criticism, try lots of different things, challenge yourself and give everything a go, but don't hide who you really are because you think you need to fit into a generic system. You will hear differing opinions on your talents and skills. This is a reflection of the industry you are entering, which is full of subjective viewpoints. Reviews of your performance may vary greatly and there will be people who admire your work but also those who may not rate it so highly. Don't get lost in trying to please everyone. Be yourself, don't lose who you are. If in doubt, always listen to your gut feeling about who to trust and who to believe.

'It's not enough to have talent – you have to have a talent for your talent.' – *Stella Adler*

People always ask me whether a certain school is better than another and what the top schools are. I can't really answer those questions because it depends on the individual's needs and that particular year of students, classes, teachers, outside directors, productions, and so on. Of course there are certain training establishments that pop up regularly in theatre programmes and have long-standing reputations. I have spoken to many different people who have attended lots of different drama schools. Some had good things to report on their training establishment, while others had only bad things to say. Some felt they belonged and were guided, others did not and had teachers who did not support them properly.

> **TIP!**
>
> Don't try and search for the perfect training place. It does not exist and your training will be full of highs and lows, whichever course you choose.

Your friend may be attending a particular course and loving it, you may follow suit and not feel you fit in at all. Visit schools, speak to tutors and students there and try and get an insight into the life of a school/course. I recommend choosing a course that introduces you to many different acting methods (Meisner, Stanislavsky, and so on), rather than focuses on just one method so you can make an informed decision about what works best for you. Different actors prefer different ways to approach and study a part. There's no right or best way to prepare for a role so long as the outcome is convincing and the actor feels comfortable. You want to be able to experiment as much as possible. Follow your gut instinct to find a training place that's right for you, one that you feel will best contribute to your journey as a performer.

'Nobody "becomes" a character. You can't act unless you are who you are.' – *Marlon Brando*

Why train at drama school?
If drama school can be such a mixed bag of experiences, why do I still recommend that you attend one? Well, in my opinion in most cases the positives still largely outweigh any possible negative experiences and it is impossible to find a course of any kind for any subject, be it drama, pottery or maths, with which you will be completely happy. Drama schools vary in what they offer and how strongly they assist their students in the variety of fields they cover. There are so many different courses to choose from. So, what benefits can be gained from attending an accredited drama school and why do I still recommend this option? Here's why:

★ Training in all fields important to the performer – different methods of acting, voice, movement, singing, dance, history of theatre, screen, radio, learning the studies of various acting practitioners, accents and much more – is on offer. Some people need more help than others in certain areas and a good school will class you appropriately and give you more help where needed; it will also push you to achieve more in areas where you are ahead of others and perhaps have more natural ability. For example, well-respected MT (musical theatre) courses stream their dance classes so that each student attends the class best suited to their level.

★ A showcase for your skills – at the end of your training you will be able to perform your strengths and abilities to a select audience of industry professionals, who offer representation or work if they are interested in you. This is a vital opportunity as often it's not about the best person getting the job but the one lucky enough to be seen in the first place.

★ You'll gain a knowledge of how best to show off your talent in speech, song and dance in auditions, how to communicate with industry professionals, how to prepare for an audition, how to handle yourself professionally, how to write your CV, a covering letter, even how to choose a photo.

★ The opportunity to practise performing in all shapes and forms in front of different types of audiences and to learn that making mistakes is part of the process.

★ Contacts: Outside directors, masterclasses, workshop leaders and fellow students. This can be the beginning of an extensive network of connections, a vital tool for any performer. Remember you are far more than just someone who gets up on stage and plays a part. At the same time you have to be your own business, publicity manager, agent (if you don't have one), accountant (if you can't afford one) and much, much more.

★ Following a three-year BA course, you get full Equity membership on graduation.

★ Gaining a deeper knowledge of yourself as a performer: Knowing your strengths and weaknesses, what you need to work on and gaining in confidence in yourself as a person and a performer.

★ A knowledge of the business jargon in terms of acting, dance, singing and staging; extensive practice in performance with and without a public audience, how to exit and enter a stage, how to behave in a rehearsal, how to approach a text, and so on.

Drama school is basically a compendium of all the basics you need to know as a professional actor entering the industry. It's a chance to practise in a non-judgemental setting and to be seen and noticed by people you might otherwise escape when performing to the public.

TIP!

In terms of singing I strongly recommend you see one of the very renowned teachers in the industry for a vocal assessment before you start training. Choose someone who teaches the cream of the crop in the industry, a person who really knows their stuff. If possible, go for a London-based teacher because the most reputable teachers are based there, most of the industry 'big stuff' happens there and they are close to Pinewood Studios and West End theatres. Invest in this financially, it's worth it! Visit them at regular intervals throughout your training to make sure your school's teaching methods benefit you and your singing style. Most schools advise against seeing tutors not related to the course and visiting classes outside as they feel it will confuse students. However, from my own personal experience I learned the hard way that having an outside opinion can sometimes be a refreshing and important voice of truth. I urge you to seek outside vocal advice regularly, especially if you have any concerns about your voice.

Some common misconceptions
★ It's impossible to guarantee yourself work through going to drama school.

★ You don't attend a course to learn how to act as such. Instead, you learn how to act better. The purpose of training is learning how to be the best actor possible with your own individual talent. Acting is a natural gift – you are either born with it or not. While a good school can nurture and help you develop, no school can work miracles and supply you with something for which you didn't have a natural aptitude in the first place.

★ There's no guarantee you'll find agent representation at the final showcase.

★ Top ten drama schools simply don't exist and neither does an official league table although there are unofficial top schools with longstanding reputations. They are generally well received in the business and attract certain industry individuals at showcases and public productions.

★ You won't be a finished performer when you graduate. This is only the start of your journey as an artist and you will have to put in time and effort to continue developing your skills every day of your life as a professional long after completing your training.

Training: London versus other parts of Great Britain
In London you are in the hub of one of the world's major entertainment capitals with all its benefits and opportunities. London agents can come and see all shows open to the public as well as your showcase. This is a plus as some agents see several shows and then at the end of the year, they make up their minds based on a variety of performances about who they would like to take on.

Most professional castings (especially for musical theatre) happen in London and the South. These are easier for you to access in your final year/term when you are allowed/ready to attend them. However, it entails expensive living costs.

Outside London, living costs are usually much cheaper. Training can be to an equally high a standard as in London. Cities such as Manchester and Glasgow tend to have a lively arts scene. However, most agents are located in London (some will have offices in London and elsewhere, but these are rare), so they won't be able to see your shows when they're open to the public. If the school does not have a showcase in London, agents and industry professionals from the South will not come and see you.

Should I go to drama school, and which one?

Accredited or non-accredited, what does this mean?

The Conference of Drama Schools (CDS – www.drama.ac.uk) is an organisation comprising Britain's 22 leading drama schools. Courses offered include acting, musical theatre, directing and technical theatre. The National Council of Drama Training (NCDT) accredits courses (not schools) guaranteeing a certain standard of training. To quote the National Council of Drama Training website (www.ncdt.co.uk): 'Accreditation aims to give students confidence that the courses they choose are recognised by the drama profession as being relevant to the purposes of their employment and that the profession has confidence that the people they employ who have completed these courses have the skills and attributes required for the continuing health of the industry'.

The NCDT accredits mainly three-year courses, not postgrads or other one- and two-year courses. It's impossible to say that all unaccredited courses are automatically bad, so research classes, teachers and their general reputation in the industry. Visit schools: some have refused accreditation to keep their own idea of timetabling rather than follow NCDT guidelines as to types of classes and distribution of hours between subjects. For more details visit www.ncdt.co.uk/guide.asp

Another way to check the status and how your school is received in the industry is to read the Ofsted reports (www.ofsted.gov.uk), which are usually very thorough and detailed and should give a good first impression. Also, check out the CDS website to download a free booklet *Official Guide to Vocational Courses for Drama and Technical Training*.

> **TIP!**
>
> Have a look at *The Independent Schools Yearbook*, which provides comprehensive reports on all accredited drama schools. Available at www.acblack.com/Catalogue

A levels versus B Tech

Drama schools usually require A level (or equivalent qualification), B Tech or similar qualifications for you to apply for a place. It seems many people can't get out of school fast enough to start training and performing! *See also* pages 22–25 for more detail on this subject. I would be hard pressed to lecture you about school – I myself couldn't wait to leave, thinking it was a terrible bore. I am sure you must have heard it all before but school is important: You need a good education to secure a future, good grades are vital, and so on. In my opinion, all this is true. Study to the best of your academic talents and the more options you have for later, the better. You never know what's going to happen. You may have an accident and never dance again or lose your voice through illness. If you are academically inclined, definitely take your A levels.

Don't think you'll never use this knowledge – English, in particular, can come in very handy. Acting is about language and communication. You never know what might happen and being a good performer means more than just studying drama and singing all day. There are also some very good B Tech options available and some schools offer a combination of A level/B Tech qualifications. Also, consider what specialist schools have to offer: www.standards.dfes.gov.uk/specialistschools

Some B Tech courses won't leave you all university course options, however. You may think attending university is the furthest thing from your mind at the moment but keep your options open. If you are academically capable of handling A-levels and you learn well academically then I would advise this route. A-level Theatre Studies is largely a theoretical course and the practical element can be quite small, so pursue lots of practical experience outside your course. The B Tech Performing Arts course is designed to be more practical and interactive rather than studying on your own. There are two courses: the First Diploma, a one-year foundation for those who do not have the requisite GCSE qualifications and the National Diploma for those who do. It depends entirely on which type of studying suits you best. Have a look at http://www.edexcel.org.uk for course details and what they specifically offer.

TIP!

Have a good balance of subjects. By all means choose a course such as drama or music, but select something unrelated to performing, too. Even if you just want to temp while waiting for that next performing job, many employers still want to see subjects such as English and maths at A-level standard on your CV.

Do my school grades matter?

How well you do at school won't affect your success as a performer and good school grades won't give you bonus points when applying to drama school as this doesn't interest them. Keep in mind that most drama schools have minimum A level or equivalent requirements (usually two A-level grades at C) that must be achieved for you to be considered for a place. Most drama schools are now connected to universities, hence they have to comply with some academic entry regulations. While school grades are definitely important for most other type of career, I recommend you study to the best of your ability as you can only gain from this.

One-, two- or three-year: Which course is best?

This depends totally on the individual. Some need more training time than others. Keep in mind that one-year (postgraduate) courses can be extremely tough and intense as schools literally squeeze three years into one. If you have never danced before, a year of postgraduate dance training may not be enough to bring you up to the required professional standard. Full equity status is usually only guaranteed upon completion of a three-year degree course (check with individual schools).

Degree, MA or Diploma?

Will you be more successful as a performer with a degree on your CV? No, casting directors really couldn't care less so long as you can do the job. A degree is useful, should you wish to pursue any postgraduate study or for work that is non-performance related. Many jobs nowadays require a degree, even some temporary office work.

Postgrads – do I need a relevant BA degree?

Many schools state on their websites that you need a relevant first degree to qualify for their postgraduate course. In practice, this is not always the case, so check with the schools individually. I know postgrads who were accepted without any first degree or who had degrees in sciences, work experience in banking or other varied backgrounds. Don't assume that if you have not done drama at university you are not eligible for a postgraduate drama school course. The amount and type of experience you have to offer varies from person to person. Ultimately what counts is how your audition goes on the day. Do not be put off if you think your experience is limited, the schools will let you know if they recommend a longer course or more experience.

I can't decide which school to pick

This can be quite a complicated decision, especially if you feel connected to several schools. Talk to former and current students, staff who work/have worked there. Go and view the schools. Do you like the area the school is located in? Is it safe? Ask them for an example of a timetable so you can compare what different courses have to offer. Find out where their showcases/public performances are held and go and view some, if possible. Check out facilities like dance studios and rehearsal rooms. Are private singing /Alexander technique lessons included in the course fee? Do you have to pay for any extras? How is each school received in the industry? Read their Ofsted reports (*see also* page 17). The reputation of a school can often be a deciding factor for students but remember that even if Judi Dench or Anthony Hopkins went to your chosen school, there's no guarantee that you will be equally successful just by attending the same training ground. After listening to what everyone has to say and contemplating all that you have observed, go with your gut feeling.

'Coughing in the theatre is not a respiratory ailment. It is a criticism.' – *Alan Jay Lerner*

If I attend an MT course instead of an acting course, will my acting skills be weaker? Will I miss out on acting classes that I might need?
Some of you who want to work in MT are worried that an MT course will be too focused on dance and singing, and that you will miss out on acting opportunities. There is no formula to success but I believe that if you choose the right type of MT course incorporating all-important elements of training, your acting potential and work opportunities should not be limited. Different MT courses offer different classes: Some are better than others and some offer more acting opportunities than others. Ask for timetables to look at what is on offer or find out more at the open days and speak to current or former students – this is where the research aspect comes in. If you make the choice to study MT, in my opinion choose a course that offers more or equally as many hours acting in ratio to singing and dance hours. At some schools the first year of an MT course is spent performing plays and only towards the end of that year do students take part in a 'song and dance' type of performance. Renowned MT courses will place a strong emphasis on the acting element, though, as this is the basis of MT. Whether MT or acting, it's important that you make the choice according to what works best for you.

Amount of class hours
MT courses at schools like GSA and Mountview in London's Wood Green offer almost all the hours available on straight acting courses at the same school. Usually, you will not miss out on acting classes at these schools. In addition to a general acting schedule, singing and dance training hours are added on top of acting. This means that people on the MT courses at such schools generally have longer hours than their acting counterparts because they do all the classes that the straight acting courses do, plus the song and dance aspect (ballet barre in the mornings, private singing lesson, dance and so on). Note that schools and courses vary in hours, so check schedules to see what is on offer.

More acting classes will not necessarily make you a better actor
Acting is the basis of all MT performances, so it's important to have the talent and skills to act, above anything else. However, it is simply not true that doing more acting classes will make you a better actor. Different people have different needs. It's not just the theoretical hours on a timetable that make you a better performer, but also the amount of performance experience you receive during your training. This kind of experience is often offered to the same extent on both straight acting and MT courses, as students do exactly the same amount of shows per year including final year/term shows.

> **TIP!**
>
> Some three-year MT courses also incorporate a final-year play, while many acting courses perform a final-year musical. Again, check with individual schools for details. Most basics, such as Shakespeare, modern plays, and so on, are covered well on renowned MT courses.

Camera training and radio
You will receive a good amount of camera training on MT courses, which should not really differ in hours to the acting course. At many schools, you will have the opportunity to do a show reel in your third year/third term on both courses. Radio is one field most MT courses do not cover and if you want to study this, you will have to find an extra course.

If you attend a well-recognised MT course, you should not miss out on any acting classes and opportunities. It is also interesting to see that the first years of GSA's MT and Acting courses are very similar. Some students decide at the end of their first year whether they feel more suited to the acting or the MT option. This may be something to keep in mind if you are unsure which course to choose.

Will I be able to play acting parts if trained in MT? Will casting directors for non-MT related work take me seriously?
Absolutely. Graduates from renowned MT courses have worked extensively in film, television and on the stage in plays. I could list countless examples. The renowned MT courses in the country train their students for all types of work, not just MT.

Will I be able to work in musical theatre, not having attended an MT course?
Yes, but it depends on your talent and skill in the singing and dance

department. If you have been dancing and singing since a young age you may be skilled to a professional level and not need to attend a full-time MT course. Personally, I think an MT course is very beneficial from a versatility point of view – the more you can do, the more jobs you can audition for, and the higher the possibility of you finding regular work. If you have the talent, why not exploit it? There are also some agents now who only take on actors who have song and dance skills because they can put them up for more work as the business gets more and more overcrowded.

MT courses don't just teach you how to sing and dance. On top of this, you learn how to handle professional MT auditions, what to sing and why, how to build a song repertoire, how to group sing in a musical and where to place your voice in a chorus (so that it does not stick out when it is not supposed to), music theory (so you can sight read during a rehearsal and don't hold everyone else up trying to get your line) and then actually being able to sing that harmony while everyone else around you sings something completely different. All these skills need to be learned and practised, although some may have a very good natural instinct and need much less training than others, in which case you may not need to attend a full-time MT course. Drama school should prepare you for everything and many different kinds of performing work. Make your choice based on your own needs and talents. If unsure, apply for both and let the schools make a decision of where to place you.

> **TIP!**
>
> It is also possible to switch from acting to an MT course (and vice versa) at the end of your first year if you are attending a school that offers both. Not all MT courses are the same and offer the same amount of acting training. Do your research before you make a decision.

What age is best to attend drama school?

> 'You are as young as your faith, as old as your doubt; as young as your self-confidence, as old as your fear; as young as your hope, as old as your despair.' – *Douglas MacArthur*

There is no definite answer to this question as everyone is different and matures individually. From personal experience, however, and as someone who started training at the age of 18, I am tempted to suggest that you wait until you are two or three years older. This is not simply due to the fact that many drama schools state on their websites that they prefer the 'more mature applicant', although it is certainly a pattern to be noticed among training establishments and which should not be ignored as they have their reasons. One thing is for certain, though, your career is not over if you don't get a place at drama school at the age of 18. In this fast-paced world many young people believe they have to achieve success and fulfil their dreams *now*, and the sooner the better. Think about it, though: Will it really make you happy in the long run to attend training at such a young age? Are you ready for what's to come? Many of you also want to get into drama school as quickly as possible as you think it means a life doing what you love every day of the week. I can totally relate to this attitude, as at the age of 18 I couldn't think of anything better and couldn't wait to leave school. Looking back, I think I missed out on some aspects, as I was simply not ready emotionally and also unprepared for the intensity of training.

But it all sound like so much fun

While I don't wish to say that drama school isn't fun, it's also very tough and has rough stages and parts. It's not for the weak-willed or fainthearted. Sometimes the idea of acting, singing and dancing all day can be deceptive – there's a lot more to it. There's a lot of pressure and after all, you are preparing for a profession and being trained to do a job.

> **TIP!**
>
> Drama school can also open up many emotional issues and this is why it can be helpful to be a few years older so you have more maturity to deal with them.

Why would I personally advise to wait a bit?

Generally speaking, the difference in maturity between someone who is 18 years old instead of 21 is quite noticeable. Going straight from school to drama school gives you no time to experience life on your own. This is not necessarily to be a better performer but to be more rounded and sure as a person, to build up an adult's confidence. Otherwise you go from one institution to another, joining a very competitive lifelong rat race at a very young age without having done anything else. Starting your training that little bit older has the following benefits:

1. You can get other qualifications under your belt for your second career (which most actors will need as they will be unemployed at least part of the time), should you want to.

2. You can move out of home, do something totally different with your life and see if, after all that, you still want to be a professional performer.

3. Some people do nothing but perform all their life and drama school seems a natural progression. Some end up questioning themselves: Is this really what I want to do, or is it all I think I can do? A girl in my year who had been performing professionally since a very young age once said to me, 'I cannot even write or read properly, this is all I was ever taught to do. I never had a full proper education.' I am not saying everyone ends up feeling this way, but it is possible.

Going to drama school is never a waste of time even if you decide against acting as a profession but some graduates aged 20 or 21 get very disillusioned if it doesn't all happen immediately. Here's an example of a scenario: After finishing school and doing amateur and youth theatre plus various classes you are immediately offered a place at the drama school of your choice. You enjoy your time there and do well, get an agent at 20 or 21 straight from your showcase – and then suddenly, the work doesn't happen. There's nothing, just rejection after rejection. Audition after audition, and no one wants to give you a job. This is very, very hard to suddenly be confronted with because you can't help but think why? Everything was going so well, I have always been successful! If you had experienced a year or two years or so between education and drama school then maybe you wouldn't feel performing is your only life and that it defines you. You wouldn't feel so much of a failure because you would have other things to look back on and say: 'Hey, yes, but I achieved this and that, remember?' It's psychological. It is important to have a life outside performing. Also, you will be those important couple of years older and better equipped to prepare yourself for the demands of the course and the pressure of the industry. I went straight from A levels to drama school and had no time to prepare myself for what I was getting into (a summer course can be quite deceptive although I do strongly recommend it). It really hit me, and many others, hard that first year. Those who had already done a university course and were 20–21 years old were much calmer about the whole process and they all said they were glad they'd waited till they were older.

Many people go to university before attending drama school; it does not count against you at all. All that matters in terms of you getting a place at drama school is how you perform on the day of the audition. University is a very different experience to drama school and not necessarily second choice. You can still do dance/singing lessons while at university and perform in amateur/youth theatre. Many people do. You also do not have to study acting or drama. Instead, you can study something totally different which may enrich you for the future. Going to university is not always about a back-up plan. It may simply be that you enjoy learning and studying. This may be beneficial to later performances later, who knows? Plenty of people who are actors also studied something else and have degrees in other subjects. That doesn't mean they are not dedicated to their craft, simply that they are following lots of different interests. Some even went back to study at university after drama school.

It's important to be broadminded in this profession.

> **TIP!**
>
> Performing is not about thinking about acting all day long and drama school from the age of five, it's about real life, what makes you the person you are and how that can make you a truthful performer.

You can be extremely dedicated to acting and performing in university theatre while doing a completely different degree (like Emma Thompson or Stephen Fry who both went to Cambridge University). This dual life may actually make some people better performers because they have a balanced life. I knew some people at drama school who studied English or finance and then went on to drama school for three years. They are extremely committed and now working successfully in the industry, and more so than some of their peers who never had their minds on anything but acting.

Not everyone is ready to go to drama school at 18. Some people have issues to deal with before they can dedicate themselves fully. They may have some growing up to do. Others need time to find their dreams, not everyone knows what they want to do with the rest of their life by the age of 18. Being an older drama school student does not necessarily make you a weaker performer or less committed. Some people need time to think about what they want. It's not a crime to not know exactly where you will be at 30 when you are 16 or 18. Above all, don't rush into anything. Go with your gut feeling and don't do anything just because you think you should. If you can, get professional advice from people in the industry. You may be ready for drama school at 18 and you may not.

The application process for schools
What time of year is best to apply for drama school?
Most schools audition from September until June. For those schools that give out places as they audition, it may be wise to apply early when there are still plenty of places available for different types of performer. As the year fills up,

the head of course may have already made offers to four other blonde sopranos and people of the same casting type may be rejected to make sure there's a good variety of talents and looks within the year. This is important when casting final term/year productions and for group dynamics. Some schools also have cut-off dates by which time your applications should be sent in (usually these are in January). For example, if you wanted to start in September 2009, it's best to send out applications in autumn 2008 with a view to getting an audition in winter 2008/9. That way, you'll also have more time to choose between schools, should you be made several offers.

TIP!

Have all your speeches and songs ready *before* you send off your audition application. You may get an audition date as early as a week or two after you sent off your forms! Try not to change your audition date unless you really have to, or it can get complicated. Many schools also ask you to give dates when you are available and/or unavailable to audition.

How many schools should I try for?
I recommend you audition for as many as you can afford; six seems to be a good average number and also a UCAS (University and Colleges Admissions Service) requirement. The more auditions you do, the greater your choice of offers and the higher the probability that you receive an offer at all. If you can, make sure you go and view schools on Open Days; also speak to current/past students. Don't just rely on a prospectus – they can look very nice but you only really know what a school is like if you have seen it for yourself. Also, don't be too set on a specific school. Have your favourites but be aware that competition is strong and you may well not get an offer from your preferred place of training. Sometimes actually attending a school can be very different from your impressions of auditioning there. I recommend auditioning for your first choice schools last so you have already had some audition experience and feel more confident.

Waiting lists/reserve places
Schools make offers at various stages. Some offer places every month or every time they have an audition day, while others wait until they have seen everyone and make offers at the end of the audition year. It depends on the school. If you are offered a waiting or reserve list place, you are on a list of second choice candidates. This means that if one of the people who have been offered a place

declines for whatever reason (lack of funding, they prefer another school, and so on), you will be offered their place instead. It's impossible to find out exactly where you are placed on the list, only the panel will know. Also, it can take until the August before the course starts (usually in the September or October) for all places to be distributed so if you are a wait-list student, you may literally be in for a long wait! Some schools also have shortlists, meaning you are kept on hold until all auditions for that year have taken place, at which point the school decides whom to make the offer to.

Drama schools who request CVs

Some schools ask you to send a CV as well as/instead of a personal statement. This is a performance CV, so jobs such as waitressing, bartending, gardening or helping out in an old people's home are irrelevant.

Drama school references

This is nothing to worry about, schools simply want a reference so they can ask questions about you as a person and a performer to gain a clearer picture of your skills and talents. Do not put down friends or family members. Singing, dance and drama teachers are good choices, as are amateur theatre directors or musical directors, a longstanding professional (not necessarily in the performance industry) family friend and even your A-level drama teacher. Do not submit references if they are not requested.

> **TIP!**
>
> Filling out the forms can seem a confusing and complicated procedure so take a photocopy (or print off two copies) first so you can make mistakes on your draft before copying a final version on to the actual form. For most schools you will need to print off forms from their website although UCAS is now online. When filling out your application form, leave anything that mentions 'for office use only' blank. Do not staple together. Use paperclips. Remember to photocopy your application and send it by special delivery so that it is guaranteed to get there. Do not ring drama schools until at least four weeks after your application was sent off. If your application arrives after a school's deadline, it may be sent back to you.

Feedback following rejection

Usually there is simply not enough time or staff to evaluate every applicant's audition in written report form and send you feedback, as there can be up to

3,000 applicants per year per school. Some schools offer to send you a tick box sheet upon request about how you did at the audition. This is, of course, a very basic evaluation as tick boxes cannot fully represent you as an actor but it may give you some indication as to where your weaknesses lie and what you need to improve. I was lucky enough to be given personal feedback by GSA at the time because I had formed a strong connection with some tutors during the summer course.

Deposits/waiting for better offers

Once you have accepted a place, schools will ask you for a deposit to guarantee your place on the course. This usually consists of the fee of your final term of your course, which at the time of writing was around £3,000–£4,000. Should you decide to leave the course early, often your deposit will not be reimbursed, so make sure you check with your particular school beforehand. If you have received several offers and cannot make up your mind, keep the CDS deadline in mind. Once you have accepted a place and paid a deposit to one school, usually you won't be able to get this back. Check with individual schools, this is just a general outline. Please note that CDS guidelines state that you cannot accept more than one place at the same time!

TIP!

If you have been offered a place but are holding out for a possible better offer, make sure you don't lose your place at the first school because you forgot about their confirmation deadline.

Re-applying to drama school after being rejected

It is common to pursue a second year of drama school auditions. Many applicants are rejected in their first year of auditions due to the amount of competition or because applicants did not know how to present themselves and their talents so their chosen schools were unable to see their potential. Being rejected does not necessarily mean you don't have what it takes. Some people have third or even fourth years of drama school auditions until they gain a place. Dustin Hoffman apparently auditioned *seven* times for The Actor's Studio in New York City before being offered a place! It is totally up to you how many years you wish to try for, but a second year of drama school auditions has become almost the norm now as the industry becomes more and more popular.

Re-applying next year for 'better offers'

It is entirely up to you whether you want to decline your place and try again for a different school next year. My personal recommendation would be that you don't accept an offer if you don't really, really want to go. You need to be 100 per cent committed to get the most out of your training and in most cases it's just too expensive to do on a whim.

> **TIP!**
>
> When you re-apply for a course/school for which you have auditioned before, your former audition will often not be taken into consideration. This means that if you got to the third round in your first year or were offered a place, there's no guarantee you will get equally as far or be offered a place again!

Postponing an offer

Sometimes people wish to keep an offer on hold for a year due to lack of funding, because they don't feel ready, to try for other schools they prefer, or for other personal reasons. This can be possible but check with each school on their rules and regulations for this scenario. It may be more difficult if you have also received an offer of funding (or a DADA – Dance & Drama Award).

Photos for drama school applications

These do not have to be professionally taken. A photo from a photo booth such as the one in your passport is totally fine, and it can be colour or black and white. If the school asks for a full-length shot, again it does not have to be professional photo but a photo booth head shot will not be enough for this. All application photos are used for admin purposes only and so that they can put a face to the name on an application form.

> **TIP!**
>
> Put your name on the back of any photos in case they become separated from the rest of your application.

Personal statements for drama school applications – I'm no good at writing!

First of all, perfect personal statements don't exist. What may sound good written by someone else could be totally inappropriate for you, your style and your particular strengths and experiences. So don't get anyone else to write your statement for you because you are scared of getting it wrong even though the idea may seem tempting!

> 'Sometimes I think my writing sounds like I walked out of the room and left the typewriter running.' – *Gene Fowler*

Why do drama schools want a personal statement?

It is true that a good writer does not necessarily make a good performer. The key is that drama schools are not looking for great writers. They want people who are able to express themselves and their ideas. There is some truth in the fact that if you don't make a decent effort with your statement, you may not even get an audition as some drama schools do make the first cut after reading your personal statement. Why? Because they are trying to find some way of reducing the huge number of applicants and get those people seen who, on paper at least, seem to fit the requirements, such as age, have done some kind of performing before, have references from teacher/director, and so on. A personal statement can be simply written (if you are dyslexic, always use spell check) as long as a general enthusiasm comes through, even if the wording is not great and you are not the best writer. They are looking for people who are willing to make an effort and express themselves as this is a large part of being a performer.

> **TIP!**
>
> Many drama school courses now have degree status and are directly connected to a university, hence they have to justify their intake on an academic level. A lot of the schools now run their application system through UCAS, which has always demanded a personal statement as part of their procedure.

Help, how do I begin?

★ Don't make it too long, a page at the most.

★ If possible, type your personal statement. Should the space on the application form seem too small, put 'see attachment' in the space and attach your personal statement printed on A4 paper at the back.

★ If you don't know how to start, sum yourself up in three words for your first sentence.

★ Give two or three sentences of your performance experience, but don't make a list. You have to do that anyway on many application forms for schools and they can read it there. Pick out one particular performance that influenced you most and say why and what you learned.

★ State why you want to go to drama school, what appeals to you about acting/performing (why you want to devote your life to it) and state why you want to attend the particular school you are applying for.

★ Say what you enjoy doing outside performing. If you like reading, be specific about the kind of books you enjoy. Have you built schools in India, tutored younger pupils at your school, worked in an old people's home, got any work experience at all? What has shaped you as a person?

★ What parts do you see yourself playing?

★ Do you have any special skills? If so, what are they?

★ Favourite playwright, play, actor and why? Mention your idols and why you look up to them.

★ What do you think makes you unique as a performer, what are your strengths, what do you feel you need to work on?

★ Brevity is a key factor. Don't ramble on, be precise and to the point.

Generally speaking, be specific! Everyone applying to drama school has a passion to perform, probably 80 per cent of applicants will write that. State the plays that have stuck in your mind and why. Maybe there's a character you would really like to play. Perhaps say what made you feel connected to a character you have performed in the past, what was it about that certain play/musical/etc. that really got to you. What was it you found interesting to work on, what particular part of performing did you conquer? Giving detail makes you different and tutors/panels may remember you of something in particular. Think about it. About 2,000 or so people per year apply to each drama school. Almost everyone will write about their A levels, love of performing, going to see plays, that it's their dream to be in the West End or in a film, the amateur work they have done, NYMT (National Youth Music Theatre), and so on. On top of this, find something that makes it *your* personal statement. It's not enough to say what you enjoy about performing, schools need to see that you have done something about it and have actually practised your craft in some shape or form already.

Not all applicants get to attend an interview. Out of everyone who auditions maybe a quarter will get the opportunity to be interviewed, if that. Out of one of my drama school auditions consisting of 100 people on the day, only three were seen for interview, namely those who made it to the final round. Some schools such as RADA ask personal questions in the first round but this does not apply to all drama school auditions.

Auditioning for schools
Preparing for drama school auditions and when to start
Since there is no perfect way to prepare, this is just a basic outline. I suggest you start educating yourself and practising your craft as soon as you have decided you would like to train. Even if you are very young, you can still take part in school productions, amateur/youth theatre and attend children's classes/workshops in singing and dance. Read plays, go and see productions of all kinds. Don't forget to make school your priority, though, and to have a social life too. Going from one class to the next will not necessarily make you the best performer, it's important to keep a balance and have fun with friends. In terms of the actual preparation of material for drama school auditions, I recommend you begin to read, watch, listen and research for pieces at least a couple of months before you send off your application forms. This will give you enough time to try out, learn and digest a variety of speeches and songs.

Go and see schools. If you are auditioning for an MT (musical theatre) course, I recommend that you regularly attend weekly dance classes at least six months before applying, if you are not dancing already (which I definitely recommend).

Consider possible interview questions: Why do you want to train as an actor? What can you bring to this profession? Why have you chosen to apply for this particular course?

Audition fee
Remember, you are paying the panel and their school for their time and work in assessing you and your talent as you would for any other service. This also includes admin fees, such as sending you the relevant forms and information material. Never send your audition fee as cash in the post.

Drama and singing exams
Exams such as singing exams offered by London's Guildhall and the Royal Academy, as well as the LAMDA (London Academy of Music & Dramatic

Arts) acting exams, can be useful to gain a good musical understanding (sight reading, sight singing) and practise performing speeches. Even though schools may glance at your application and register that you have completed these, this usually has no relevance whatsoever as to whether or not you are offered a place. Grade As in all your exams do not confirm that you are a good actor or singer, although they do suggest you have a certain musical and artistic technical knowledge. These exams can be beneficial but not mandatory. *See also* page 294 for details and links if you wish to pursue exams.

Waiting to hear from drama school after auditioning
Some schools will send you a letter stating whether you have been successful or not within two weeks of your audition. Others may write to you a week after your initial audition – GSA (Guildhall School of Acting) is very quick, for example. These are the schools offering places regularly throughout the year. If they are part of UCAS, you will find out whether or not you have been successful when UCAS generally release their results. Some schools may not send you a letter until a couple of months after your initial audition (final audition, if there are recalls) even if they are not part of UCAS, simply because they may be overwhelmed with applications and paperwork and not have sufficient staff to complete it all. Phone the school if at least double the amount of time they claim you need to wait for a reply has passed. Due to lack of admin staff and a general bombardment of applications, schools are often delayed in responding.

What days do drama schools hold auditions?
Some have set first round days such as every first Thursday of the month; others do weekend workshops. It really depends on the school and you will have to request details individually.

Drama school auditions – the day itself
This varies from school to school. Some schools hold just one day while others have a recall weekend or even three or four recalls (like RADA – Royal Academy of Dramatic Art). You may be asked simply to present one or two speeches for the first round and then come back for work on your speeches, workshops, group work, and so on on another day if you are successful. Check with individual schools for their audition procedures. Generally, all drama school auditions will include the following (order may vary):
★ Acting courses: A vocal and or physical warm-up, presenting your speeches (usually at least two), possibly a singing audition (singing a solo or singing in a group), working on your speeches with a panel or tutor, improvisation,

group work, an acting workshop/class, a voice workshop, a movement (not dance) class and possibly an interview. Some schools may also want to see a devised piece. *See also* pages 35–36.

★ MT courses: A vocal and or physical warm-up, a jazz class where you learn and have to present a routine and which also includes 'across the room' leaps, kicks, turns, and so on. Possibly a ballet barre and/or a tap class depending on the course. A movement class, group acting, an improvisation class. Presenting your speech or speeches, presenting your solo or songs. Possibly an interview, a group singing class, a physio (to check if you are physically capable of handling the course), a written or oral test in which you are asked basic questions about musical theatre.

A tour of the school is sometimes included in the audition day.

> ### TIP!
>
> Some schools ask you to sing your songs/do your speeches in front of each other; others have you present them individually with just the panel in the room. It depends entirely on the school and is not something you should worry about. Best to get used to this, as it is usually common practice training at drama school.

★ Speeches: See pages 206–217 for advice on what to choose, how to present, and so on.

★ Songs: Confirm with the schools themselves and/or read their audition guidelines for length of songs and styles. Usually they ask for a contrast, namely an up-tempo/character song and a ballad (slow). Some MT courses may accept pop or similar material for an audition, although classical and operatic material is usually not accepted. *See also* the singing chapter and Appendices for the songs to avoid/recommended song lists, sheet music and the backing track section, 'Types of musical theatre songs and preparing for your singing audition' as well as 'What belongs in an MT repertoire' for advice on how to present your sheet music and what possible composers to look at for material. For more information and to see if you are prepared, try the test on pages 37–42.

Auditioning with an injury/illness

If you are really inhibited vocally and/or physically, always try to reschedule your audition. Should this be impossible, you should make sure the school is aware of your situation. It is OK not to throw yourself around the floor if you are recovering from a sprained ankle, for example, but the school should know about it in advance, so they don't think you are inhibited for any other reasons.

Devised pieces for drama school – what's that all about?

'Don't think you're funny. It'll never work if you think you're funny.' – *George Abbott*

This sounds either terribly confusing or simply terrifying! Some drama schools (such as LIPA – Liverpool Institute of Performing Arts) ask applicants to devise a piece of about two to three minutes in addition to presenting their speeches/songs. But what does that mean, and what are they looking for? Panels want to see a performer who is truthful, honest, energetic, creative, imaginative, dedicated and totally committed to their choices. They are not looking for a perfect performance. Rather, they want to see what you as an actor have to offer as opposed to the next person auditioning. Don't be scared, you have nothing to lose. I know exactly how you feel. Initially, I was terrified about doing a five-minute stand-up performance at drama school in my first year, which is a similar type of exercise but looking back, it was one of the best things I ever did and people still remember it today! You can make a huge impact with your piece of just a few minutes. Make use of this opportunity and don't shy away from it. This is the first step towards giving a convincing performance: being bold and brave enough to present something of yourself. If you can do this, you can do anything.

OK, but how do I start, what do I choose and do I have to be funny?
Don't panic. This is not a test to embarrass you. See it as an opportunity to create anything you like!

> **TIP!**
>
> Think of something that is really important to you as a subject matter and/or something that shows off your greatest strengths.

I don't think you can really do anything wrong here so long as you commit to your choices, put truth and energy into what you say and do, and succeed in 'performing' some kind of message or journey. This does not have to be deep and meaningful (although it can be, of course), but it has to say something personal about you, something that makes you stand out from the rest of the crowd. Maybe it's a piece of fiction you wrote yourself, perhaps something to do with your life, there are so many possibilities, so many options. I suggest you make a list of shows, plays, personalities, issues of any kind (world or personal) that appeal to you/are important to you and why. Then write a list of things you definitely do not want to do, such as, ballet, juggling, singing, doing accents, mime, clowning, and so on. This should narrow it down quite a bit and give you an idea of what matters to you and how you feel comfortable presenting it. You don't necessarily need to script the whole thing if writing really isn't your strength. Your performance can even be entirely without speech.

To give you a few examples of what I mean, these are a few stand-up routines I have seen from fellow students at drama school:

★ American girl talking about adapting to British culture, imitating a few stereotypes and speaking of her frustrations about fitting in.

★ Girl giving her own acted-out account of her relatives having sex next door, acting it from the point of view of a five-year-old (the age the girl was at that time).

★ A guy performing a mini political puppet show with five different puppets manipulated by only himself.

★ A girl dressing up in total costume as an old woman in a wheelchair who is drunk and bends her limbs in crazy fashion to get more drink as she is stuck in a wheelchair (the limbs were fake and attached to the girl's body).

★ A guy dressing up in ballet costume and dancing *Swan Lake* to a tape recorder (keep in mind that this particular guy was far from a dancer, being overweight and half-bald). He did not focus on the comic element of his scene but instead concentrated on the sheer frustration of someone trying to master dance with two left feet. It was a reflection of his own feelings and because he was so dedicated he managed to change the initial reaction of laughter following his entrance in a pink tutu. The audience began to relate to the feelings of frustration and anger of the character he had created. I thought it was quite an achievement for a five-minute performance – and without the character speaking a single word.

As Henry Irving said on his deathbed, 'Dying is easy, comedy is difficult.' I could go on and on with examples but I think this may have given you some ideas and reassured you that there is no right or wrong performance, only a brave, truthful and committed one.

Are you ready for your drama school auditions?

'Opening night: The night before the play is ready to open.'
– *George Jean Nathan*

Drama school auditions, could anything be scarier? Are you prepared enough? Find out with this simple test (the answers are at the end).

1. Audition speeches: it's one week before your first drama school audition, where do you stand?

a) Hmm, well… I know I'm doing something from Shakespeare, not sure which play… *Midsummer Night's Dream*? Will buy an audition monologue book tomorrow. Not sure what the guidelines are for my school and what I have to do, guess I should find out. I'll speedlearn my speeches three days before the audition and if I don't know them that well, just fake it. After all, it's the personality that counts, it doesn't matter if I don't know the pieces perfectly.

b) I've read various plays throughout the year and seen different productions, browsed through websites. I've chosen five or six speeches from that process about two or three months ago which I know backwards and have rehearsed a couple of times with a helpful professional in the business and also worked on myself. I've familiarised myself with the school's speech requirements and have gone through the lists of speeches they recommend and state as material not to be used. Since it's a week before the audition there's no point altering the way I approach them now, I need to trust myself and my choices, and just go for it on the day and follow any direction the panel may give me. Any friends who may say the speech is a bad idea or who were rejected with the same speech are not comparable to me. I'm a totally different person and schools react differently to speeches. I plan to do the speech that I feel like doing on the day or possibly what the panel requests to hear.

c) I sleep with Simon Dunmore's *An Actor's Guide to Getting Work* under my pillow every night and have highlighted and marked or written at the side of the pages throughout the whole book so it's barely legible and I know the book backwards. I chose my 20 speeches a year ago, each of which I prepared with an audition tutor once a week for a whole year. I've been reciting my audition speeches 24/7 for the past six months and think about nothing else. I try a new way of doing them at least once a day, asking everyone and anyone I meet what they think. I go through lists and lists of drama school 'no no' lists or 'recommended' lists over and over to see if I've missed anything. I panic when I hear from friends that a speech I think is similar to mine was not liked by a drama school panel or those friends were rejected. I panic when I think of which of my 20 speeches to choose on the day. What if someone has the same speech?

2. Audition songs – as above, it's one week to go so where do you stand?

a) I don't know that many songs so best to stick with something familiar, 'On My Own' from *Les Mis* will be fine and everyone loves it so the panel's bound to like that. A second song? Hmm... Christina Aguillera's recent single sounds quite fun, I think I'll go to Chappels the day before my audition and buy the sheet music. I'm either taking my music along in its original book or as dirty and crumpled loose papers, but who cares, performers are creative, not tidy, right? Not sure if the song is in my range, or too long or too short, but as long as I enjoy it, it should be OK, right? One of the top notes in 'On My Own' sounds a bit screechy but I'm sure the panel won't hear that – they'll be tired from seeing loads of applicants anyway so won't be that attentive.

b) I have a singing teacher who suggested a couple of songs to me. Apart from that I also did some research myself. I've picked three to four songs that are a mixture of composers, styles and tempos and made sure they're no longer than two to three minutes long. Also, that they suit my voice and are not too high/low for me, and so I have some to choose from on the day of each audition. I've prepared a 16-bar version of each song in case the panel runs out of time and asks for this. All my sheet music is photocopied and taped together neatly and marked with a pencil and highlighter clearly. I've rehearsed these plenty with a teacher and on my own and made definite character choices. I've thought about intentions and emotions in the song and the lyrics. I've also thought and practised the technical aspect of the songs but am now concentrating on the performing side for the audition. As it's now a week before the audition I'm going to rest and take care of my voice and make sure it's in top form for the audition.

c) Songs? I have a whole book of possible songs that I've collected since I was 13! Everything from Jason Robert Brown to Sondheim to Ivor Novello; also have some opera (Puccini) and an R&B number in there, you just never know! I've been to five different singing teachers and rehearsed five different ways of performing them in detail just in case so I have five different options in case the girl before me sings the same song and stands a similar way to what I had planned. All my music has been specially hand printed by my friend's computer music printing programme, anything to make a good impression and stand out. I've rehearsed all my gestures in absolute detail and know exactly how many inches my hand will be from my face at every note of the song. I've learned all the composers' life stories by heart and know when their shows last ran in the West End. I've trained for years to be able to belt out that top note in my songs and to make sure every intonation and breath will be perfect.

3. It's the evening before your audition, so what are you going to wear?

a) Um...black track suit bottoms, comfy trainers and a T-shirt? I haven't really thought about it. Want to be comfy and not feel weird because I'm wearing something different to everyone else. Oops, tracksuit bottoms have some stains, oh well, it's not the way you look that counts, it's your talent, right?

b) Something comfortable that stretches and accents my positive features. Something clean, ironed and well presented. Nothing ripped or missing buttons. An outfit that represents my particular style as a person and is of a colour that highlights my features. No big logos on my clothing! Not all black, unless stated in the audition guidelines. I'm wearing a support bra (if female). I've taken along a change of clothes for the movement/dance workshops. Dance outfit: Girls – depends on the school I'm auditioning for. Usually leotard and tights or jazz pants and leotard/tight-fitting top. Proper and suitable dance shoes are important. All black isn't necessary, unless audition rule. Guys: Jazz pants, fitted T-shirt. I will wear some make-up (girls) but not over the top, just to highlight my features. My hair is washed, not falling in my face and hiding my eyes.

c) I have six different outfits all specially bought for the auditions. Lots of very low-cut tops (if you've got it, flaunt it!) and a tiny miniskirt. Will just have to watch it when I do the group work or miss out on some things. I have a personal stylist coming round each morning to do my make-up and hair. I'm putting my hair in curlers and doing stage make-up, everything to look your best, right?

> ### TIP!
>
> I recommend removing all jewellery and piercings for drama school auditions. This includes wristwatches, if you are doing a movement/dance audition. Anything that might get caught in people's hair or be a hazard in any way should be removed for everyone's safety. Also, having a piercing in certain body parts can be distracting to the audition panel – you don't want them watching your tongue ring in fascination and forgetting about you! Also, you'll find it's school policy at most drama schools and similar training establishments to remove the above mentioned items during class and rehearsals.

4. So, how did you choose the drama schools you're auditioning for?

a) Just typed in drama school under Google and a few came up. Chose the ones in my area so I can comfortably go from home as I'm too scared to leave my hometown. I don't know that much about the schools but I'll find out when I do the audition, right?

b) I made a list of what I want to gain from my training and looked at all the schools' websites/prospectuses offering this. I gathered opinions from people who work/train/have trained there. I visited the schools on an open day (if they had one) and asked questions. I chose schools that have lots of hours of practical work, one-to-one training sessions and a final-year showcase in London.

c) Duh! RADA, LAMDA and Bristol Old Vic, of course! They're the best schools around and I've been told there's no point applying to second best, right? Plus Peters Fraser & Dunlop goes to their agent showcase.

5. You're auditioning for an MT course but you're not really a dancer, so how have you prepared your dance?

a) I haven't done any but my singing and acting is bound to blow them away. They can't expect you to be good at everything, right?

b) I'm not primarily a dancer but I have done regular jazz and ballet for the past two years and worked on my speed at picking up routines, flexibility and dance terminology. If I can't do a step I'll just have energy, be alert and smile and not look at my feet. Getting a step wrong isn't the end of the world as long as I have a positive presence.

c) I've been dancing so much I barely have time to breathe and I'm totally frustrated that I'm still so bad at it and still can't do the splits! I've lost all confidence and am bound to get everything wrong. I'll hide at the back and hope no one notices me!

6. What are you going to concentrate on in the audition, how are you going to behave?

a) Um... like I do at home and with my friends? I'm supposed to be me, right?

b) I'll do my best and be alert, energetic, open and positive and look focused. I'll be a good group member in the group exercises and give as well as take. I'll be imaginative, brave and not afraid to take risks and just go for it. I'll not play for laughs. In the dance audition I'll make sure I'm well placed and everyone can see me. Making mistakes is part of life so if I forget a line I'll just ask the panel if I can start over, it's not a crime. I'll take my time before doing my speech/song and not let anyone rush me. I'll not talk during someone else's audition and generally stay away from too much gossiping and giggling. I will not at any time put myself down as a performer or tell the panel I am nervous. I'll not play my pieces at the panel unless the writing requests so or I am directed to do so.

c) I'm going to try and make no mistakes and do exactly what the panel tells me. I'll make sure I tell them I'm supernervous when I enter the room. I'd be mortified if I forgot a line in my speech/song or looked stupid. I hope I can make the panel laugh with my comedy and will try and be really funny. If they don't laugh, I'm sure I'll *die*! I'll smile and make eye contact with the panel the whole time so they know I'm really there with them.

7. Interview - how have you prepared?

a) I didn't even know there was one.

b) I've thought about why I want to be a performer and what appeals to me about that particular school/course. I've thought about why I chose my speeches and songs, how they show the best of me and what character choices I've made. I've thought about actors/actresses I admire or dislike and why. I've thought about recent productions I've seen and what I would change about them and why. I've read up on the most recent theatre news and most important directors, playwrights, plays, and so on. I've thought about what I would do if I wasn't a performer. I have thought about what I would bring to the profession and why I would be a valuable member of this school. I have thought about what makes me stand out, my strengths as a performer and what I need to work on. I've thought about what kind of things I would like to work on when I graduate (classical plays, television/film, MT, try directing, TIE (Theatre in Education), and so on) or maybe I simply don't know yet.

c) I've written out all my answers to any possible question that may come up and learnt them by heart. If they ask me something I didn't prepare for, I don't know what I'll do!

Answers: Well, I hope everyone picked B!

> **TIP!**
>
> Take a look at 'An Applicant's Guide to Auditioning and Interviewing at Dance and Drama Schools' on www.ncdt.co.uk/apply.asp

How do I pay for my training?

'There's no money in poetry, but then there's no poetry in money, either.' – Robert Graves

At the time of writing full-time drama school training can cost approximately £30,000 in tuition alone for a three-year course if you have to pay the full fees and this *excludes* living costs. This means that most full-time acting and MT (including postgrad) courses cost roughly £10,000 a year. Unless you were born with a silver spoon in your mouth or are extremely lucky, you will probably have to try and find someone else to pay for your training.

So, what can I do?
1. Most three-year accredited courses are government maintained or state funded. All UK and EU students are eligible and can have access to student loans (the maximum amount in 2004 was £4,000 for the duration of the course) and can apply for help with the student fee contribution (£3,000 in 2006/7 and £3,070 in 2007/8; visit the NCDT website for current details). Note that if you have received funding from the government for a previous course (such as university), you will most probably not be eligible for this. Check with your Local Education Authority (LEA) and also visit www.dfes.gov.uk/studentsupport.

2. DADA (Dance & Drama Awards) is another option. However, this only applies to independent schools, which are part of this scheme. Up to 58 per cent of students on courses at schools following this scheme are given such an award. Both UK and EU nationals qualify for application but not students outside the EU. Often drama schools hold further recalls/separate auditions to decide which students offered places that year also deserve a DADA award. Some schools will have more DADAs available than others. You will usually find out quite late in the year whether or not you have been successful in this regard as most schools wait until all auditions for the year have been completed. Your financial situation will be taken into consideration and may influence whether or not you are eligible. These awards may be given to students on one-, two- or three-year courses and you will receive a National Diploma in Professional Acting from Trinity College London.

> ### TIP!
>
> Students who have previously received financial help for higher education are still eligible to apply for a DADA award. This means that if you attended a three-year university course and received financial aid during your time there, you can still apply for a DADA.

Per annum all your tuition fees will be covered except the usual university fees (at the time of writing, these are a maximum of £3,000 annually if your parents earn less than £20,000 a year). You will not have to pay any of this until after your training and payments are subject to the same rules as 'maintenance loans'. If your parents earn less, you will not have to pay anything at all towards your fees. You are eligible to apply for hardship grants regarding your living expenses, as you are not eligible for a student loan when accepting a DADA.

To find out more information regarding DADAs, contact Manchester Education Authority on 0161 234 7021 or email fund4study@notes.manchester.gov.uk. In Ireland, contact the Department for Education and Learning in Belfast on 02890 257 735. If you are an EU student but not UK or Irish national, contact The Department for Education and Skills EU Means Testing Team on 01325 391 199. In Scotland, contact the Student Awards Agency for Scotland on 0131 476 8212 or www.student-support-saas.gov.uk.

3. Contact your local drama schools to see if they have any privately funded special scholarships available that are separate from the funding methods described above. Many will hold auditions for these throughout your training.

4. Contact charities, trusts and foundations. This requires research and

planning. Don't contact every possible charity or organisation in the country. Make sure you are eligible for their funding/match their interests. See below for details of where to access a list of charities online and also look at www.tactactors.org and www.scholarship-search.org.

5. Career development loans from your bank – for further information, call the DfES on 0800 585 505 or visit www.lifelonglearning.co.uk. The first repayment is usually due five years after graduation.

6. The Mackintosh Foundation (020 7637 8866) usually gives out grants up to £10,000.

7. Try Thomas Wall Trust (UK nationals only). Call 0207 638 1753 or visit www.thomaswalltrust.org.uk. The maximum value is £1,000 per annum, both part- and full-time courses are eligible and applications have to be made from 1 January each year.

8. *The Stage* newspaper scholarships (www.thestage.co.uk) – one full scholarship covering all fees awarded per annum is granted by audition.

9. Try family contacts and larger institutions such as banks. Should your parent work for a bank, for example, you may be eligible for funding as many such companies, law firms and other large (global) organisations provide funding schemes for offspring.

10. Contact well-known actors and directors, especially if they are patrons of/attended the school you wish to audition for/have been offered a place at. It is worth following this route as these people do read your requests (a girl in my year at drama school received £2,000 from a very well known actress). Make sure you prepare your application carefully and that it looks profession-al and *different* – after all, these people receive hundreds of requests per year. Campaigns, websites and performances to collect money for drama school funding are some of the ideas I have come across over the years.

TIP!

Have a look at Andrew Piper's website (a Bristol Old Vic acting graduate) that goes into more detail under the 'Bristol' and then 'advice' section: www.asharp.dircon.co.uk/index2.htm

Overseas students (non EU)

Most likely, you will not be eligible for any government funding and will have to pay full fees for all courses. Please seek financial support in your home country.

Students with disabilities

Contact SKILL (National Bureau for Students with Disabilities) for further information: Information Service: 0800 328 5050 (freephone) and 020 7657 2337 (open Tuesdays, 11.30–1.30pm and Thursdays, 1.30–3.30pm). Visit www.skill.org.uk.

Postgraduate students

Most of the time there will be none or little government funding available (although you are eligible for DADAs) and you will need to find financial support privately. Contact your LEA (Local Education Authority) for more detail. You may also be eligible for a career development loan, which is interest free and does not have to be paid back until your course is completed. For more info, check out www.direct.gov.uk/en/EducationAndLearning/Adult Learning/CareerDevelopmentLoans/index.htm.

The Arts and Humanities Research Council may also have funding available that is suitable for a performance-related course: www.ahrc.ac.uk/apply/post-graduate.asp.

TIP!

> Most drama schools will want to see written proof that you can pay for your course (or at least the first year/term) before you are allowed to attend. Start looking for funding before you are offered a place – this procedure can take time. For a list of organisations to contact and ask for advice, study the NCDT (National Council of Drama Training) fund factsheet on www.ncdt.co.uk/facts.asp. See also the Conference of Drama Schools help section on funding: http://sites.stocksphere.com/cds/files/CDS%20Guide%202007%20R EVISED.pdf (go to section 8 – Information about funding and section 10 – useful contacts and funding contacts).

The Training Process and your Transition from Graduate to Professional

★

My first professional audition

I was still at drama school in the middle of my third year when one morning a bunch of girls with that week's copy of *The Stage* came into the college canteen and started chattering about the upcoming *Les Miserables* open auditions. I had never been to a professional audition, let alone an open one although I had heard many off-putting stories. Various groups started to form of students who were going to try their luck. I decided to go it alone.

On the day of the audition I left the house at 7.00am, hoping to join the queue in front of the theatre at about 8.00am. Nearing the theatre, I was hit by a mob of excited girls (separate audition days for male and female) and realised I had to go almost all the way to the tube station from which I had just arrived to join them at the end of the queue. After collecting my number sticker at the front, I spent the first hour waiting in silence and listening to the various conversations around me. 'Is this your first time at an open?' 'Oh yes, usually my agent gets me seen but this time they said all their audition slots were full.' 'Mum, I'm scared. Will it be like *Pop Idol*?' 'Oh my God, can you see that girl in the front dressed like Eponine, how ridiculous!' 'I didn't bring a photo and CV, will they kick me out?' After a while I started to make conversation with the girl behind me. She was a recent LIPA (London Institute of Performing Arts) graduate and we found we had much in common. As time passed the theatre came in sight again and after three hours finally we reached the beginning of the queue – only to be given a ticket with a time at which to return and queue some more. Despite this slight let down, we were extremely glad to escape to a café – in typical London style it had started to rain down like buckets.

Returning, we were finally allowed to enter the theatre through the stage door and like cattle were slowly herded up flights of stairs and through various rooms. Emotions and tensions were on a high. While many girls were on the phone receiving last minute encouragement from friends and loved ones, others were frantically trying to decide what to sing and yet a different group of girls were crying in their mothers' arms. I noticed with surprise that the number of people giving support was almost equal to the number of girls actually auditioning that day. Now separated from my audition accomplice, I sat between two mirrors and someone's costumes trying to focus while surrounded by noise. A man began to hand out forms for us to complete and collected CVs and photos while taking our names. I sensed things were speeding up and sure enough, the next waiting area was backstage in the theatre itself. We were lined up according to our arrival numbers. Separated by a black backstage curtain, we could clearly hear the sound of singing and the booming exclamations of 'Next!' For some girls the pressure was too much, they simply left and ran out of the theatre. Others trembled in silence, yet still more waited in the arms of mothers, grandmothers and even backstage crew.

Finally, after seven hours of anticipation it was my turn. My name was announced and I walked on the stage, handed my music to the pianist and tried to smile. Blinded by the spotlights I couldn't make out the panel but concentrated on keeping my eyes focused on the centre of the theatre while I started singing. After about eight bars a loud 'thank you' finished my audition. Deflated, I turned round and started walking off the stage. 'Hold on a minute, come back here!' In a daze I turned round to face the glaring lights again. 'We want to see you again, we will give you a call regarding a date.' The pianist pressed my sheet music into my hands and I was rushed off stage. But the reality of a recall had not quite hit me when the mob of still-waiting girls started racing towards me. 'Oh my God, you got a recall! What did you sing? What did you do? Tell us what to do!' They were clawing at me frantically, looking at me in desperation as they waited for an answer to guarantee them the same ticket to the next step of this process. I was like Charlie Bucket who found a golden ticket. A stagehand grabbed me by the arm and pushed me through a black door back out on to the street. In a daze I looked around at the people rushing past me, feeling like Alice in Wonderland just thrown back into real life from the rabbit hole. Did all that really just happen?

After a few days of waiting beside the phone at home, the call came. I was told I would be sent some music from the show and given a date to return to the actual *Les Miserables* theatre (at the time the Palace Theatre). When the music arrived, I noticed I had been sent chorus songs and Fantine's big solo. It seems that I was being considered for a major role! I called my mother in anticipation and spent days and nights listening to, living and breathing *Les Miserables* and Fantine.

The day of the recall I arrived to a quiet theatre and was placed in my own waiting room (the chorus dressing room) near the stage. What a difference to the crowds of the week earlier! After just ten minutes to myself, I was asked to the stage. I was so nervous I was in tunnel vision mode and didn't pay attention to my surroundings. I saw a cannon, some barricades and the famous cobblestones but then there was a loud thud as I tripped flat on my face in the middle of the stage. Immediately I felt the sensation of a large black mark forming on my right arm and for a split second I almost forgot where I was. I was so embarrassed I had no idea what to say or do so I just scrambled to my feet and stood there as if it was the most normal thing in the world to fall at the feet of those auditioning me. Fortunately the panel did not seem in the least fazed and asked me to proceed with my songs. Head still spinning and barely hearing their directions or the piano intro, I made a tentative attempt at 'Lovely Ladies' followed by a confused 'I Dreamed A Dream'.

Somehow I got through the singing, remembered all my lyrics and was re-directed in Fantine's number when they asked for 'more focus'. The environment, the fall, I was completely thrown out of my usual comfort zone and as much as I tried, focus was just not happening. They thanked me for coming and sent me home. Although I didn't receive a further recall for *Les Mis*, I had learned the true meaning of the words 'the show must go on'.

Preparation for drama school training

'It is up to us to give ourselves recognition. If we wait for it to come from others, we feel resentful when it doesn't, and when it does, we may well reject it.' – Spencer Tracy

After stressful and emotional months of nail-biting auditions, the unbelievable happens and you are offered a place. After the initial celebrating, you may suddenly start to think wow, what next? How do I prepare so I'm well equipped for the beginning of term? Personally, I had absolutely no idea what to expect, so apart from buying the listed dancewear items, I didn't give my training much thought until two weeks or so before the start of term. Suddenly I realised I did not have a place to live. I decided to call up numbers on the list of temporary accommodation sent to me by the college. Most of them were fully booked by this point, so I was stuck with the YMCA. I remember arriving there barely 24 hours before the start of my course with two suitcases and not much more. It seemed a scary and grotty place: in the middle of the night I was woken up by two drug dealers having a massive punch-up in front of my door! Consequently, I was too scared to stay out late during Freshers Week as I didn't want to return to the YMCA when it was too dark and no staff were around, so I missed out on most of the first few important social events. I lasted five days at the YMCA before moving into a friend's room, where I was forced to crash on the floor with sofa pillows in between desperately trying to find a permanent place to live. Mine is not the only such story. There are always people who get stuck with finding accommodation. I remember we had someone in my year who spent a few nights in his car!

Finding somewhere to live

Schools often send you a list of supposedly decent temporary accommodation. Be wary of these suggestions, as I know from experience that they are not always good or safe and can also be expensive. This includes halls.

> **TIP!**
>
> I personally recommend that you move into a shared house/flat, halls or find a host family *before* the start of your first term.

Move in a couple of days beforehand, not the night before. Don't stay in a B&B and wait till you have made some friends. I made that mistake. It's not a good idea – you won't have time to think about moving and settling in once your term has started. The emotional and physical turmoil of those first few weeks takes a while to get used to and it's so good if you can go home in the evenings to a place that's yours, where you know everyone and you feel comfortable. Also, you'll already start to integrate into your school if you spend a week or so with your housemates, meaning your first few days will be less daunting and you'll have others to refer to if you have any questions. You'll also have company to walk home from the pub and to accompany you to all the fresher parties, which is why it's good to live with second years that are usually responsible for organising such events. It's also nice to have friends to turn to, especially if you are living away from home for the first time.

I recommend living with a mix of people rather than just students from your course/year. Remember that you will be with these people ten–twelve hours a day, five days a week anyway at college. Living together might be too close for comfort (as I have seen in past experiences). One person from your course is fine, but try to have some second and third years, which can be really helpful if you need advice; also actors or musical theatre students (depending on which course you choose). Living with tech students is also a great balance, I found. A mix of sexes is also a good idea; same-sex houses are usually not too good in my experience.

Most schools have open days where you can meet others also looking for accommodation and/or an accommodation notice board. Many schools, such as East 15 near Loughton, Essex, also offer accommodation online. Go to these notice boards before the summer holidays begin and during the summer. Good accommodation goes fast, so try and secure a place as soon as possible. Those in shared places know quite early on who is moving and who will be staying, that is, third years will leave, and so on, and will need a replacement. We used to put up a notice looking for a new housemate in June and would have new students for that year's autumn intake calling from early July! Try and view a few places so you get a good idea of what's on offer.

Make sure you know what you can afford. Ask the housemates exactly how much they spend on water, gas, electricity, TV licence and phone per month/quarter. In terms of council tax, as a student you are not liable for this. However, make sure you are living in a student-only house. Once you have at least one non-student residing with you, all of you become liable for council tax. You may be eligible for a discount, though. For more information, refer to www.adviceguide.org.uk/index/life/tax/council_tax.htm

Check out the level of tidiness in the house. Has a kitty been set up for loo roll, milk and other general expenses? Do they have a rota or does everyone just do whatever they want in terms of cleaning? Is there a washing machine and microwave? Does the central heating work? I recommend you ask a parent to accompany you to any viewing. It's not uncommon and most of the time they are the ones paying for it anyway, and they may well have the experience you lack when looking for the right kind of rental accommodation. If moving into new accommodation, check whether the house is furnished or unfurnished before you commit. If furniture needs to be bought, make sure everyone is happy with what is needed. Also, discuss Broadband, Sky, and so on. Often people have very different priorities and ideas here, so it's best to be clear what you want, need and can afford.

Normal rental contracts run for a year and will have a six months' break clause after the first six months, after which you or the landlord can give two or three months' notice. This can vary. Usually if someone moves out of your house/flat share the rest of you will be responsible for paying the full rent each month despite that person leaving. You are usually not all on separate contracts. Make sure you check details before you sign. Most landlords will do an inventory and it is usually your responsibility to pay for one when you move out; also to pay for anything that has been damaged or lost. The inventory only gets done when a whole group moves out of a house, not just one individual leaving a room. You will almost certainly have to pay a deposit too (usually six weeks' rent) and this will be returned to you once the inventory has been checked and you move out. Landlords use the deposit as a safety net in case you do not pay your rent or anything in the house gets lost or damaged.

Make sure you also calculate the amount and cost of travel to your accommodation as this can make a big difference. For example, whether you can walk everywhere for free or will have to use the tube if studying in London. Even if they do a student discount – which you have to apply for *before* buying your Oyster card – make sure you send off the forms in August of the year you start studying. You will need to send in a form signed by the school as proof of your student status. Download this from the Oyster website or ask for a hard copy at any London tube station.

What do I need to bring?

Don't take your entire room from home! Do take items such as a television/DVD player, sheets, towels and personal belongings that you know will be important to you – particular books, CDs, stuffed animals and, of course, your own laptop or computer, if possible. Remember you are creating a new home away from home.

TIP!

It usually goes down well if you ask the house into which you are moving if they need anything to see if you can contribute. Student houses *always* need something! Some sort of computer comes in extremely handy, especially with printer and internet access because college computers are often overcrowded and slow, while the printers are almost always out of order. If you can invest in some sort of computer/printer set-up to take to college, then do so. You'll be extremely glad you did as you'll be doing a lot of research for projects, shows, class, etc.

Take lots of good, comfy and, especially, warm clothes (most schools save on heating and are always freezing cold). You won't have to dress up for college – you can get away with jogging bottoms and trainers, if you wish. You'll be on the floor a lot. Make-up is also not necessary. Usually, it's a case of the less, the better, though some make-up is fine, of course, and some drama schools (especially those with dance-oriented MT courses) may take the opposite view and require you to wear a certain amount of make-up for class. I recommend you keep jewellery out of college – for many classes you will have to remove it anyway. Make sure you buy everything on the list you receive from the college; there is a reason for everything on there. The list usually mentions character shoes for girls (buy shoes from a mid-price range, cheap will break quickly and expensive might get stolen). The right shoes are a must-have, as are practice skirts. If your college offers such a service, send them your measurements. Prices may seem expensive but anything you buy or try to make yourself most probably won't be quite what the college envisioned. In my experience, most female students have their practice skirts made and a bit of a uniform look will be going on, so you may not want to stand out. I would not pay more than say £35 (at the time of writing) on a practice skirt. Kneepads for MT students are also a worthwhile investment.

Many drama schools will want you to wear black leotards and tights (or tight pants, vests and jockstraps if you are a male) for all dance and movement classes. Everyone panics about this initially but the shock wears off quite quickly. The idea of leotard and mirrors may give you cold sweats right now but remember you are not alone and everyone will probably feel just as uncomfortable at first. Make sure you wear in your dance shoes before you start the course or it could be painful. MT students should definitely buy capezios (*see* page 254) for jazz as well as soft jazz shoes and make sure you have the correct taps fitted on your tap shoes. Don't do a cheap job; it pays to invest as your shoes will be in constant use and you won't want to spend time and money getting new ones all the time. This does not apply to ballet shoes: buy the cheapest ones as they will wear through quickly, expensive or not. I had to get a new pair every three months or so (and they looked a real state by that time!) and I tried everything from the cheapest to the most expensive kind.

> **TIP!**
>
> Joining the student union is also worthwhile as you can get discounts at London's theatre showbiz shop Dresscircle (*see* page 279), on your Oyster card, at the cinema, theatre, etc.

Make sure you also buy some sort of recording device. MP3 players/iPods are very common now and a fantastic investment, though admittedly expensive. A good old-fashioned Dictaphone should also do the trick.

Living costs

As a student in London, at the time of writing at the very least you will need £8,000 per annum (£12,000 is better) to survive and be able to pay for the basics (travel, rent, bills, food, and so on). For any extras like clothes, drama school related reading material, dancewear, outings to the pub, theatre tickets, you will need to allow extra. I personally think that right now you need about £1,000 per month to be able to live as a student in London without going into debt. This sum includes a double bedroom in a house/flat share with three or four others. If you share with more people, live in zone 5/6, are happy with a box room and OK with giving your social/night life a miss or enjoying it much less frequently, then you can get away with lower costs. Outside London costs may be a lot cheaper. Save money by taking advantage of discounts on food at supermarkets and buy fresh fruit and vegetables from market stalls. Consider ways of increasing your income (see page 55). Keep a record of how much you spend, even if it's just pencil scribbles in a notebook, and check your balance regularly online, through phonebank or at the cashpoint.

Further tips
On the MT courses many students tend to go to the gym on top of college hours. You don't have to do this but it seems to be fashionable. How these people all afford it, I don't know, but some gyms do two for one, student and couple offers, etc.

Never leave anything lying around at college. Sadly, a lot of stealing goes on because often people don't have the money to buy their own stuff (worn-through ballet shoes are tolerated but only to a degree because after a while you really cannot dance in them anymore). I must have had five sweaters, several pairs of shoes and various other items stolen during my training.

Definitely keep up physical exercise, dance and some sort of vocal training the summer before you start training. Don't let it all go and be totally lax when you begin the term. If you are already used to regular exercise it won't be so tough. Also, you won't look so out of shape in dance class compared to everyone else.

See shows, plays and read books. Get yourself in the right frame of mind for full-time training. This isn't like school where you have a summer vacation, don't think about it till the morning of your first day and then slowly get back into it. Training never stops and should be continuous although of course everyone has two weeks or so summer break when they should wipe all concerns from their mind.

Remember to register with a local GP in your new area unless you live so close to home that you can use the same one. One of my housemates caught a terrible stomach bug and suffered in his room for days on end – he couldn't get an appointment with an NHS doctor as he hadn't already registered with one. Remember to find a dentist and optician too.

What should I expect when starting drama school?
Expect to feel very tired, emotionally and physically, for the first two months or so. The intense, sudden physical and emotional regime takes a bit of getting used to.

Expect that many people will go out to the pub every night, enjoy too much booze, get to bed far too late and face the music in the morning! This will calm down later when they usually stop as soon as they realise the course and the tutors mean business and they need to focus to survive.

Don't complain about the work load or physical strain. Just get on with it! Unless you have injured yourself, of course, in which case you should see your head of dance or head of movement.

Drama school is not like university where you can relax in bed with a lie-in after partying hard the night before. Expect very long hours, few breaks, a tight regime with serious deadlines and consequences, but also an enormous amount of possibilities, very inspiring people and the opportunity to be amazingly creative.

Expect to feel that many things don't make sense and some tutors and classes/exercises are confusing. Don't worry, it will all fall into place later. Many of these things take time to digest. Just trust it for now and go with the flow.

Go for it from day one! The initial week or so people have some time to settle in but your training starts from day one and so does the marking or rather, the observations of the tutors.

TIP!

> Whatever you do, don't be afraid to make mistakes, just go for it, be energetic and daring. Try and get on with people in your group or at least respect them. Above all, have a good time and don't be intimidated by anyone. You have as much right to be there as the next person.

Don't be scared of your tutors. I know some may seem intimidating and egos are always flying around but remember that you are *paying* them to do a job. You're not doing them a favour by attending their classes. They are the ones doing you a service.

Many colleges expect you to sign in a few minutes before the beginning of your first class of the day. If you are not signed in on time, you won't be allowed to attend *any* classes that day. All the colleges are extremely strict about this. If you miss a vital class that way, it will be entirely your fault and not the secretary's for not letting you in. It's quite common to see drama school admin staff being bribed with everything from chocolate to massages to give terrified students the chance to sign in, even after arriving late.

> **TIP!**
>
> Most of the time, such bribing does not work. Believe me, I tried!

Absence is usually heavily looked down upon. Even with a cold, a fever, or stomach flu, most people keep going. Being ill is usually not an excuse for non-attendance unless you break your foot or something equally inhibiting. Most teachers consider their classes far too important to be missed due to something as 'petty' as a chest infection. Seriously, try not to be absent. If you really feel awful, then go in, suffer silently and let everyone see how awful you feel and if the teacher sees fit, they will send you home. Even though it sounds unhealthy and spreads illness, this is not an uncommon attitude and you will be respected for trying. I remember coming in with a particularly bad case of the flu with a high temperature. That day I took part in the 'quieter' lessons and was told to lie on the floor and watch at the side during movement class. Schools have a notice board where everyone's absence and the reason why is listed for everyone else to see. At some colleges, if you miss more than three full days a term you might be called into the office of your head of course to explain yourself and could be given a warning.

Don't panic! No-one's out to get you. As long as they see you doing your best and working hard then people will be supportive. If there is one available, make use of the college counsellor, who is confidential. It's OK to go and see him/her; the large majority of students make use of this service at least once during their time training. Drama school can be tough as it opens up many personal issues so don't be afraid to confront them. And don't let anyone bully you either. Challenge anyone who seems to have issues with you.

Be sociable. Go out with people after college. Don't hide in your room or spend your entire time with your head stuck in a book, taking notes about what you learned from class. There's a definite time and use in keeping a training diary but also a time for socialising with your fellow students.

Working part-time while at drama school

This is a hard call. I remember some of my fellow students having to beg tutors to leave rehearsals early so they could make it to their temp job in time. On top of the many, intensive training hours, holding down a regular part-time job can feel like an impossible burden. But you are not alone. About half of all drama school students take on extra work at some point while attending drama school. For those attending three-year courses the first year seems to be the easiest for this as the hours are not quite as long as in the second year. In the third year hours are a lot more scattered due to rehearsals, and so on and it can be difficult to stick to a job with set hours. Most students I have met worked as part-time ushers or in a supermarket or other big department store, usually on evening and weekend shifts. There are various other jobs you can do, like teaching or tutoring, giving music instrument lessons, etc.

> **TIP!**
>
> Some drama schools pay students to spend time with and show around applicants on audition days or to accompany people on open days – these are often weekends so don't clash with classes. And some also pay first years if they usher the third-year shows.

Your time at drama school: tips and advice

★ Don't let anyone make you feel as if you shouldn't be there. You were offered a place so the school believes in your talent and potential. You have as much right as the next person for attention and tuition.

★ If you are uncomfortable with your singing teacher, talk to your head of course about it. Assess why you are having problems relating to the teaching methods of that person. If you feel uncomfortable, are not progressing or have other viable reasons to change, you have the right to ask for a different singing teacher at your school.

★ Think ahead, be disciplined and get organised. Put together items such as photos, CVs, and so on in plenty of time. Consider your audition material and work on this from day one. Don't waste an entire term at the pub! Make use of facilities like the radio and recording room, use dance studios for extra practice if you think you need it. Use the library – it's free. Too few people make use of the large sheet music selections there and the opportunity to borrow plays.

★ Don't be afraid to ask questions. If you are having trouble fitting in or generally with the course, talk to someone about it. It's your right.

★ Be pleasant and cordial but don't worry about what other people are doing. They have their challenges and you have yours. Everyone has different things they need to work on at drama school.

★ Showcase – make sure you choose your showcase scene partner(s) with plenty of time to rehearse. If you have a favourite person you would like to work with, make sure you secure that partnership well in advance. For three-year students I would advise mentally choosing a partner (or partners) and having a selection of relevant showcase material at the end of your second year. The third year will fly by! I ended up having to do a monologue at my showcase because there was an uneven number in my year and there was no one left to partner me.

★ Don't worry if agents don't approach you straight after a performance of your showcase or other show. Most will phone you from their office at a later date or after they have seen you perform in several productions. It's common for drama school students to race out to the foyer after one of their performances to check how many CVs/photos were taken. How many people picked up your CV is irrelevant, however – all you need is that one agent/casting person to believe in you.

TIP!

> It's not always the lead performer in a show who piques the casting directors' or agents' interest. I have known chorus members dancing in the background or playing small speaking roles receive interest from agents or casting people after they have seen their performance. Don't think you are not being observed if you don't have the lead.

★ Whenever you're given the opportunity to work with an outside director, attend a master class or ask for advice from a casting director and others, make sure you know who they are. Research their credits and background, so you come across as knowledgeable. Some of them may even test you on the spot and you'll look foolish if you don't have the right answers. How can you fully take advantage of such an opportunity if you know nothing about someone's background?

Professional work while you train

Most schools will have policies on how to deal with this matter and many of them do not encourage professional outside engagements during your training. It's possible to work during the holidays in productions and I know of several cases during my own training where this was allowed. However, make sure you check with the school first before signing any contracts.

Professional auditions while training at drama school

Most schools won't allow you to audition professionally until you are in your final training year/term, when you are permitted and encouraged to attend open calls for experience and to write off to casting directors to be seen.

Leaving drama school early to start professional work

There are cases where students are successful during their final year/term auditions and are made an offer of work while still training. This is quite a rare occurrence but it does happen. It's totally up to you whether you take up the offer or complete your training. Most schools recommend you do not leave before your showcase and stress the importance of completing at least half of your final year/term. If you do leave early, schools can use your first professional job as your final performance to grade you (instead of a final year/term show or the showcase) so you can still be awarded your degree/diploma/MA. Some schools will even fly out to foreign countries for this procedure, should the job take place abroad.

Writing to casting directors and agents while at drama school

There's no point in writing to anyone until you can issue an invitation to a professional public performance. Usually, the entire cast of your production will collectively write off submissions to agents and casting directors. These submissions consist of a covering letter from the group as well as a photocopied A4 sheet of paper with mini versions of everyone's photo with their name below. For the showcase, your publicity department (or similar) usually send out invitations to industry professionals of all kinds including a booklet with names, photos and CVs of all the graduates in your year. Generally, while at drama school I would not worry about writing to individual agents as long as you are doing a group cast mail out for each production (this can be far more effective). In terms of casting directors, write only in response to advertisements you see in PCR (*Production Casting Report*), and so on, and only once you have started your third year or final term, if doing a one-year course.

What next after graduation?

Just after graduating from drama school was one of the toughest times of my life. Going from the extreme adrenaline and stress of a showcase and/or final year shows, not to mention at least a year of intensive training and long hours to nothing to do is very strange. I remember sitting in my bedroom after the last night of my final year show and literally saying out loud, 'What do I do next?' I felt very empty and lost – although I had found an agent, I had no job to go to. Very few people leave drama school and go straight into a job. It can happen but usually about 5–10 per cent of the year, if that, leave their training early for work or have work immediately when they have finished. The Actors Centre offers an anual bursary of £2,000 for recent drama school graduates who have completed a two- or three-year full-time NCDT/CDS accredited course. To apply and for more information, go to www.actors centre.co.uk/alanbatesbursary.htm.

'If opportunity doesn't knock, build a door.' – *Milton Berle*

First step

Get a (temporary) job. This is where previous work experience or a qualification comes in useful (*see also* pages 122–129). You'll need to find a way not only to pay your rent and bills but also the cost of singing/dance lessons, workshops, etc. to keep yourself in shape between jobs and on the ball mentally and physically for auditions.

> **TIP!**
>
> The main reason why many people quit this business or move back home is because they can't afford it, particularly the cost of living in or around London.

I didn't get an agent from the showcase, is my career over?

Not in the least! Remember drama school was the basic stepping stone and you are now at the beginning of a long road. The number of people who sign with an agent after completing their training varies hugely from year to school. In my year everyone except about two students found representation, in other years it was a lot less, while in other schools only a few people found representation. This really depends on all kinds of things and there are no set rules. What's important to keep in mind, however, is the fact that not all agent-client relationships established after training work out. A lot of people get an agent from their showcase but leave them again as things didn't work out and consequently they do not find alternative representation as quickly. You might not have had any interest from an agent who saw you perform at drama school, but you may get an agent, say six months or even a year or two later, and stay with them for life. After all, not all agents are good ones. Personally, I believe only a few agents in the UK really know what they are doing and have the contacts claimed by others. There are no rules in this business.

How can I attract an agent if they weren't interested in my performance at my drama school showcase/shows?

Writing to them is one way. Send your CV, photo and demo CD/show reel/voice-over CD to those you already know accept applications and suit your particular talents. I suggest recording as many drama school performances as you are allowed to (and that you feel are worth recording) as they can then be edited and turned into a show reel. If it looks professional and they are interested in your initial photo, agents will look at and listen to what is sent them. Agents who did not attend your showcase/performances at drama school can be reached this way. Your school should have a record of which agents attend their showcases and public shows.

TIP!

Get a list from the marketing department and write to agents who did *not* attend any of your performances. The others will have taken note of you and/or your details and contact you, should they be interested. Remember the more detail you send about yourself, the easier it is for an agent to observe and assess your talent and style. Also, try and include an invitation to a performance of yours (see below). Check out *The Actors Yearbook* for details on how specific agents prefer to be contacted, what to send off and what they are looking for – a very helpful section on this subject is included. Also *Contacts* (most schools will have a copy in their library). Read on to view examples of covering letters and how to put together a professional application.

Perform, act, create

This is not just to continue your development as a performer but also a way to network (many jobs are cast by the 'who do you know who could play this part?' method). Also, to make contacts and to attract agents without the usual writing-off method – other members of your cast may ask their agents to attend, giving you a chance to be seen by them too and to network. Try fringe, workshops, student films, whatever comes your way. Most of this will be unpaid, so assess whether or not it is worth your while to commit to it. Consider the following:

★ Where will the performances be held?

★ Will the standard be high enough for me to invite potential agents?

★ Do I get on with the director?

★ Will it be reviewed?

★ What is the standard of my co-performers?

★ Do I have a decent part(s)?

★ Is the play/musical/writing good?

★ How much pay will I lose out on by committing? Can I afford it?

★ What else is involved and am I just performing or also painting scenery, washing costumes, etc?

How much work you do for free is up to you but it should not form the basis of a CV. In general I am not a fan of the idea that an actor should not be paid like anyone else who does a job. However, there's so much competition out there now that people are begging to do *any* kind of work even for free, just so they can put something on their CV. If you say no, then there will be 50 others queuing behind you, happy to take the work in your place. Realistically, at some point almost every performer has to do some free work. Sadly, it's almost become common practice. The Actors Centre in London (*see* page 281) offers workshops culminating in public performances in which you can take part, but they are expensive. It may be complicated to combine this with your temp job but it's very common for actors to do both – perform and work during the day (or night) to pay for it. This can be exhausting but it's what people do. Even established performers work for free occasionally just to keep their foot in the door.

A little while back, I was given the opportunity to perform in a reading of a musical at the Sadlers Wells Theatre in London. Since it was unpaid, I had to find some way of keeping my finances running and fitting all this around rehearsals and performances. I decided take the bull by the horns and ask my office temp job at the time whether I could have flexible hours. Considering I was temping at an investment bank, I was sure they would say I was crazy as being present for long hours on end is vital to the job. Miraculously, they sympathised with my dilemma. The deal: Office job 7.30–10.30am, rehearsing 11.00am–4.00pm, then back to the office job for 5.00–9.00pm. For the next two weeks, all I did was to rehearse, work, cram some food in between and sleep. I felt a bit like Robin Williams' character in the film *Mrs Doubtfire*, walking in and out of completely different environments requiring opposite personas. It takes some time to zone back into the atmosphere of a trading floor when you've just rehearsed a song and dance number for four hours! Apart from singing (by accident) in the midst of a group of very puzzled looking chairmen in a lift one afternoon and turning up to rehearsal in my office suit twice as I had forgotten to get changed, I managed this masquerade quite well – for a while. One day, my body simply gave up and I got a very bad case of flu. I had no choice but to call in sick for rehearsals, quit my office temp job and recover, grumbling in bed for the next week with a high temperature. Luckily, I was well enough for opening night but by that time I had passed my bug round to most of the cast, who in turn passed it on to their friends and acquaintances within the industry. Rumour has it that my bug even made it all the way to Judi Dench and the Haymarket (where she was rehearsing *Hayfever* at the time) and stopped her performing the first previews. This could just be all in my imagination, though.

Writing off to casting directors and theatre companies

> **TIP!**
>
> *Don't* call and ask what they're casting.

If you do write off, avoid writing general letters. It's best to write if you know something is definitely casting. Better still, write off for a specific part for which you know you are suitable and always write to a specific person. People do get seen from writing these letters, I've seen it happen. If you really suit the part and your application is professional, people will pay attention. For help with cover letters *see also* pages 82–84 and check out *The Actor's Yearbook* for listings of rep companies and similar to write to and when it's best to do so. Some companies accept general submissions but only at specific times of year, so check their websites. Personally, I wouldn't include a stamped addressed envelope unless so stated as many casting directors keep your details for reference.

Going to opens
I know this can be a horrible waiting game but if you don't have an agent you haven't much choice and occasionally they do recall people if you show promise, talent and have the right look. I myself was once recalled from a large *Les Miserables* open.

Keep learning
Don't assume the learning part is over just because drama school has finished. You're just starting out! Continue to read, watch, go and see theatre productions of all kinds, dance and sing regularly, keep your game up. I know this can be expensive and it's a constant vicious circle to find the money somewhere to pay for all these expensive lessons but if you can do it, then do so and it will pay off. After many years, I am now able to put 'intermediate

dance' on my CV, simply by attending London's Pineapple Studio on a regular basis and this has opened up more casting doors for me. The Actors Centre has plenty of workshops of all kinds that you can attend; it also has a green room and other areas where you can meet people and network. This is also a good way to keep yourself busy if your temp job is mundane. There's nothing like a good class to look forward to while photocopying…

> **TIP!**
>
> If you invite agents to your performances, remember to offer to pay for their tickets. It's also a good idea to ask other cast members if their agents will be attending as they too may see you and show interest.

Council tax and income tax
Remember you are now liable for council tax so check if you want to stay in your current home if sharing (this may be difficult if some of you are now liable while others remain students and don't want to pay, *see also* page 50). Council tax can be paid in monthly instalments or a one-off annual payment. You will get a discount if you are living with students or living alone.

For advice on registering as self-employed and paying income tax, *see also* pages 152–160.

The Practicalities of Getting Seen for Work

★

'I don't make mistakes, I have unintentional improvisations.'
– Andy Darr

Castings are not always what they seem

One morning I was lounging in bed after the closing night of one of my third-year shows at drama school when a phone call suddenly interrupted my blissful daydreams. 'Hello, this is Graham from the casting office at the BBC. We saw your show last night and would like to invite you to an audition for *Holby City*.' I was not amused. It was barely 9.00am, so far too early for friends to be playing pranks. I laughed down the phone: 'Yeah right, sure.' No response and then 'Is this Jennifer Reischel?' I was taken aback by the seriousness of the tone. 'Um…yes, it is.' 'Well then, please do get your diary out and put in 12 noon for Thursday in three days time at BBC Elstree Studios. If you are interested in attending that is!' I listened in embarrassment while he rattled off the address and the names of the people I would be seeing.

On the way there I got horribly lost. All signs leading to Elstree Studios seemed to point in opposite directions. It was like Alice in Wonderland: go this way; no, go that way; this way please; no, the other direction! Out of breath, I arrived in front of the huge iron gates. The security guard barely gave me a look, so to get myself noticed I ended up having to yell my name above the chattering autograph hunters. Mr Security looked at me dubiously, but then made a quick phone call. The side gate opened and I was let in, ushered into an open-air electric type vehicle and swiftly driven to my required building. We whizzed past a playground and I caught a brief glance of Parkinson, sitting on a bench and mumbling to himself over a script. The 'car' stopped with a jerk. I was shown into a waiting area and handed a script to familiarise myself while waiting for my turn. I gazed at the pages of dialogue. Nothing made the slightest sense and I felt as if I was reading a professional medical report! I could just about make out that the nurse (my character) was flirting with the head surgeon (the other character in the scene) over a discussion of intravascular thrombosis and other terrifying terms.

Silently I practised the words, thinking that maybe I should ask for a dictionary. All the other aspiring *Holby City* nurses waiting to show off their flirting techniques through medical babble seemed to be utterly at ease, breezily reading through their papers, fanning themselves with their copy of the thrombosis discussion after a mere glance at their lines. I don't think I need to elaborate on the outcome of this audition – let's just say that from that day onwards I included a dictionary in my essential audition kit and I hope that particular screen test never resurfaces!

A year later I was asked to audition for *Footballer's Wives*: 'Lesbian tennis player, the secret girlfriend of one of the main characters, Cat Deeley look-alike, sporty, attractive, confident'. Well, I could mostly identify with that! 'The Method' has never really made much sense to me so I avoided spending the next few days hitting tennis balls against a wall just to 'get into the part'. Instead, I just let this audition happen as I was asked to prepare nothing in advance. I arrived to find a script and a comfortable waiting area. Minutes later, a black girl entered the room. She too was handed the same script and gave me a puzzled look on reading the 'Cat Deeley' description out loud! I shrugged. A little later, a Chinese girl arrived and then a redhead. They all mused over 'Cat Deeley' in puzzled silence. 'Margaret will see you now,' I was told. I heard nothing back after my audition.

A few months later I was asked back to Three Mill Lane, the then casting home of *Footballers Wives*, to read for a different character. This time I really thought I had nailed it. The breakdown sounded exactly like me. Well, except for the lesbian part (once again)! I walked into the waiting area in my Audrey Hepburn style outfit and sifted through my script with confidence. The door opened and a girl was sent out who had just been seen for the same part that I was up for. She was wearing the shortest mini skirt I have ever seen. It was almost a belt!

Once more, the waiting room filled up, with tall, leggy girls, all wearing mini skirts that Twiggy would have been proud to own back in the Sixties. Was I missing something? I read through my breakdown of the character again. 'Stylish, classically dressed, think Audrey Hepburn or Grace Kelly'. The words 'mini skirt' could not be found. I looked up only to see yet another little number walk in. Again, the audition was fine but I didn't get the part. And the lesson I've learned from all this? *Never* assume that because you look/dress exactly like the breakdown of a character that this is the look that will result in the final casting choice. Don't try to pre-empt a casting, don't try to be clever, just go in as *you*. Either they'll take to your look – or they won't.

Agents

> 'An actor returns home one night to find his wife dishevelled and in distress. Wife: "Your agent was here and tried to make love to me." Actor: "Joe was *here*? Did he leave a message?"'

When I was training, I knew absolutely nothing about agents or how to choose one. Back then *The Actors Yearbook* was not in existence. There was general gossip about which agent had apparently found work for former graduates and which famous people certain agents had on their books but generally, most people didn't have a clue what to expect. After my showcase I received calls from six agents stating their interest. Common sense told me it was probably a good idea to visit them all and gather opinions and points of view on my career. During interviews I had no real idea what to ask so I ended up letting the agents do most of the talking. I discovered opinions varied greatly with regard to what field I could – and should – work in. Finally, I called my drama school's marketing department for help. After hearing many stories about why each agent I visited was a bad choice (so and so had never got a job through them; the agent dropped certain people after a year on their books) I discovered that (a) there is no perfect agent and (b) I would have to make up my own mind when choosing an agent and go with my gut feeling.

A submission to an agent includes:

★ A covering letter (never more than a page).

★ Your CV (again, try and stick to one page).

★ A professional 25 x 20cm (10 x 8in) black and white photo head shot (not a holiday or photo booth picture or one taken by a friend).

★ A singing or voice-over demo or show reel (if you have any of these, see pages 106–116).

★ If applicable, an invitation to a production in which you are taking part.

★ A stamped addressed envelope so your details and material can be returned if the agent is not interested.

A good agent will only take you on if they have (a) met you in person at their offices and (b) are able to see you perform somewhere and/or can see a show reel or listen to a demo CD. Otherwise how can they judge your talent and skills and whether you are suitable for their books?

> **TIP!**
>
> You are more likely to get a response if you include an invitation to a performance in the vicinity of the agent's office (in London this usually means in the West End or very close by) and/or include a professional singing demo and/or show reel.

Most agents will want to go and see drama school showcases/performances, professional performances, fringe work, professionally organised showcases and similar. They rarely attend amateur performances although it does happen, especially with new agents who are just starting out. Some may audition you in their offices (more common for children's agents) but usually they will want to see more.

As you may already know, all professional UK agents are listed in *Contacts*. After receiving your copy you may well sit down on your couch to flick through only to realise there seem to be hundreds of agents to write to. Great, you might think but how on earth do I know which of them are any good, what they are like and which ones might be interested in me? What if I pick the wrong ones to write to?

How do I know which agents to contact?

Do your research first! Your best bet is to start with *The Actors Yearbook*, which includes a section on agents, details on the agency such as the number of clients, the type of clients, when it was first established and most importantly who wants to be contacted and how (mail/phone/email). Opinions on whether it's OK to phone up an agent and ask whether they are taking new submissions vary. Some agents state that they receive twenty or so phone calls a day and they may say no simply to get rid of you. Such agents prefer details by mail, some will accept emails (make sure your details are attached!). Others state that they prefer a call as they feel throwing away expensive photos is a waste of money and they can gauge potential new clients through a quick conversation and let them know whether or not to send in their details. Not all agents are listed in the yearbook but there are a good enough number to give you an idea of the situation. Other ways to find suitable agents to write to include asking around in the profession and checking out agents' websites to see their client lists (do they have anyone like you already on their books?); also to research agencies' backgrounds. There's no point in getting in touch with every single agent in *Contacts* as not all of them will be relevant to what you are looking for in a representation.

TIP!
An entry in *Contacts* does not mean they're any good as an agent! *Contacts* is a directory not a list of recommended agents. If an agent doesn't have a website it doesn't necessarily mean they're no good. Some very established agents don't feel the need for a website and run their business very successfully without one.

So how do I know if an agent is any good?

The agent-client relationship is a delicate one but the most important thing that actors often don't realise is that *they* are employing the agent and not vice versa. Granted, agents have the upper hand with a huge pool of talent from which to choose and make offers but ultimately the actor decides whether to take on or decline representation. You trust someone with your career and pay a percentage of your earnings in return for their services. It's like hiring a lawyer or an accountant. Choose carefully, ask questions and research the background of agencies. Don't fall into the easy trap of accepting an offer of representation simply to have an agent because for most actors getting an agent seems to be the equivalent of finding the Holy Grail. It's important to find someone willing to put in the work for you however well known you – or they – may be. An agent is no use to you if they sign you up then never think of you again. This can happen when most of their other clients are working ('keeping them in the green') so they don't have to invest effort in out-of-work clients. In the long run, you need someone who believes in you and your talent. This is very difficult to assess, especially when you are just starting out. Below are a few tips for finding a respectable agent for screen/stage acting, singing and dance work (not extra work):

★ They *won't* ask for upfront fees (including annual fees) for any other directories or web pages. For further details, including legal advice on this issue, visit the Equity website.

★ They *won't* expect you to use their photographer, their show reel/demo tape/voice-over facilities as part of any deal to take you on their books.

★ They *will* work in an actual office where they will meet you (not just work from a website or a PO Box).

★ They *will* have access to *Spotlight* and do all castings through this. They'll also read PCR, *The Stage* and all other related publications regularly.

★ They *will* come and see you in shows unless they are very out of the way.

★ They *will* assist you in (but won't pay for) creating a show reel, demo CD or voice-over tape.

★ They *will* take 10–20 per cent commission depending on the type of work.

★ They *will* have an excellent understanding of contracts.

★ They *won't* say that by joining their agency you are also obliged to join a drama school/class/any other sort of workshop that is 'part of their agency' and requires you to pay them money.

★ They *won't* work on a 'first come, first served' basis for any auditions or jobs. To give you an example, the conduct of whichever client responds to the agent's text first gets the audition/job is highly inappropriate.

★ They *will* have a clear focus rather than stating 'we represent actors, singers, dancers, models, presenters, magicians, etc.'

★ They *may* lend you money for reprint photos, etc. to be deducted later from your earnings (some agents will do this and others won't, it depends).

★ They *will* believe in you and they will understand that this business can take time. And they won't let you go if you haven't made them x amount of cash after a certain time. Instead they'll keep you on and submit you regardless of how many jobs you have had, unless your personal behaviour or manners have received negative comments or the chemistry between you and them is not good due to a clash of personalities, etc.

★ They *will* have strong personal contacts within the industry and will constantly aspire to keep and improve on these.

★ They *will* pay regular visits to shows and showcases.

★ They *will* dedicate an equal amount of attention to their established names as well as new clients.

★ They *will* keep their promises and not make empty ones such as 'I can definitely get you work' and they'll stay professional at all times.

★ They will *never* put you up for anything for which you are unsuitable. They'll also check with you before submitting you if they are unsure of your feelings about nude/topless work in films, homosexual parts, etc.

★ They *will* make professional excuses for you without embarrassing you if you don't want to take on a particular job or attend an audition (for example, if the job is unpaid or the agent has had bad feedback from this company before).

★ They *will* handle all aspects of communication for you. Anyone who approaches you directly should be referred to your agent.

★ They *will* be in their office Monday to Friday during normal working hours.

★ They *will* keep a record (usually a folder) of submissions and will be able to let you know the most recent jobs for which you were submitted.

★ They *will* pay you immediately (within 14 days is your legal right) for any work unless this is delayed through no fault of the agent and they will send you written confirmation through the post.

★ If necessary, they *will* recommend an accountant and/or lawyer to you.

★ If the timing is right and they know those involved well enough, they *will* try and ask for audition feedback.

★ They *will* give you a detailed description of your audition: the people involved, where it will take place, what you need to bring, etc.

★ They *will* want to speak to you after the audition to hear from you how you thought the audition went.

★ They *will* speak to you immediately you call up unless they are busy. In which case they will call you back later that day or the following one and not just let the assistant deal with you or ignore your call.

★ They will *never* shout at you or be impolite.

★ They *will* be happy for you to visit them at an arranged time and *will* listen to any concerns and answer any questions.

★ They *will* be happy to meet any parents involved.

★ They *will* see you perform in something before they take you on and possibly audition you in the office/rehearsal room, see a show reel or hear a demo CD.

★ They *will* encourage you to interview them as much as they interview you during the first meeting.

★ They *will* let you choose your own photographer and advise you with this (they'll have possible contacts in this department). Later, they'll advise which photo to pick from the contact sheet.

★ They *will* let you know when your repros have run out and they need you to order new ones for future submissions.

★ They *will strongly* recommend you are listed in *Spotlight* (the large majority of castings are now done through this service).

★ They *will* be discreet and confidential and never talk negatively about you to anyone in the industry.

★ They *will* have a clear picture of your skills (vocal range, dance expertise, musical instruments, etc.) and weaknesses, preferences, personality and your performance history so they will be able to recommend you accordingly.

★ They *will* actually know who you are when you call!

★ They *won't* have more clients on their books than they can handle (anything up to 100 people if more than one agent is involved or the agent has assistants). Big agencies such as ICM (International Creative Management) have a lot more clients but they also have separate agents to deal with them. The ratio between agent and number of clients has to be good.

★ They *won't* have similar clients on their books who may clash for work.

★ They *won't* talk negatively or divulge any gossip/personal about any of their clients to you.

★ They *will* be your sole representation for performance-related work although you may have a separate agent for modelling and/or voice-over work.

> **TIP!**
>
> Contact Equity to see if the agent you are interested in/has shown an interest in you has been blacklisted for any reason or if you are experiencing problems with your agent.

Dos and don'ts for handling your agent

Do:
★ Call/pop by the office regularly (maybe every three or four weeks or so – ring first!) just to see how things are going.

★ Have intelligent and important questions prepared when you first meet them.

★ Say you are interviewing various agents to make a decision about representation.

★ Pay for your agents' tickets when they come and see you perform.

★ Ask for help with photos, show reel, CD, etc.

★ Call your agent if you know you will be late for an audition so they can notify those involved.

★ Keep your agent up to date regarding your availability to work (let them know if you go on holiday, etc.).

★ Call your agent after the audition to talk about how it went.

★ Consult your agent before making drastic changes to your appearance (hair cuts and colourings) as this may change your casting type.

Don't:
★ Call every day.

★ Constantly ask what you have been put up for, whether there are any auditions happening, why you have not had any work.

★ Ask whether *Harry Potter* is finally auditioning.

★ Involve your agent in any personal problems unless they affect your work and/or you need serious help, are ill, etc.

★ Badmouth your agent to other people in the industry unless you have a very good reason to do so and even then it's best to keep it to yourself. You never know who may be listening and this is a small industry.

★ Change your agent just because you have not had any work for x amount of time. Check how many jobs you have been put up for, how many auditions you have actually had and in front of whom. It's not always the agent's fault if you do not have work. For example, if you have been seen for five shows and two television castings that year in front of important casting people then the agent is doing their job.

★ Reject an agent simply because they will not give you a written contract. Some do, others don't. If they don't give you a piece of paper to sign, it doesn't mean they are not professional. If you are unsure of an agent or the agent is very new, check to see if they are blacklisted on the Equity website for bad conduct (usually not paying up) before you go on their books.

What if I have several agents to choose from?
If you have a choice of agents who are interested in representing you, interview them all first then make your decision. I recommend waiting until after your showcase if you are at drama school before choosing an agent. If they are seriously interested in you, they will understand and will wait for you.

> **TIP!**
>
> Remember to inform the agents whose representation you wish to decline. A simple letter stating you have chosen a different representative and thanking them for their time and advice is usually the best way. It will pay to stay on good terms with them – you never know when you may need to change agents again and will want to return to their original offer!

Why do I pay my agent even if I found the work myself?
Your agent's job is not to get you work – that's your role. The agent's task is to give you the opportunity to be *seen* for work opportunities. He/she invests time and money daily on trying to get you seen for work, sending out your details by mail or email and making phone calls on your behalf. Once you have a job the agent negotiates the deal then sorts out your contract and if the job is a long-running one, he/she will assist you with anything that occurs during the contract. Agents do a lot of 'silent work' that we as clients never really see.

Co-operative agencies
These are agencies run by actors for actors and usually without getting paid. It's a matter of becoming a part of a group of actors that (a) either could not find representation or (b) were dissatisfied with their representation. I know some producers who will not deal with co-operative agents as they say they do not want to speak to the actors themselves and they prefer someone who is independent. Also, sometimes actors cannot be as committed to finding work for others as they can for themselves. It's a personal decision whether you find a co-operative agency you feel you can trust and you think works well for its members or whether you pursue finding an independent agent. These agencies may charge joining fees which are legitimate as you are all piling together for the admin costs as everyone works for each other.

Does it matter if I'm with a famous agent or should I choose an agent that's not so well established?
Here, the key factor is whether the agent has the contacts. Can they pick up the phone, ask to speak to Cameron Mackintosh, for example, and actually get to talk to him? Are they able to get through to the people who really matter? Do they have a good reputation with producers and casting people? Of course most new agents won't have this kind of power at first (although there are always exceptions) and so established agents are often preferred. However, famous agencies sometimes concentrate more on their well-known clients, especially if a very large agency, and may possibly not invest as much time in you as a new client. There are still some excellent well-known agents who treat all clients equally so it's best not to generalise and to find out what works for you by interviewing individual agents. Also, casting directors dislike agents who send along literally everyone on their books for a casting as it wastes time. It's much preferred that the agent reads the breakdown and submits only those clients who fully fit the brief. Although you can ask around for advice on this, at first you will have to make up your own mind and go with your gut feeling.

Leaving an agent

If you want to leave your agent, be honest about it. Let them know why. Maybe you've decided to give up the business. If you wish to find a new agent, be discreet because agents know and talk to each other.

What to ask your agent during the interview

★ Why do you want to represent me (rather than the 50 other actors appearing in my showcase)?

★ Who else do you represent (if the information is not already available on their website and this also applies to other questions below) and how many clients are on your books?

★ Do you focus on any particular field in the industry (TV, musical theatre, etc.)?

★ What kind of work do you see me doing? It's important for an agent not to limit you but also to be honest about your casting type.

★ Is my photo appropriate? Does it show me off to my best advantage?

★ Do I need to change my CV at all?

★ Should I state my real age?

★ Will I need to sign a contract and do you have a draft you could show me?

★ What is the agency's history and when was it first established?

★ What are your rates of commission?

★ How do you feel about unpaid work, TIE, etc?

An agent may think you are talented but not want to take you on at that moment as they may already have someone similar on their books or perhaps they have too many clients to look after. Don't take it personally; it's business. Thank them for their time and advice.

I have been to an interview with an agent but not heard back since

You may attend an agent interview where the agent states that they will be in touch, but then they never call. It may be that the agent has decided against taking you on for the reasons mentioned above or they may have simply forgotten due to pressure of other business. The best way to remind an agent of your presence is to send them a letter thanking them for the interview and their advice (by mail is usually best), and also to invite them to any of your upcoming performances. This is also possible if quite some time has passed. It may be that an agent sees you for interview and for various reasons he/she decides not to take you on. Six months later, though, the situation may be different and a reminder letter with an invitation to a performance of yours may be all that is needed to pique their interest again and remind them of you and your work.

> ### TIP!
>
> Once you have accepted an offer of representation, always remember to keep looking for work yourself. Representation won't solve all your problems and it's only an aid in getting you seen. Not all agents are good agents. Also, think about your personal connection with the agent you choose. It's not a matter of liking the agent as a friend but feeling you can talk freely to them about any professional and (possibly) personal issues that are relevant to your work.

Presentation: your CV and photograph

'Resume: a written exaggeration of only the good things a person has done in the past, as well as a wish list of the qualities a person would like to have.' – Bo Bennett

I remember the very first professional CV I ever sent off. I was 17 years old, by coincidence I had just discovered PCR and thought it would be rather a good idea to put myself up for a few castings. At the time I had had no professional experience so I filled my CV up with school credits and even invented some roles I had never played! I typed three pages of it, going all the way back to nursery school days when I played a little drummer boy at age three. I printed it on pink paper. I didn't know what a professional photo was, so I attached a holiday snapshot of myself in a bikini and a (bad) photocopy of one of my black and white modelling test shots. I waited for weeks for a response and funnily enough I never received a reply.

A professional performer's CV usually resembles the following layout... Make sure your name is the first thing that catches the eye. Putting it in bold at the top of the page is a good idea and fancy writing and colour are also OK if not too over the top.

Part 1 – Personal
Contact telephone (mobile), build (slim, petite, large, medium), height, eye and hair colour, email address. Your address and home phone number if you wish but these are not mandatory. Personally I do not recommend adding them for security reasons. Your agent's contact details, Spotlight Number (*see also* pages 200–201), etc. are usually safer. State if you are an Equity member. You do not have to label this section 'personal', just give the information.

Part 2 - Training
Add any official training you have had. If you have not been to drama school include voice lessons with singing teachers (give their names), drama courses, Stagecoach Theatre Arts (www.stagecoach.co.uk), summer courses, dance training at Pineapple, etc.

Part 3 - Work experience
Usually this involves professional experience. I recommend you include amateur dramatic musicals/plays under a separate heading. If you have attended a drama school include the major productions (not more than three or four) in which you performed. Give the name of the production, where it took place, the year, the director (musical director and choreographer for musicals) and the part you played. Arrange this in order starting with most recent experience first. Separate into stage (theatre and cabaret) and screen (film and TV work).

Part 4 – Skills
★ Singing range, type of voice (soprano, mezzo, alto) and your range (lower F to top C, for example).

★ Dance standard: Ballet, tap, jazz, etc. (basic, intermediate, advanced).

★ Any musical instruments and your proficiency (basic, intermediate, advanced).

★ Include grade exams for all the above if you have done singing exams, LAMDA exams, dance exams (also Latin and ballroom) or other drama exams.

★ Languages.

★ Computer skills.

★ Driving licence (only if you have a full clean one).

★ Stage combat skills (only if taken a full course), miming skills, voice-over skills (only if you have a voice-over demo).

★ Accents (only if you can really do them well and convincingly!).

★ Any other extra special skills such as juggling, baton twirling, fire eating, etc.

If you can afford it, use nice, thick paper. You can print your photo on to your CV as well as attaching it but if you do so, make sure you use really good paper and an excellent printer so the photo looks halfway decent.

I would recommend against stapling items. Use paperclips instead so your items can be separated for filing without damage. In my experience it's better to place a little sticker with your name on the back of the photo, rather than writing it on the actual shot. I advise against printing your name above your head shot but it all comes down to personal taste. I think it distracts from the photo and you can line up the photo on top of the CV under your name (as the photo is smaller than the CV) so your name is perfectly visible above the photo without anything being printed on or above the actual print.

> **TIP!**
>
> Age – you do not have to state your real age or birth date if you think it may damage your chances. Instead, include your playing age (*see also* pages 185–186).

Common CV mistakes

★ Too long. Stick to one page, especially if starting out.

★ Try not to abbreviate – spell out everyone's name in full.

★ Don't get too creative or colourful. Keep it simple! You are not a media graduate who has to display their computer graphic skills.

★ Don't fill your CV up with exam results; leave out any A level and equivalent grades – they are unimportant at this stage.

★ Avoid the words 'CV' and 'resume'.

★ Don't lie or exaggerate. You'll be found out.

★ Don't include professional acting credits gained as a child unless you think they are valid.

Your photo

'There are no rules for good photographs, there are only good photographs.' – *Ansel Adams*

During my third year at drama school I was extremely low on cash and thought it would be clever to scan the phone book for a photographer who would do my head shot on the cheap. He charged £40 for a short session outdoors under a bridge. The man I chose was not only (a) extremely dodgy and kept asking me very personal questions but (b) the photos were useless. Embarrassingly enough they were on the board outside my third-year productions (and attached to my CV) until I got an agent who told me to change my photo ('what a ridiculous excuse for a head shot!'). For some reason my drama school thought they were fine and suitable even though they looked nothing like me.

> **TIP!**
>
> Spend as much as you can afford to get the best photo you can. Work a few more hours in your part-time job to hire a decent photographer. Your photo is an important key in getting seen for castings. I know of unknown actors who have been seen for major productions such as the new Bond movie simply based on their *Spotlight* photo. So don't opt for second best: invest in your photo. This is not the time to cut costs.

Choosing a photographer

Check out any possible photographer's work first before booking a session. The best place to look is in the annual *Spotlight* books. You can view these for free at most drama schools, in your agent's offices, at local libraries or at the *Spotlight* offices in Leicester Square, London (*see also* pages 200–201). The offices are usually open from 10.00am–5.30pm, Monday to Friday. *Spotlight* also has over 50 photographer's portfolios available for you to browse through. Another way to look at a photographer's work is through their website and examples can be found in the photographers' listings in *Contacts*. You can ask a photographer for samples too. *Always* choose a professional who has experience of shooting actors, not a friend or relative who claims to be good at it. Ask how many pictures they will take. Make sure they take head shots and maybe five or so full-length, if those are what you want although they are rarely requested by casting offices. I recommend studio rather than outdoors as it tends to look a lot more professional and the lighting is usually miles better unless you choose a renowned (and very expensive) photographer. As a very rough guideline – and at the time of writing – I would say that you will have to pay about £150 in London for a decent photo session.

> **TIP!**
>
> Make sure the photographer takes 'head and shoulder' shots rather than just your face as these can often be over-lit and too close up.

During the session

★ Act naturally, don't pose. This is not a modelling session and actors' photos tend to be real life rather than glamorous. The photographer will ask you to hold a position when they need you to. Just be yourself. Try variations such as smiling with your mouth open, mouth closed, semi-profile, straight to camera, serious, etc. so you have a good variety of shots. You don't want 50 shots all looking almost the same. A good photographer should be able to get a repertoire of poses out of you without you thinking about it too much, though.

★ If female, try your hair up and down if you can – or make a definite choice beforehand, should changing styles take up too much session time. Make sure your hair is out of your face and wear glasses if you usually do so.

★ I recommend staying away from accessories unless it's something unobtrusive like ear studs.

★ Make-up: Stage make-up is not needed here. Normal going out make-up is fine but don't go without make-up or the lighting will swallow you. Guys: You can wear a theatre make-up base if you want. I would not recommend anything further than an under-eye concealer (great for both sexes).

★ Clothes: Make sure your neckline is flattering. Collars are really best for guys, while girls have more options. No patterns or big logos, though. Stay away from sleeveless and strapless; also neon colours. Go for something single-coloured if you can. I would also avoid leather or denim jackets. These are a bit too casual and often they have sloppy collars that don't photograph well.

Choosing your photo(s)

The contact sheets (usually three or four A4 sheets that are a compendium of all your photos in thumbnail version) will arrive in the post a few days after your session. You then need to pick the ones you like best. Usually the photographer has three or four included in the session price but you can always pay extra for more if you wish. These will be blown up to 25 x 20cm (10 x 8in) format for you to take a closer look and then make your final choice. Once you have picked a few images from the contact sheets, ring your photographer and give him/her the numbers of those particular photos. They will then send enlarged formats of your choices through the post.

TIP!

Try not to pick your own photos. Let professionals, such as your photographer, agent, casting people or your drama school tutor, help you. Ask anyone who sees actors' photos on a regular basis and understands their purpose. Family and friends, especially your mother, are just too close!

Looking cute is not necessarily the desired effect to sell you. Of course you have to like the photo too but we are usually our worst enemy at picking photos as we see ourselves the wrong way round in the mirror. Therefore we're often surprised and sometimes even perturbed by the initial photos. Imitations of celebrity headshots that are often glamorous and 'special' are not what you need when starting out. Special backgrounds or interesting head poses won't catch the eye of an agent or casting director: they want to see *you*, not a clever camera effect. More than anything the photo has to look like you so that when you walk into an audition the panel doesn't look surprised when you don't resemble the photo they hold in their hands.

A good idea is to choose two or three photos. Go for one serious one, one where you're smiling, maybe one that makes you look younger – or even older. I wouldn't pick more than three definitive ones though. Once you have chosen your final photo(s), you will need to have reproductions (copies) done to send out to potential employers, casting directors and agents. Never send out originals! I suggest you order about 50 at a time, at size 25 x 20cm (10 x 8in) and black and white. Traditionally, colour is not really used in the UK. For a list of companies offering this service, see *Contacts*. Prices may vary. If applying for work in America then a different set of photos is necessary (*see also* page 198).

Digital photography is becoming more popular. Often the photographer will shoot three rolls of film in an hour. After each film, you look at the photos on a computer together, say what you like/dislike and these things can be miraculously ironed out with the help of technology.

> **TIP!**
>
> *Always* use reproductions ('repros') in your submissions. Photocopying your photo is not a good option – it won't be anywhere near as good as the quality of an actual photo. Print a small replica of your photo in the top left- or right-hand corner of your CV if you wish.

Covering letters

Please note that there is no perfect cover letter and different people respond in different ways to the letters you write. Below is the vital information you need to include when writing to casting directors and agents followed by some general examples of letters.

★ Always address your letter to an actual person, never to Sir/Madam. Also not 'Dear Trevor' – always write out the person's full name and make sure you research who is responsible/in charge.

★ Make sure all spelling and grammar has been checked.

★ Unless you have amazing handwriting, the letter should be typed.

★ Include a stamped, self-addressed envelope so your details can be returned if the relevant person is not interested.

★ Avoid pleading phrases such as 'I have written to you before' or 'I really need work', 'It would be great if you replied'. Also, never be rude or pressing.

★ Don't be too casual or friendly: you are writing a business letter.

★ Make it short, definitely not more than a page. A paragraph or two is sufficient so don't ramble on.

★ Don't list all your credits; they can be viewed on your CV.

★ Do include your address and name at the top of the letter and use headed notepaper if you can and/or attractive paper. This shows you are a professional.

★ Do include an interesting personal fact about yourself such as 'I have recently played the part of Dolly Levi in a production of *Hello, Dolly!* with the NYMT'.

Here is an example of a letter to an agent:

Dear Dallas Smith,

I am writing to you regarding professional representation and would like to request a meeting.

Version 1: Having recently completed playing Barnaby in a production of *Hello, Dolly!* with the National Youth Theatre/Glasgow Amateur Theatre/City Lit School, I feel that I am now ready to embark on a career as a professional performer.

or
Version 2: Having recently completed a three-year BA degree in Musical Theatre at Arts Educational School culminating with a final performance as Mrs Lovett in the musical *Sweeney Todd*, I am particularly skilled in tap dancing and soprano singing.

or
Version 3: I am currently/will be appearing as Dolly Levi in a production of *Hello Dolly!* at the Jermyn Street Theatre from Monday, 10 January until Saturday, 15 January 2008 inclusive and invite you to a performance on a date convenient for yourself.

I have included my CV and photo/show reel/demo CD for your review and am available for interview at any time.

Yours sincerely,

(Signature)
(Plus name typed in capital letters afterwards.)

And now for an example of a letter to a casting director:

Dear Trevor Jackson,

Version 1: I am writing to you to request an audition for the part of Cosette in the West End production of *Les Miserables*.

or
Version 2: I am writing to request an audition for the West End production of *Mary Poppins*. I believe I possess the necessary performance skills to be suitable for this show as my dance is of intermediate level and I have a lyrical soprano vocal tone with range lower G to top E, belt to E.

(Add an interesting fact about yourself, recent credit, recent drama school graduation, etc.)

I have included my CV and photo/show reel/demo CD for your review and am available for interview at any time.

Yours sincerely,

(Signature)
(Plus name typed in capital letters afterwards.)

TIP!

The examples above include the basics and are not to be copied word for word! You have to find your own style and your own individual skills and facts to help you stand out. Some people think you need to add clever gimmicks to stand out. On his website, director and drama school practitioner Simon Dunmore lists a few such examples of applications he has received over the years. These gags may seem like a funny idea at the time but in reality they are often just a waste of people's time and make you look less professional.

Getting an agent/professional work if you've not been to drama school

Is it possible to get professional work without going to drama school and/or having an agent? Yes it is, although I have also spoken to people who did not attend full-time training and have found this can be a hindrance when applying to agents and professional work, especially for MT. There are always examples of people who succeed, however. Whether they are in the majority or not may be another matter but if you want to give it a go, try the following:

★ Write off to agents with a professional performance CV and photo.

★ Take part in amateur and youth theatre and invite agents to your performances.

★ Go to open auditions or apply to theatre rep companies directly. See *The Actors Yearbook* for a list and how/when to contact these. (Many announce castings on their websites so it pays to check regularly.)

★ Write to casting directors, although general submissions are not usually a good idea. It's better to apply for a specific production and/or part.

★ Take part in student films, compile a show reel and send it off to agents.

★ Make a demo CD (*see also* pages 106–112) and send it off with cover letter, CV and photo.

★ Arrange your own showcase consisting of scenes, songs and speeches with other performers in your position and invite agents and casting people to attend. Choose a venue situated near a majority of agents' offices. This requires a lot of organisation and you will also have to pay to rent the venue, hire a technical crew, ushers, pay for printing invitations and sending them out, as well as sometimes checking out the copyright on speeches. Make sure your showcase is as professional as possible.

TIP!

Alternatively send your submission to an organisation such as Debut Productions (www.debutproductions.co.uk), a London based theatre-company specialising in the production of actor showcases. They now arrange showcases in Manchester too. Be sure to check exactly what you are paying for and what you will receive in return.

Professional auditions: the lowdown

Where are professional auditions advertised?

About 90–95 per cent of all professional auditions are advertised out of sight from the general public. Either a casting breakdown will be sent to agents only, who can then submit their clients for appropriate parts, or auditions will take place through so-called 'in-house' casting. This means the relevant casting director contacts the agent representation of certain performers they already have in mind for a part to see if they are interested and available for the production. Casting directors also attend drama school showcases to find suitable actors. Without an agent and/or such a reputation that people actually approach *you* for work rather than vice versa, finding out about auditions is by word of mouth. Speak to friends and other industry professionals who may be kind enough to let you know if something is casting, and check certain theatre companies' websites regularly to see if you suit any of the upcoming castings. You can then apply for these in writing. Theatre companies and venues publishing castings publicly on the internet are:

Birmingham Rep: www.birmingham-rep.co.uk/core_asp/casting.asp
Derby Playhouse: www.derbyplayhouse.co.uk/casting.html
Greenwich Theatre (London): www.greenwichtheatre.org.uk/casting.html
Hull Truck Company: http://hulltruck.co.uk/website/casting.php
Pitlochry Festival Theatre: www.pitlochry.org.uk/page133.php
Royal Exchange Manchester: www.royalexchangecasting.co.uk/index2.html
Steven Joseph Theatre (Scarborough): www.sjt.uk.com/vacancies.asp

Other places where some open calls and other auditions are sometimes advertised for everyone to view and apply for are *PCR*, *The Stage* (newspaper and on their website), *Castweb*, *Castnet* and *Castingcallpro* (see below for more details on these services). However, these are very rarely castings for West End musicals, feature films, television, and the so-called big jobs. Instead you will find opportunities for TIE, cruise ships, music groups, student films, fringe/similar, unpaid and profit-share work as well as the occasional commercial and television/film casting. To be considered you will need to have agent representation and/or write off to casting directors and companies (as stated above).

Audition seasons

There are certain times in the business that are are popular casting seasons. These tend to be mid-January until the end of May and mid-September until the end of November. Summer months and over Christmas tend to be quieter – especially July, August and December. This does not mean that auditions never take place during those particular months – they do, just generally not as frequently as during the other months I have found.

TIP!

You should never be asked to pay to attend a professional audition. In addition, there should be no need to call a premium phone number or text your number to get seen or receive information on a casting. Exceptions: The new reality TV productions, more recently *Grease*, *Joseph* and *The Sound of Music*. If in doubt about the nature of a production or audition, always contact Equity for advice.

What actually happens at a professional audition?

'Theatre is life, film is art, television is furniture.'
– *Author unknown*

Musical theatre: West End and tours

Musical theatre productions can incorporate up to 10 or 12 rounds of auditions, especially for new shows like *Wicked* or *Lord of the Rings*. The average number of audition rounds for a West End or tour audition when replacing casts such as *Les Miserables*, *Phantom*, etc. is usually three or, more often than not, four.

Private dance auditions

Depending on the show, you will either sing or dance first. For shows such as *Cats*, *Saturday Night Fever*, *Anything Goes*, dancing is often first. Whether dancing is first, second or third, the procedure is always the same: this is a general outline. Though variations are always possible, the description below has been accurate for 99 per cent of my MT auditions.

A dance audition involves you turning up with the required shoes (jazz, ballet, tap, character or all, depending on what they ask you to bring), learning a routine (often from the show) and then presenting it to a panel. The routine will usually be about one minute long, maybe shorter. You can also be taught several routines – one tap, one jazz, and so on – depending on the amount of dance in the show. While learning the routine, the panel is often already in the room and will watch how you cope. On many occasions, there will be about 30 people or so learning the routine on either a stage or in a dance studio/room and the person teaching you is often the choreographer or dance captain of the show. Usually they will switch people at the back to the front (and vice versa) so everyone gets a chance to see the routine clearly.

Full dance shows usually give you about 10–15 minutes to learn a routine. In shows where dance is secondary and the people being seen are not primarily dancers this time frame can be longer, up to half an hour in some cases.

TIP!

There are usually *no* warm-ups before the dance audition and you are expected to warm up yourself.

Once time learning the routine is up, you will be asked to present it in front of the panel and to perform it. All this without the person who taught you dancing with you, meaning you have to know what you are doing as there is no one to watch. If you are lucky, you may have a mirror in front of you, which helps. Usually groups of 4 present (the panel chooses which group you are in and where you stand) and sometimes pairs. Dress varies from jazz pants to leotards and tights, although they ask for figure-hugging clothes rather than loose so they can see your shape – make sure your hair is out of your face, too.

For some shows (like the recent West End production of *My Fair Lady*) there will be two dance auditions, one for the 'singers and actors' and the other for the 'dancers' of the show. The singer/actor audition will be a simplified version of the dancers' routine. Sometimes one knows in advance that there are two dance streams, sometimes one doesn't. Sometimes they tell you immediately who they would like to stay for the next round from the group and sometimes they don't. Sometimes they may also ask you to improvise – like dancing to nightclub music (*Mamma Mia*).

At dance auditions for dancers in musicals, often many people already know the routine for the well-known musicals such as *Chicago*, etc., as they are taught the major ones while training at dance-college. During open dance auditions the rooms are usually very crowded and the procedure happens as above. However they are generally much more rushed and also the crowds can be much larger, with up to 100 people dancing at the same time in one room.

Private singing auditions
Usually you will be asked to prepare two contrasting songs in the style of the show, sometimes just one song.

> **TIP!**
>
> *Never* sing from the show for which you are auditioning unless asked to do so (typical in the USA) or sent music to learn. UK casting people prefer your own choice of song for the first round. That way they can judge your creativity, see what you have to offer in terms of acting and singing and how you might fit into the show.

The panel may ask for two songs initially but often you end up singing only one song (usually of your choice) due to lack of time. The song should be no longer than two or three minutes and should show your singing range and a character. Before starting your audition, you briefly explain your music to the pianist. Mention any repeats, change of key signature, anything they need to know to make their (and your) life easier. Once you have completed your song(s) the panel will thank you for coming (hopefully) and that will be it. Very rarely do they immediately say they want to see you again or hand you music from the show to learn although it does happen sometimes. Some performers who are known, have done quite a bit of work or know the casting director, musical director or director, may skip the first round and be immediately sent music to learn from the show for the part(s) for which the panel thinks they are suitable.

At the singing audition the panel may randomly and spontaneously spring the 'Do you have a monologue?' question on you. You may sometimes sing and dance on the same day but this is quite rare and more common for touring productions than West End ones. If the panel decide they like you after hearing you sing, they may ask you to do a monologue but they may not have a script ready for you to read. It's advisable to have at least three monologues of your own ready (classical, drama and a comedy) for these situations so that you can choose accordingly.

Further recalls

The first recall after your initial audition will either involve the dance (if you sang first) or singing (if you danced first), or being sent music/script from the show. You will then be asked to come back and perform the song/excerpts and read the script from the show. This time you may be given direction and be re-directed so it is good to be ready for anything.

Any other recalls after this may involve more songs from the show or other random songs, other scenes, reading with other potential cast members, being asked to do another dance audition, and so on. This varies from person to person; also from show to show. You may skip recalls and go straight to the final recall (this has happened to me). It all depends.

Auditioning in a theatre

Usually you will wait in a little waiting area just off stage until you are introduced to go on, or in the wings, meaning you can often listen to but not see the people auditioning before you. Singing auditions never happen in front of other potential candidates, but dance auditions do, as you learn the routine in a group. Unless you happen to be Elaine Paige...

Auditioning in a room

There will be a waiting area outside and people sometimes chat to each other depending on how nervous they feel and how they deal with their nerves. Beware of funny echo sounds being 'sung back to you', especially if auditioning at Pineapple. I remember doing an audition for *Footloose* there – and hearing every second line sung back at me by the room! Needless to say, I was totally put off.

> **TIP!**
>
> Be sure to tell the person organising the audition that you have arrived so they can cross you off their list or you may wait ages if no one knows you are present!

Some shows, like *Les Miserables*, have a 'final workshop day' where they spend a few hours with all the potential new cast members left from all the recalls and do a whole morning/afternoon of physical workshops: group songs, group scenes, and so on. After this final audition workshop usually half of those who attended are eliminated, while the other half are offered a contract. Other shows may not involve a dance audition at all (*Woman in White, Les Miserables* and *Phantom* unless ballet chorus). Some MT panels tape your auditions if the main casting people are abroad (foreign shows often do this). You may even be asked to prepare a song in the native language of a foreign MT audition – German is popular.

Private play auditions
You will:

★ Be sent a script from the show and asked to learn a specific part(s).

★ Be asked to prepare a monologue (or several).

★ Not be asked to prepare anything but just turn up and cold-read a script given to you there and then.

★ You may not be asked to read anything at all, simply be interviewed about your past work, the last plays you have seen, etc.

You may then be asked to read scenes other than those you prepared, do more monologues, be re-directed, asked to read with other cast members or potential cast members, be interviewed, and so on. There is no set number of rounds here really; it depends totally on the situation. You may go once and get the part immediately or else you may be recalled several times. It's not so set in stone as the MT audition.

Private film auditions

As above, the difference being that if given a script you may be filmed, often in strong close-up. Usually you will be asked to do several takes and be directed/re-directed. Do *not* play to the camera unless asked to. The interview is often not filmed although it may be filmed if they want to screen test you to see if you work on camera.

Private television auditions

Once again, as above. Many television auditions seem to favour interviews rather than anything else as a first stage (*Footballers Wives* and *Holby City* spring to mind). You will be asked if you have seen the programme and for your thoughts on it, so be prepared. It also pays off – more than play or MT auditions – to be dressed similarly to the character you are up for. Often the decision as to whether or not you are suitable is made three seconds after you enter the room. Naturalistic casting is popular. The interview is often not filmed although it can also be if, again, they want to screen test you and see if you work on camera.

Private tv/internet/commercial auditions

You can rarely ever prepare for these and usually they are at very short notice as in sometimes you get a call on the day itself. Usually you are told very little, maybe what the commercial is for, a little bit about the character, and so on. but it's mostly guesswork really. Sometimes you can literally turn up and know nothing. Come dressed as much as you can in character. If no specifications are given, dress smart-casual – jeans are usually fine. Again, 95 per cent of the time your audition will be taped.

A lot of improvisation goes on here. Sometimes you are given a script and then asked to improvise according to that, and often with props. Sometimes you literally walk in and they will say 'Pretend you're calling your friend on a mobile and she is telling you about breaking up with her boyfriend', or 'Pretend you're a washing machine and have a heavy load that is annoying you' (yes, it *can* happen!). I would say about 50 per cent of auditions are carried out alone while the other half are with other potential actors. You may switch parts within the audition or play the various parts. It can last 30 seconds or 20 minutes. They may also direct you or ask you to play scenes in different ways. I have found it's best to be spontaneous, on the ball, happy to improvise and good with quick situation changes.

> ### TIP!
> You may be given a form to fill in at the beginning where they may want your statistics (chest, waist, hips, shoe size, height, weight, etc.). It's good to be familiar with these or at least to have them noted down somewhere so you always have them to hand. Before filming starts they may very well ask you to say your name and agent to the camera and do profile shots of your face, meaning you turn your head left and right. This may also happen in TV/film auditions.

Open auditions

These usually involve a lot of waiting. It pays to turn up about two hours beforehand, especially for the big MT auditions – and still you will be left to wait quite a while. If you turn up late then very probably you will not get seen at all as the queue will be too long. Depending on the show, you will either sing or dance first. Dancing usually involves learning a quick routine from the show. Rooms are often tightly squashed and you will have little time to learn the routine. For singing, they usually want to hear sixteen bars of a song in the style of the show although it is common for them to stop you after as little as eight bars. The panel know exactly what they want and can make up their mind the moment you walk in before you have even opened your mouth to sing whether or not you are what they are looking for.

> ### TIP!
> While in the queue you will be asked to fill out a form with your personal details and once into the building, you will be asked to hand this, your CV and professional photo to one of the assistants. This gives the panel more of an indication of your past performance history and skills. Often, panels tell people immediately whether they have a recall or not and will state that they will be in touch.

Panto auditions

These are similar to the MT audition. If you are asked to dance first, this will be like the dance audition described above. Should you be asked to sing, it will also be as described above. At first auditions people are sometimes given scripts or songs from the show to sight-read. They may also ask you to improvise certain situations. Again, at panto auditions people are sometimes told on the spot whether or not they will be seen again.

How long in advance will I know about an audition?

The average is about four to seven days I have found and the longest is about three weeks. The shortest – next day or on the day itself, as can also happen for MT auditions, meaning you need to get audition songs ready in a couple of hours or have a repertoire prepared beforehand (highly recommended).

When do I hear back from an audition?

Usually if you have not been successful, you will hear nothing at all, not even a 'no'. *See also* page 4.

What do I do if the panel ignores me?

If the panel seem uninterested, are talking, sleeping, eating or on the phone during your audition, try not to worry! This does not mean they are not listening and that you are not doing well. Just keep going and pay no attention. An unresponsive panel does not mean you are a bad performer. Some panels are just generally grumpy or happen to look bored. This may have nothing to do with you personally. Here are two experiences of my own:

During my audition for the musical version of *Romeo and Juliet*, one panel member noisily ate a sandwich during my first song, and then proceeded to take a phone call, talking to his friend about an upcoming golf game throughout my second song. I thought I had blown it but I ended up being recalled.

While auditioning for a German version of *Night of the Musicals*, I encountered a particularly unwilling panel consisting of one grumpy and tired-looking elderly man. Upon entering the room he never opened his eyes or spoke once except to ask what I was going to sing. I started my rendition of 'I Don't Know How to Love Him', which I had been asked to prepare in advance. After 16 or so bars I was cut off with a wave. The pianist smiled apologetically and asked 'Mr Grumpy' whether he would like to hear another number. He was cut off with a wave, followed by a second wave out the door aimed at me. 'Mr Grumpy's' eyes were still closed. I exited in a daze.

The little book of audition contacts

It really pays off to keep a record of every production and person you audition for. As the years go by and information adds up, you *will* forget details. There's nothing so annoying as knowing a particular name or company rings a bell but you cannot remember where you have heard it before or where you have met them.

Professional auditions – how should I prepare and behave?

'The secret of success in life is for a man to be ready for his opportunity when it comes.' – Benjamin Disraeli

Most actors don't like auditioning. It may come as a surprise to you, though, that many panels are equally anxious about the process. It has happened to me several times that the person holding the audition has actually said words to the effect of 'I wish I could cast you all' and apologised for having to see us in this manner. Directors, musical directors, casting people and other professionals given the job to cast a production have a big responsibility. They are expected to discover the next great, unknown talent from seeing people for just a few minutes at a time and most importantly, to choose the best performer from the hundreds, sometimes thousands of applications they receive.

It's inevitable therefore that they may sometimes miss somebody or simply forget to see a suitable candidate. The last thing a producer wants is to realise throughout rehearsal (or worse yet when already in performance) that his/her production has been badly cast. Bad casting can cost financially as well as in reputations, and it's vital that the best person for the job is found. The only way possible is to invite potential actors who seem suitable on paper for an audition and to see what they can do. Sometimes casting directors will contact someone they know and have seen work that they believe may be suitable for a specific role. However, it is almost inevitable that this person will still have to come in for an audition, if only to meet and get the OK from the remaining production team. It's no wonder producers often go for the safe option and choose performers who have already proven themselves (and are a likeable household name), simply to make their life easier and/or secure some sort of guarantee that the production will be a success. Unknown quantities are a gamble and sometimes one they simply cannot afford.

> **TIP!**
>
> When you walk into an audition, the panel will always want you to do well. They are always on your side. Besides, it makes their life easier if you get the part!

The panel will want you to be that special person they have been looking for so they can stop their search, go home, relax and feel good that they have found you. They need an actor who connects with an audience, exudes natural confidence in their talent and skills, is secure in themselves, happy to work with other people, knows his/her strengths and weaknesses and will deliver consistently. They also want someone with a 'can-do' attitude, who is open to constructive criticism and will work hard to achieve the best result possible. Those who show no energy and come across as unsure, timid, unwilling to commit and explore, and show little dedication to a project can cost time and money not to mention emotional turmoil. The key to a successful audition is to exude the talent, skill and all those personal positive qualities that will make the panel feel like they can trust you with the job. Basically, give them the confidence to hire you. How can you achieve this? Apart from choosing great audition material that will help the panel see your potential, how can you make them feel secure that you are the best person for the job? Here are some tips:

★ Punctuality is vital. Arrive early so you can get used to the audition venue and space and don't have to rush into the audition. If you are running late, call your agent (or the people directly if you don't have one) to let them know.

★ Take some bottled water along and maybe something to keep you entertained while waiting – an iPod or a book, something related to the production is always good. If you see anything lying around in the room related to the production, pick it up and read it. Even if it's the script you already know/have learned by heart. Look interested in the production for which you are being seen – you never know who may be watching.

★ Very probably there will be others waiting with you to audition. Remember they are competing with you for the same job. Don't let them intimidate you. They may try and dissuade you from singing certain songs or doing certain audition pieces – 'What are you singing?', 'Oh, I'm already singing that'. Keep things friendly and pleasant, but don't let anyone bully you into being scared or changing your audition pieces. It has happened to me quite a few times that people have tried to put me off my song because they panicked when they found out they were doing the same one. Do have a chat though as everyone is in the same boat and probably just as nervous as you.

★ Be polite to everyone. You never know if the person you are speaking to is important. Also people usually want to hire good group members and actors willing to try and get on with everyone to a certain extent rather than someone who is a complete loner or very self-centred.

★ Make sure you wear appropriate clothing. Your outfit should be comfortable and easy to move in. Costumes are not needed (unless stated in the audition ad or your agent tells you so). For period productions a suit for a man and for a woman a long skirt, a shirt or something with a collar and buttons as well as heels are always a good idea. Find clothing appropriate to the part for which you are being seen. If the character is a rock singer, obviously don't turn up in a suit. As a female, if you are auditioning for the part of a stripper in Cy Coleman's *The Life*, for example, don't wear a flowery summer dress. Equally, don't sport a tight mini skirt if singing for Laurey in *Oklahoma!* I would generally avoid trainers unless they really do suit the casting. Usually some neutral footwear works best, I have found. Try not to go in all black if you are auditioning in a theatre as you will literally be swallowed into the blackness and all that will stick out is your head. Well, that's the way it looks to the panel sitting 15–20 rows away from the stage. Girls: do wear some make-up as bright stage lights can make your features disappear. Most importantly, dress 'nicely'. See this as a chance to show off your best features. Don't look as if you have just got out of bed and put on an old track suit that needs a wash – unless of course the part requires it. For MT auditions, always bring dancewear.

★ Be careful when using perfume or cologne. You don't want to send anyone out of the room in a sneezing fit!

★ Don't be afraid to set up your audition space once you are in the room or on the stage. If there is a chair present, but you are going to stand for your audition, ask if you can move it out of the way. Don't try to work around it; be in control of your audition.

TIP!

Grab a chair if you need one but don't rely on one being in the room. Making your speech/song dependent on a prop or piece of furniture can totally throw you.

★ It's OK to be nervous. Try to relax by getting used to your surroundings and breathing deeply. A smile also helps as it immediately engages and energises.

★ If no information for the audition is given, keep your monologue to no more than two minutes. Most directors can tell in that time if they are interested. Have several pieces prepared in case they ask to see more.

★ Definitely do not ask if you will be called back. The casting director will let you know – that you can be sure of. If you do get called back, it can be a good idea to wear the same outfit as during your first audition so they remember who you are. Clothing can act as a trigger in their minds. It's also advisable to prepare the same songs as your first audition as well as some additional ones, including material sent by the casting panel.

★ Be prepared for anything – talking like a dog or cat, imitating an old person's voice or a young person's voice, or talking with foreign accents. Often panels want to see how you deal with taking direction of any kind.

★ Be prepared to deliver your monologue or song in a different way to the one you are used to. Some panels may start to direct you in different ways to how you interpret your audition piece.

★ Remember to thank the panel before you leave – and don't forget the accompanist.

★ Prepare to wait: auditions almost always run overtime and they may want you to stick around for a call-back some time later. Don't say you need to leave to get to your temp job! If you have a part-time or day job, arrange time off in advance or quit the job altogether if it's a really fantastic part and you feel strongly about it.

★ If you are sent a script, always learn the lines or familiarise yourself with the song even if you are not told to do so specifically. If anything, it helps you feel more confident and you will look professional.

★ If there is a camera in the room then unless asked to play to the camera, always play to the person who is reading/performing the other character(s). This is who you are listening and responding to.

★ Do ask clear and simple questions if you are unsure of what you are being asked to do. However, don't ask what you should be doing ('Shall I sing my second song now?'), the panel will let you know what they require.

★ It's a good idea to always know who wrote the song you're singing and what show it's from. You want to appear as knowledgeable as possible when asked questions at your auditions.

★ Whenever possible, bring several choices for your musical audition's first song, and ask the panel to choose between them. They may ask you to pick so be ready to make an on-the-spot decision if you are asked to do so. This will help ensure that you're singing what they want to hear and it gives the people to whom you're auditioning input into your performance as well. Make sure, though, that you know *all* the songs well.

★ Remember your audition starts as soon as you walk through the front door or on to the stage. Some people are even cast on first impressions alone – even if not, those first moments can sometimes play a huge part in the casting process.

Be prepared to answer a few questions about yourself after doing your pieces. These may include:

★ What have you done recently? Answer truthfully about your work. If you have not worked for a while, don't worry. They probably won't ask you and if they do ask then it will not necessarily go against you. Discuss with your agent in advance how best to answer that question if you have been out of work for a long time.

★ What did you last see at the theatre and how would you improve it? This is a tricky one. Don't slag anyone off! The person sitting on the panel might well have had something to do with that production and may be the choreographer of the show you are up for. Try to be diplomatic, such as for *Guys and Dolls*: 'I really enjoyed it but would have preferred a reprise of *Rocking The Boat* as I liked it so much.'

★ Why did you choose this song/piece? Who wrote it? Where is it from? Have an answer ready – and *don't* look at your music to find out the composer or where the song is from.

★ Why would you be suitable for this part? Which part would you like to play? Again, be honest and mention a lead role, if you feel you are suitable but have good reasons. Choosing a part you are nothing like just because it is the main part can be fatal.

★ How is your dance? Another tricky one if you are not a good dancer – basic jazz/tap/ballet. If you cannot dance at all say, 'I can move.'

★ Can you sing? Be honest about your range as they may very well test you on the spot. Only put down notes you can hit 100 per cent every time, even under stress.

★ Have you prepared a monologue? They may ask you this at a singing audition. If you have not prepared one (although you always should, just in case) then be honest and say so. Don't try and stumble through something painfully and totally embarrass yourself. Sometimes a panel will give you 10 minutes or so to go away and think about a monologue to then come back and perform.

★ Why did you choose that speech/song? Don't worry; you haven't done anything wrong! Panels are genuinely interested in your answer either because it's so vastly different from how you seem or because they are interested in you and want to know what you are like as a person. Continuing the audition on a more personal level is usually the next step. Make sure you have an answer prepared and never say someone else chose it for you! Elaborate on why you thought this piece suits you and is suitable for that particular audition.

★ State clearly what speech you are doing or what you are singing. They will ask you what you are doing; say 'I am singing such and such from this show' or 'I am doing this character from this play'. Phrases such as 'I am going to try and sing' can seem tentative or negative. Appear confident in your choices. If the panel asks what choices you have brought along, list them.

★ When you enter the room/stage stand in the middle of the room, not too far to the back and not too close to the panel. Give them and yourself space. Approaching the panel (for handshakes, etc.) is not a good idea unless they come up to you or ask you to come to them. Stand there until they tell you what to do.

> **TIP!**
>
> Some stages/rooms may have an 'x' to mark the point where you should stand.

★ Some film auditions may be a simple interview after you have been given a briefing of the character. Be honest and answer precisely the question that was asked. Don't ramble on. At the end often you will get an opportunity to ask your own questions. Have at least one question ready so you seem open and interested in the process. Often you may be asked: 'Is there anything else I should know about you?' Think of an interesting fact or experience that may contribute to why you are suitable for the show/film/part. Having no questions prepared may make you seem uninterested and/or that you have not researched this particular casting.

★ Sometimes nerves can make you feel you have to rush into your pieces. Instead take your time starting a speech or song. Allow a few seconds to focus and *breathe*.

★ Warm up. If anything, it will help you focus.

★ Focus your speech/song on a point in the wall or auditorium directly above the panel's head and don't make eye contact with them.

★ Don't worry if you suddenly freeze or go blank. It's OK to make mistakes. Just ask if you can start again.

★ Never discuss your payment at an audition. It's your agent's job to follow up and negotiate on your behalf once they have made you an offer.

★ Try not to think about the audition once it's over. Analysing what you did/did not do won't help and will only aggravate you. What's done is done. If you don't get cast and never hear again this does *not* necessarily mean you are a bad performer or that they did not like your audition. Don't blame yourself or anyone else: just move on. I know this is easier said than done and I have been guilty of the above, but I can honestly say that it has never been helpful for me to think that way.

★ Being ill is human and nothing to be ashamed of. However, telling the panel (or anyone at the audition) that you are ill/have the flu/a cold, etc. when you walk into the audition is not necessary. The panel can tell if your singing sounds hoarse or your top notes are weak and will either (a) mention it and ask if you have a cold or are ill. You can then reply truthfully. Or (b), they will say, 'We see you are ill and we will call you/send you some music to learn for the recall when you are well again.' At my *Miss Saigon* audition a girl went in to sing for Kim and she could barely speak, her cold was so bad. She bravely got through half her song before the panel told her to go back to bed and that they would send her songs from the show for the recall in two weeks' time. If you feel too ill to attend an audition and are worried that (a) you cannot sing/speak at all or that (b) the casting people won't see you in the best light then don't go and try to reschedule. It's human to be sick once in a while and as annoying as it can be to miss an audition, if you are ill you are ill.

TIP!

The fact that you turned up at all means the panel will expect you to audition to the best of your ability without excuses.

★ Select material suitable for your playing age – make sure the song/speech fits your age and type.

★ If you are at an MT audition, don't select material written before 1900 unless you are performing a classical piece for something like *Phantom Of The Opera*.

★ Stay away from props unless advised otherwise.

★ Do your research. Find out as much about the job, production and company as you can beforehand, including storyline, characters, songs, director, what else the company have produced, and so on. Get as full a picture as possible of the audition. Directors, casting directors, fellow performers, etc. who have had successful careers will want you to know about them. You may come across as ignorant or not very professional if you don't appreciate the background of some of the best-known persons in our industry. Remember some professionals have egos and will expect you to know who they are.

★ Go to every audition you are asked to attend, even if you think you are completely unsuitable and don't understand why the production team have called you in. It doesn't matter what you think, *they* think you might be suitable. Even if you end up feeling totally out of place, you may ring a bell in their minds for another production they are looking to cast in the future. The original casting breakdown may state they are looking for a tall brunette but you might walk in as a petite redhead, only to totally blow them away! Worst case scenario: you do a good audition, they decide you are not suitable but keep you on file for reference. I have known people being called back for other jobs this way – it happens.

★ Always take along a copy of your CV and photo just in case.

★ Try not to let any personal worries or concerns affect your audition negatively. I know this can be difficult from personal experience but try to create a separation between daily life and the state of mind when you audition. This is where it pays off to arrive early so you can re-direct your focus.

> **TIP!**
>
> Make sure you are fully capable of all the skills required for that particular audition. This is where it's important to be truthful regarding your CV. For example, if it says on your CV that you are a proficient tap dancer and this is not true then you may look very foolish and make a very bad impression if you cannot show off this skill in an audition. If tap is nowhere listed on your CV but the production team ask for it in the audition then just be honest and say you are not trained in this type of dance. Ultimately it's the casting director's mistake for asking you to attend when you do not have the required skills listed on your CV. On the other hand, they may be fully aware of the fact that tap is not in your repertoire but wished to see you anyway. That's just something to keep in mind.

'It's the writer's job to make the play interesting. It is the actor's job to make the performance truthful.'
– *David Mamet*

Cold readings

'Having talent is like having blue eyes. You don't admire a man for the colour of his eyes. I admire a man for what he does with his talent.' – *Anthony Quinn*

Some productions may require you to audition in the form of a 'cold reading'. This means performing a scene while holding a script in your hand to refer to, which you will have had little or no time to prepare beforehand. Your scene partner may either be a member of the panel, or another actor who has already been cast in the production or is also auditioning. I have found cold readings to be especially popular for television auditions and new plays. On arrival at the audition, you may sometimes be given a script to look over for a few minutes before being seen by the casting panel and then asked to read. Another form of cold reading involves being presented with a script while you are already in the audition (for example, just after performing your song or monologue). You may then be given a bit of time to leave the room/stage, familiarise yourself with the text while the panel sees other actors and return 10–15 minutes later to present the scene.

Reading are a useful way of auditioning because production members get a glimpse of your acting style and they can work out whether you suit any of the parts in the production and how you take direction when asked to read in different ways, with different accents, and so on.

How can I prepare for this?
First of all, don't panic! The panel will not expect you to deliver a perfect piece, especially if you were not given any information about the work beforehand or it is a new and unknown. You are there to do a *reading*, not deliver an award winning performance.

★ The panel *won't* expect you to learn the piece by heart in just a few minutes. They are simply looking for a general inkling of how your style and personality might suit the material and character.

★ If you know you are auditioning for a specific production where the script has been published, get a copy, read it and familiarise yourself with the language and different characters.

★ Don't bury your head in the script, look up! The panel want to see your face and to see how you react as much as 'act'. If you are scared of losing your place, keep your thumb on the lines. Hold your script with one hand so the other is free to become part of your performance.

★ Practise cold readings with friends at home if this kind of auditioning worries you.

★ If you are dyslexic, do let the panel know before you read. This will not be seen as 'making an excuse', it is merely informing people why you may not be as confident at reading as others.

★ Panel members reading lines with you are *not* actors, so don't be put off if they sound monotone or generally quite 'neutral'. At this point, the panel is focusing on *you*, not how good your reading partner is.

★ Remember to project if you are in a theatre.

★ Take your time. Due to nerves, some actors tend to speed up their delivery. Think about what you are saying, listen to your reading partner and react accordingly.

★ If given a script on arrival or asked to go away and look it over, read the scene through several times and concentrate on understanding the essence of it, rather than trying to memorise specific lines. Feel free to write down notes at the side. Make character choices or choices as to your delivery. Even if they are not what the panel envisage, you will have shown your personal interpretation of that character and scene, and what you would bring to the part. Bring something to the table, anything! If they don't think your choices are suitable and want you to try something else, the panel will redirect you and ask you to try other ways of acting the scene. See it as a positive sign. If the panel were not interested in you, they would not bother to hear you try other interpretations.

★ Don't be afraid to use both your body or the audition space. Gesture if you feel so inclined, move about if you think it is appropriate. Remember that making character choices includes your physicality as much as your voice and thought process.

> **TIP!**
>
> Cold readings are also part of the audition process at some drama schools.

Alternative auditions/performance work

Fringe work

Auditions for this are advertised in *The Stage*, *PCR*, *Castweb* and *Castnet*. Fringe work is often unpaid or profit share (meaning that if there is any money left over after the venue, printing material, and so on have been paid then the profit is shared between all). It is a good way to gain experience as an actor starting out and to make contacts and be seen. *See also* pages 60–62 for more information on this subject.

Student films

These are a useful training ground and worth considering to fill out your CV when starting out or as material for a show reel. Usually they are unpaid (sometimes travel and food will be paid, though) and are advertised in *PCR*, *The Stage*, *Castnet*, *Castweb*, *Castingcallpro* and www.mandy.com. Make sure you get a copy of the film on completion. It's a good idea to offer your services to budding directors/filmmakers and similar on the equivalent courses at your drama school, I found my first student film 'job' that way. You may just stand on a corner holding a rose and miming (like I did), but everyone has to start somewhere.

The actor/musician

This term is becoming more and more popular for musical theatre and basically involves performing, acting, singing, dancing *and* playing a musical instrument all in the same production, sometimes all at the same time. An example of this type of show was the recent touring and West End production of *Mack and Mabel*. These productions have become common because (a) they had a novelty value and (b) they save money, especially when touring. Being able to play a musical instrument is a great special (and extra) skill to have and something to promote when you apply to castings.

> **TIP!**
>
> Rose Bruford drama school in Kent (*see also* page 347) offers a BA degree course for acting/musicianship.

Amateur theatre

This can be a great training ground and definitely recommended for those starting out and wishing to gather stage experience. There are some very competent amateurs out there, some of whom are equally as talented and skilled as professional performers but have chosen to remain amateurs. The difference here is not necessarily the talent but personal mindset. Amateur performers act for fun and as a hobby, while professionals make it their life choice. There is a saying: 'Amateurs rehearse until they get it right, professionals rehearse until they cannot get it wrong'. I think there's a lot of truth in this. Ultimately, an amateur has a life outside the stage without the pressure a professional career demands. (That is not to say that a lot of politics don't go on in most amateur societies.)

While professionals of course enjoy performing, they also have to deal with a lot more than just the 'acting' part, including countless auditions, rejection and running their own business. Professional performers need a certain psychological mindset to survive in the industry and deal with all that is demanded of them. Many amateurs are unable to relate to this and/or don't possess the necessary skills themselves. Visit www.amdram.com to find a group in your local area that you can join. Most require an audition.

Reality TV

This phenomenon came into play with the popularity of *Pop Idol*, which debuted on ITV 1 on 5 October 2001. It migrated into the world of theatre in 2006 with *How Do You Solve a Problem Like Maria?*, sparking the creation of *Any Dream Will Do* and *Grease Is the Word*. No prior skills or training are required for auditioning and agents are usually kept out of this process. Some reality television open auditions require or propose dressing in character for the show.

Personal Promotion

'I have no intention of uttering my last words on the stage. Room service and a couple of depraved young women will do me quite nicely for an exit.'
– Peter O'Toole

Demo singing CDs and getting them heard

You may want to record some songs for the purpose of sending them off to an agent or casting director, or you may perhaps wish to pursue a recording contract or find a manager or agent as a professional singer. I have made demo CDs for both markets and below are some of my experiences and the things I've learned.

Decide what your demo is for

Do you want to send it to potential theatrical agents as a demo of your voice for musical theatre work or are you looking to be a recording artist? There's a big difference in your choice of style and material. You may have to do two demos if you wish to do both.

Who is it for?

As a potential recording artist, why do we do a demo and what is it? A 'demo' is basically a CD that showcases your music, style and personality and convinces A&R (artists and recording) reps (basically music industry talent scouts or the casting directors of the music world) to sign you on to a contract.

As far as musical theatre goes, this is a way for agents to hear you sing without having to go to your performance or showcase and also something they can send casting directors, and so on once you are on their books.

Determine your budget

Make sure you plan exactly how much you will spend and on what. Take into consideration time spent in studio (usually paid per hour), expenses for 'cleaning up' the demo after recording it, the cost of making copies and money spent on the cover design. At the time of writing, a really decent, professional demo easily costs about £300 pounds, and probably more. Why? Read on. Many agents and music companies *only* listen to professional demos because they have too many to choose from and because if the quality is not good enough your talent/voice may be distorted. That's not to say that you have to spend thousands and thousands, which is also ridiculous, but I would plan around £300 (depending on where you live) for three or so songs.

Here are some ways to save money:

(a) Find local companies who may be willing to support you or your band if you offer to perform at their annual Christmas party for free. Anything is worth a go.

(b) Look for scholarships and grants offered by various companies and societies for aspiring musicians through the Internet or in your local library. Write to any that seem suitable.

(c) Try these online resources: www.bmi.com/bmifoundation/index.asp and www.free-4u.com/music.htm

Selecting songs

Remember, you are not picking random songs here rather you are creating a 'mini programme' for the music pros to listen to. Create a good mix of slow and fast material that shows all you can offer. A demo is typically 10 minutes long or three to four songs as a solo singer. That's it. If they then ask for more, all the better!

> **TIP!**
>
> Bands: Don't put everything your band has written/performed on your demo or you will have nothing new in reserve if a music mogul wants to hear you live.

The order is up to you but I suggest you put your strongest piece first and another strong, polished piece at the end. Forget about long intros, it's best to get straight to the point. Choose material within your range and be sure to show off your own particular, special style. Record companies get thousands of demos a day, so make yours stand out. Copying famous artists will make you seem like a tribute performer, not a unique artist in your own right. I would not attempt singing songs made famous by Aretha, Whitney, Mariah, etc. unless you are truly up to it and a professional has told you so – or you have a completely different take on the song. Most of all, be you, be individual. You can record covers or your own material, or a mixture of both. If you are recording your own material, make sure you try it out in front of an audience first to see how it is received and try to get a professional opinion on your song-writing. Only include self-composed material if you and other music professionals really think it's excellent.

Determine your musical style. Jumping from folk to rock or from opera to pop will confuse people. Stick to one style that is you. What are your influences? Who are you like, not like? What makes you stand out? 'I have a really good, strong, high voice' is not good enough, so do a lot of people. Companies look for star quality which cannot be taught but presenting as a professional rather than as an amateur is a good start.

For a musical theatre demo, record a variety: character song, a nice ballad and a good up-tempo number. They can be well known but make sure they show range and style. I would also definitely include some type of pop song (this can be from a pop musical), as many MT shows currently require that sort of singing now.

It's possible to have your sheet music transposed, sheet music tracked from a CD you have if the music is out of print or even to record your backing track in a different key if need be. See also pages 234–238 for further information. Chappells music store (www.chappellofbondstreet.co.uk) in London sells a huge selection of backing tracks that are fine for a demo recording. Note that Chappells have moved from their original Bond Street home to Soho's Wardour Street despite their web address!

Performing someone else's work

It's rare that demos are liable for copyright; you should be fine recording someone else's work for demo purposes only.

TIP!

If you are writing your own songs, you should copyright them so that other people wanting to use your songs will need to obtain your permission to reproduce them. For help with this, visit www.copyright.gov/register and the British Music Rights website: www.bmr.org/page.

Finding a studio

Ask for recommendations from schools and also other people you know. Even www.yell.co.uk might be a good idea to look; also try *Contacts*, etc.

Interview potential studios (check if they have a website you can look at first) and arrange a visit. Ask the following questions:

★ How many mics are available and what quality are they? Go to your local music shop or call Chappells music store to find out the best mics currently available or to see if the one your studio offers is any good.

★ Ask about the location of the studio: is it next to a runway or a railway station? Find out the cost per hour.

★ Find out about the splicing costs and capabilities of the studio. Splicing is basically cleaning up your demo afterwards to remove any glitches, taking certain parts from take 2, the ending from take 5, and so on so you put together one final version of all your takes per song. The studio should have the most recent computer version for splicing. Again, call a music shop or check online in forums to find out which ones are good and which are old-fashioned.

★ Ask how quickly you will have the finished product in your hands (or in the mail) after you record. Usually a week or so is fine.

★ Before you book request an estimate of the cost of the whole project in writing. Remember you get what you pay for. Studios may do £100 a day deals but then the equipment and recording facilities will also be the equivalent.

Check out The Musician's Union or the BMI website on Google for further details on finding a good studio.

The recording event

Here are some tips for the day itself:

★ Arrive early at the studio to set up and get used to the space/people.

★ Prepare as much in advance as possible to save time and money. Have your songs all typed out and highlighted where you want to emphasise so you can put them on a music stand in front of you. You may not need them but definitely have them sitting there. If anything it looks professional. Have copies for any musicians and the sound guys. Know exactly what you want to do with the song; this is not the time to experiment. Pay attention to the technical advice of the engineers, for example how close to stand to the mic, and so on or you will have to redo takes which will cost you time and money. If you are recording with a pianist or other musicians, make sure you are rehearsed to perfection. The new environment of a studio will put you all off (it's a bit like an audition) so be really well in tune before you even turn up at the studio. And the less your demo has to be spliced, the more money you save!

★ Keep a careful eye on the time (or ask someone accompanying you) so you don't exceed your budget and have scheduled exactly how long each song will take.

> **TIP!**
>
> Warm up before you get there!

Duplicating your CD

You'll need at least 30 copies depending on who your CD is going out to. People sending to potential MT agents probably mail out a lot more demos than would-be recording artists. The cheapest way to do this is with a CD burner. If you don't have one, find a friend who has one or a library who will do the job for you at a reasonable cost. Make sure you buy blank CDs of decent quality, don't go for the cheap version. Be sure to listen to each CD before you OK it to make sure there are no glitches. There are also companies who do this. Try *Contacts* or *The Stage* classifieds; www.vocalist.org.uk is also a really good place to search.

The cover of your demo

It's really important – for bands especially – to show what you are made of. Your cover should be unique and sum you up as an artist. It should show everything that's important (your name, photos, etc.) without being overdesigned. Hiring a graphic artist is a good idea but too expensive for most budding recording artists. You can design your own cover with the help of a computer programme: http://duplication.discmakers.com although a specialist computer store will be able to give you specific advice in person. The cover doesn't have to be a work of art; it just needs to show that you have made an effort to distinguish yourself from the thousands of other potential recording artists and bands already out there.

If you are an MT performer it's not as vital as you are sending in your CV and photo, which should be fine for an agent or casting director although a good demo cover can never hurt.

Sending out your demo

For MT artists this is self-explanatory as agents and casting directors are listed in *Contacts* and *The Actors Yearbook*. But for potential recording artists it's more difficult to find the appropriate person(s) to contact. Most of the big recording companies will not even open unsolicited material (material that does not have a lawyer's or manager's official stamp on the back). Some explain on their websites what to do and where to send a demo. To find a record company who may be interested in representing you, look at artists you think are similar to you, age-wise and musically, and find out who represents them. This is usually on their website or their CD cover. Sing at open mic nights and have copies of your demo ready to hand out to potentially interested people too.

> **TIP!**
>
> Sending your demo to every record company in the country does more harm than good! Target appropriately – they have to be interested in, and represent, the sort of music you create.

Make sure you know your facts about the company, their award schemes, what they offer, etc. Once you know which company you would like to send your demo to, the next task is to establish the identity of their A&R person (the talent scout for that particular company, the middle man between the artist and the record company). This is the person to send your demo to, not Simon Fuller or the chief executive! The name of the management is usually on the CD credits of artists already represented by that company or research on the internet.

The best place to look for contact details is a publication called *Musician's & Songwriters' Yearbook 2007*, which lists essential contact names and other vital information for your demo. For further information, also have a look at *Showcase International Music Book*, which includes contact details for people in all areas of the music business. Also try www.banditnewsletter.com and www.hitquarters.com. Both these pages provide a lot of useful information for the demo sender – the latter is particularly useful because it allows you to search by artist. Also check *Contacts* for listings of agents and managers specifically for singers.

The next step is to phone all the people and companies on your list, either to ask who deals with new prospects and commissions, or to confirm that the contact name, which you have already discovered, is still current. It's best to keep a written record of all this. When you send out your demo include a SAE: if you are lucky you may get your material back!

Your demo package

★ Use a padded envelope, neatly labelled (computer printed labels are always a good idea). Include sender address.

★ Include a covering letter.

★ Enclose a professional photo of yourself or the band (for musical theatre a black and white head shot).

★ Include (of course!) your demo CD, again neatly labelled with a clearly visible list of tracks.

★ Possibly include some quotes from a recent performance, newspaper reviews, etc.

★ Include brief biography (possibly listing your musical influences and with a description of your musical style). For MT include your CV (not more than one page).

★ Include details of your website if you have one.

> **TIP!**
>
> Keep a promotion page of your music on www.myspace.com and make a note of your address on your demo and other promotional material.

★ Finally, make sure you check the spelling of everything before sending it off!

People have to be intrigued by your talent and skill as well as your professionalism and knowledge of the industry. For further reading and advice, buy a book called *How to Get into the Music Industry*. It's a really worthwhile purchase and explains everything in more detail.

> **TIP!**
>
> If you are at drama school, it's well worth using the in-house recording studio (which many drama schools now offer) to create your demo. This can be a lot cheaper and the equipment may be just as good as in an independent professional studio.

Voice-over CDs

'The voice-over is a hat you put on right now as opposed to worrying about going through wardrobe and having to look a certain way. You just got to let your voice do the talking for you.' – *Blair Underwood*

Like a show reel, demo singing CD or extra photos, a voice-over demo can be a useful instrument in getting you work – if you have the talent and natural gift for this sort of work. Not everybody does. Your demo needs to be made in a professional studio with the help of a professional voice-over company, fully edited with the appropriate music and effects that show off your voice to the best of its ability and uniqueness.

If you are attending drama school, I recommend making use of the voice-over recording facilities there to create a demo for the same reasons as demo music CDs.

What kind of vocal attributes do I need to have a chance?
Most of all, you need to have either a memorable (very unique) natural voice or in some rare cases you might have a great talent for doing a lot of different, very convincing accents or impersonations of people, or singing. Regional accents as your natural accent are popular nowadays – Scottish, Scouse, and so on. So if this is your natural accent and you have a distinctive voice, there may be a market for you out there.

What kind of voice-over work is out there?
Storytelling – CD storybooks or the classics read aloud; commercials, radio and television work; radio drama; documentaries; foreign language work (if English is not your first language).

OK, so what should I include?
Include what you are *best* at and what shows your strength, a compendium of clips of your talents. Also include on your demo any professional work you have already completed in this field. But you don't need to include an example of all the above; if you are not good at one field, choose another. Usually the companies offering voice-over demo services will provide scripts. Make sure you look through and decide on material *before* the day of recording. You do not need to memorise the material but you should still have a really good knowledge of the text.

TIP!

> Only include accents on your demo if they sound absolutely 100 per cent native. Again, only include foreign languages if you are/could pass as a native.

Stick to your age group: if they want to cast someone younger or older they will do so – there are plenty of people available for clients to choose from. Don't be afraid to be yourself.

★ The length of material depends on what you are recording. No clip should be longer than a minute and a half really. You should be able to include up to 10 tracks, with the minimum being five.

★ Microphones: There's nothing to be scared of! Professionals will guide you accordingly during your recording session. The session can take up to six hours including editing. You do not have to be present during the editing process but some actors prefer to be there and to take part in the decisions.

★ The voice-over demo-company should be able to provide you with a list of all vital contacts for this type of work so you can send your demo out after you have completed the session.

What do I have to pay?
At the time of writing usually between £200 and £500 for a decent end product and about £200 if you do a lot of the groundwork yourself. Some companies offer student/graduate rates and as many acting courses offer radio as one of their modules you may be able to do a lot of work there and save yourself money later when making your actual professional demo. Make sure the final price includes everything. Items such as VAT and hidden extras like additional charges if you run over your allotted recording time (check) all bump up the bill.

TIP!

> This is another very competitive field and not an easy way to make cash on the side. You are competing with as many people as if you were going up for a regular acting job. Also be aware that here success may take time and much depends on luck and who you know.

Animation

This usually requires a demo with extreme flexibility in voices, accents and types of characters. It is the opposite of being natural and should demonstrate great age range and vocal range; the motto here is big and bold. Voice-overs for animation are different altogether so research publications specifically written for this field.

> **TIP!**
>
> A list of voice-over agents can be found in *Contacts*.

Show reels

'The most important thing in acting is honesty. If you can fake that, you've got it made.' – *George Burns*

Agents and casting people *do* look at show reels! They are worth investing in if you are looking for representation and do not have an invitation to a current performance of yours to provide. Below are some tips on creating a professional show reel:

★ It should look professional. It's worth paying someone to edit it properly. While agents will look at show reels, often they complain the quality is poor and this has put them off the applicant.

★ It must have your name and contact details as the opening frame.

★ It should be neatly labelled.

★ It should be on DVD. Most offices now have DVD players rather than videos.

★ It is a compendium of all your best bits of acting (also singing and dance if so inclined, and presenting).

★ It should show your versatility with lots of different characters and situations, energy, types of work, etc. Don't just show clips of you playing Puck in *A Midsummer Night's Dream*! Make sure you add contrasting performances.

★ Itshould show emotional range in your acting and performance. Remember this is like an audition.

★ It can involve commercials, television, film and stage clips.

★ It should be 3–5 minutes in length – no one will watch more than that! If they are interested but not sure, they will come and see you perform or ask you for an audition.

★ It should *not* show anything that does not involve you performing on the screen.

★ It *can* include student film clips if they are well done.

★ It can also include recorded drama school and amateur performances if you are starting out – again if they are of good quality. Some casting agents have mentioned that a show reel should consist of professional credits only. On the other hand I have spoken to agents who are quite happy to look at well-presented drama school or amateur performances. As with so many instances in this industry, this is subjective and there's no definite formula.

Dancers: It's up to you really which types of dance you would like to present. Some agents prefer to see versatility while others prefer seeing you perform your strongest type of dance.

Don't worry too much about the order of the clips although it's probably a good idea to have a strong opening and closing clip. It's OK if the clips look randomly put together and don't seem to make much sense – you are not applying for a job as a filmmaker.

Most drama school courses offer the opportunity to make a show reel during your final year/term. I have found these to be of varying quality and you may very possibly have to invest in a further, better quality one. You can choose a company/course (with show reel creation as part of the course) to help you. Some are listed in *Contacts*. However, there's no guarantee of the quality of the end product and you may end up paying a lot of money for something very mediocre. View samples first before you commit.

TIP!
The Actors Centre offers special classes/courses to aid making a show reel.

What will it cost? At the time of writing, usually anything between £200 and £500, depending on how much work you do yourself and how much you prepare in advance.

Life as a Professional Performer

'It is a hopeless endeavour to attract people to a theatre unless they can be first brought to believe that they will never get in.'
– Charles Dickens

Be prepared for anything

'You need to be at Goodge Street in three hours for a commercial casting for a new webcam service, just wear jeans and a nice top'. I raced to see my office manager and asked for time off, rushed home and changed into a pair of jeans. Wading through crowds that had formed a traffic jam underground due to various tube delays I finally arrived, ducking my head to enter through a tiny door that opened into a reception about the size of my loo back at home. I crammed myself on the floor with a dozen or so other girls filling out their details on forms. Thinking I had a bit of time, I sunk back into my coat and started pondering over what to buy for dinner tonight. 'OK, it's your turn. Go straight through'. It seems the girl before me had not arrived yet so I was sent in early. Trying not to trip over hundreds of wires I made it safely to the centre of the room, which was full of bright lights and several technicians. Two very terrified-looking girls were standing at the sides giving me pitiful looks. A middle-aged man with a pencil stuck behind his ear and a 'can-do' attitude threw himself into a chair marked 'producer' and proceeded to give me the lowdown.

The scenario: I was in my bedroom, leaving someone I had met the night before in a pub a sexy webcam message. 'Make it entertaining. Hey, take some clothes off if you like'. Ooookay! Halfway through I was to be interrupted by two other girls (the big-eyed hopefuls standing at the side), who would taunt me, make fun of my message and try and take the focus away from me. No script, no further directions, just improvise away. I had no time to mull over my situation and was thrown right into the swing of things with a brisk command of 'action!'. I batted my eyelids, removed my sweater, danced alluringly to the camera, rambled on about sexy evenings and tequila in trendy bars. It seemed to go on forever. Can I please just stop now? Finally I was interrupted by two accomplices waiting at the sides for their cue.

The producer scratched his brow with the stump of a pencil. 'What do you think, Marty, useful?' Marty behind the main camera looked indecisive and said nothing. I was asked to repeat the whole scenario rolling on the floor, then pretending I was eating a banana. Then I had to hit the two poor willowy creatures on their arrival in my 'bedroom' and turn into a raving lunatic. Where was all this leading? After 45 minutes of trying to copy every television beer commercial I had ever seen, the producer finally seemed to relax. 'Well done, that was excellent. We'll be in touch.' Sadly, they weren't. But it just goes to show that in this business you should be prepared for anything! Don't think too much about what you're doing when you're thrown in the deep end, just go with your instincts and don't hold back.

What's this business really like?

Without much ado, the professional performer's life can be summed up as follows:

★ It's *not* a fair industry. Although commendable, promising yourself 'I will take the most lessons, work the hardest and look the best' may still not get you anywhere. Instead the person who went to the pub all the time, chain smokes, was late for class and nearly kicked out due to poor attendance *and* failed their dance exams may be the one who gets the starring role.

★ There are no rules that you can follow or courses to guarantee success.

★ A lot of the time success is down to luck, being in the right place in the right time and – very importantly – it's who you know (and who knows you and likes you).

★ This business *is* subjective. Casting directors will take a liking to someone walking in and may forgive little mistakes if they feel a personal connection. The most competent singer and amazing dancer may walk in and do a dazzling audition but the director or producer may not like them or they may think they have the wrong look, are too fat, too thin, too tall, etc. People can be hired simply because they are 'nice' rather than talented.

★ It's about a lot more than just talent. This industry is hard work and it's about being constantly on the ball. It also involves knowing people, having persistence and good business management as well as keeping your skills fresh all the time. But most of all, it's about luck and being given a chance to show what you can do. It is also about trends. If you don't sound/look like the current fashion then you may be fabulous but no-one will care.

★ It's harder for females as more women apply for places/roles but there are more male parts generally available. Some drama schools have therefore started to take on more male than female students to balance out this ratio.

★ Fact: There are now simply too many people all competing for a very small amount of work. This results in people offering to do literally anything to get employed even if it means working for free. The industry is also overrun with aspirants pursuing this career for the wrong reasons and thinking it's an easy route to instant fame and adoration rather than with a deeper interest in and a love for acting and the industry. These people are part of the 'I want to be a star' club, who think that being a household name will solve all their problems and make them rich and happy. The media and reality TV have made it extremely fashionable to pursue a career in the arts and also give out false impressions of what the reality profession actually involves, making a successful singing or acting career seem an achievable goal for literally anyone.

Do I have to live in London?

'I'm a skilled professional actor. Whether or not I've any talent is beside the point.' – *Michael Caine*

This all depends on the individual and what your goals are. The quality of entertainment and the standard of work can be equally good or bad across the UK. In terms of musical theatre, however, London has much more to offer – unless they are touring musicals. However, these nearly always audition in and around London. It can also be stated that the majority of auditions take place in London and the South. Most casting directors are based in the South, as are most agents. Have a look at *Contacts* to check out the ratio for yourself.

If you are from Glasgow, Manchester, Ireland, and so on, it makes sense to use your regional accent and to apply for work back home requiring such accents. This especially applies to television work. Many soaps such as *Hollyoaks* and *Coronation Street* cast in the North and the regular actors of these programmes live locally to the filming locations there. You may already have a network from home that can help you find professional work there and this is of course a great bonus.

> **TIP!**
>
> Many northern-based actors have an agent with an office in London as well as one in the North.

Is it possible to have a London agent if you are not living there? In my experience, most London agents seem to take on clients based no further away than a 90-minute commuting journey from London as they want to make sure their clients will be available to attend the casting, some of which can be at very short notice. So generally, unless your London agent has offices in the South and North, this can be tricky.

Some people find it daunting to leave home and move somewhere completely different such as a big, expensive city that's far away from their friends and family. Such individuals may feel more comfortable staying in an environment familiar to them and trying to establish a career there. It's ultimately a personal choice whether you want to sacrifice being near your family and friends to try your luck in the big bad city and hit the 'big time'. You may decide you are happy doing smaller-scale, less or simply different work, living in or near your home town and close to the people you already know.

I don't think it is possible to choose a town to work in – the industry is just too competitive. Many London-based performers regularly travel to the North with touring productions and sometimes spend more time out of London. You can't say that you'll ignore any part of the country, just be happy you have work and go where the work takes you! The fact remains that most auditions and global opportunities happen in and around London, however.

Important decisions and tools

Choosing a stage name

Your stage name is an important consideration as this is how you will be known in the profession. It's up to you whether you want to keep your own name or choose something vastly different. If in doubt, run possible name(s) past your drama school tutor or agent for a second opinion. Some people change their names as they like the idea of having a different identity, because their name is difficult to pronounce/spell or simply because their name is already taken. Check with Equity if your name is still available: as a student Equity member you can also reserve your name so no one else with the same name registers while you are training.

> **TIP!**
>
> If your name has been taken, you must choose a different name. This also applies to similar sounding and similarly spelt names to avoid confusion.

Screen or stage?

In today's competitive industry, it's impossible to limit yourself to either stage or screen work. Television screen work especially is becoming rare as reality TV gets more popular. It's fine to have a preference but you need to be open to work and training in both fields. They are very different and of course most performers will be stronger in one than the other but don't limit yourself when starting out. If attending a screen acting course, make sure it also includes relevant stage training and stage performance practice opportunities to keep your options open.

Computers and the Internet

These days an actor *must* be comfortable with the basics of a computer (Word, at least) and using the Internet. At the very least you need to be able to type a letter, print it out and find the relevant address to mail it by doing a Google search or typing in a relevant link. All castings available to the public will be posted on the Internet as will most other information that you may need. Throughout this book I regularly direct you to web links and other useful online information. Right now, computers and the Internet are the future so don't ignore them. If you don't know how to use a computer and the Internet, start *now*! Your local council may provide cheap or free courses. There are also free typing software and websites where you can practice typing.

If you want to you can establish your own website but it's not really necessary unless you have reached a certain level of fame or general household recognition, especially as your details will be on the *Spotlight* website anyway (see also pages 200–201).

Income

What can I expect to earn?

The answer to this question is complex as pay varies greatly. The Equity website supplies facts and figures for Equity minimum wages. This means that if you sign a work contract following Equity rules, your wage will have to be the minimum sum set by Equity or higher. Unfortunately, since the profession has become 'open' (meaning you are no longer required to be an Equity member to work professionally) many producers now do not use Equity contracts and therefore can often get away with paying below Equity's minimum wage. Further examples of jobs paid below Equity minimum are TIE, fringe, student films and any kind of profit-sharing productions.

Equity wage figures for opera singers and ballet dancers, singers for commercials, radio, TV, etc and theatre can be found at www.equity. org.uk/start_theatre.htm (scroll down to the latest opera and ballet minimum rates, singers rates and minimum rates for theatre). West End work is generally higher paid than touring work or jobs outside the capital. At the time of writing, the minimum weekly wage for a performer in the West End for eight shows a week is £381.13. From this figure deduct taxes, National Insurance contributions and any agent's fees (usually 10–15 per cent of your weekly wage), which leaves you with about £250 per week if your agent's fee is 15 per cent. For commercial theatre the minimum wage is currently £300 per week; for repertory theatre it is £319 per week.

For television, film, commercials, Internet and radio work, rates vary depending on what channel or company you are working for. Again, please go to www.equity.org.uk/start_theatre.htm for further details.

How do I pay the bills when I'm not acting?

'It's one of the tragic ironies of the theatre that only one man in it can count on steady work – the night watchman.'
– *Tallulah Bankhead*

Most of the time, maintaining your standard of living is the worst part about being a performer. It really can be hard to do a job that either you cannot relate to or that is completely mindnumbing just to pay the bills. The fact is, though, that at most about 10 per cent of all Equity members are constantly employed in performance-related work. Unless you are living somewhere for free or extremely cheaply (parents, for example) and have family or a partner looking after you, the cold reality is that you will have to look for other ways to keep yourself afloat while hunting for the next acting opportunity. You may still prefer to support yourself rather than to rely on someone else anyway. How you wish to do this is down to you, but there are various jobs you can do while resting. Here are some popular examples:

★ Teaching/workshop leader, etc: Good pay, this will keep your mind ticking in performance mode. However, it may also be unreliable, with a few hours here and there unless you are employed full-time at a place such as Stagecoach (see page 181). For possible openings, try places like Stagecoach and keep a lookout in The Stage recruitment section (online or paper).

★ Waitressing/bar work: The pay is not good but you can choose your hours. It's not a good idea if you are a singer as it kills your voice (having to shout in a noisy bar/restaurant). On the plus side, you may also get exta cash in the form of tips and even free meals sometimes.

★ Ushering: At the time of writing, this pays about £5.50 per hour. It can be pretty depressing to watch others perform while you yourself are out of work. However, you can choose your hours and you are in a theatre with like-minded people. Again, search *The Stage* recruitment section regularly for openings or simply drop off your CV at all theatres in person. Sometimes having a chat with the box office or other relevant staff can be helpful.

★ Call centre work: Super boring and bad wages too but again, you can choose your hours. Try call centre work with *incoming* calls (like Ticketmaster) rather than jobs where you have to make any calls yourself (which can drive you nuts). I started off that way. It's not great but you can move on to other office work as you gain work experience. Jobs are advertised in *The Stage* and on employment agency websites. Try www.secsinthecity.co.uk and www.reed.co.uk

★ Fitness instructor (gym or pool): In comparison with some of the other jobs listed here, this pays pretty well. Often you can choose your hours (although not always and sometimes you will have to get up very early). However it keeps you fit so it's a pretty good bet and you might also be allowed use of the facilities. You need a qualification for this, though. Visit www.learndirect-advice.co.uk for more information.

★ Office work: This can pay very well indeed and temporary assignments are often available, meaning you can go from job to job (therefore it does not get too boring). You can sometimes get time off for auditions, etc. if you work well on the other days or have flexible hours. I have never had a problem anyway. The letdown: it's super boring, but hey, it's temping.

Tips for office temping
At the time of writing, in London office work pays anything from £8–£16 an

hour. Rates can be lower in other parts of the country, however. You need the following skills: PC (advanced Excel, PowerPoint plus Word, if possible), Outlook (email/diary software). Maybe Lotus Notes; Access and Bloomberg are a bonus. You also need fast typing (55wpm and above), strong organisational skills, good spelling and grammar, prioritising skills, excellent time-keeping and the ability to fit in easily and remain calm under pressure. Companies also prefer people who have had some sort of office experience before.

TIP!

Visit these websites: www.secsinthecity.co.uk and www.reed.co.uk. They will tell you the exact rates for various kinds of office work and what skills you need.

Having sent off your CV electronically, agencies will contact you if they are interested in registering you. You do not have to pay them any commission as your employer pays them a percentage.

If you are reliable and good at what you do, you will almost certainly get continuous temp work and may even be given time off for auditions. Also, you can often leave a job at short notice (one day or one week's notice), which helps. There is also the option of shift office work, night work pays very well and often taxis home are provided and you can have the days off for auditions. However, it's difficult to network this way because you can't attend any mingling sort of events or meet people, which is bad as this is just as important as auditioning. I still prefer daytime office work because you have the evenings free to work on your performing career and the offices may give you time off for auditions if you work well during the other time you are there. It's more stressful but worth it.

Whatever else, always keep your agency up to date with what you are doing and why. If you have a good rapport, call them if you have problems getting time off work for an audition. But only do this if you get on with them really well. It's usually best to sort things out with your workplace direct.

Office work agencies do not train you on computer skills: they expect you to already have them when you register for work. However some offer the opportunity to improve your skills on specialist programmes in the agency's offices, free and at any time, which is worth considering. You can start as a receptionist for lower pay and work your way up the office ladder: this is the way it usually works.

> **TIP!**
>
> Improve your office computer skills by taking Excel, Word, etc. tutorials offered for free on most Windows systems and also online: www.baycongroup.com/wlesson0.htm (you will find free basic tutorials for Word, Excel and PowerPoint, as well as other useful systems).

Handling office work and agencies

Here are some useful tips to help you get the most out of office work:

★ At the beginning, register with lots of agencies to increase your chances of work, but try to become close to and stay with one agency in the end. This makes it easier to get work and also it doesn't confuse the tax office, who may decide to put you on emergency coding if you constantly change employers, as happened to me.

★ Let your agencies know that you are primarily an actor but you need temporary work to pay the bills. Although you may disappear for an audition every now and then, it won't be for more than say half a day once every two or three weeks. Be honest. They will usually be fine about it as they know they have to be a bit flexible with temps. If you are otherwise reliable and a good temp, then they won't be too concerned.

★ Very probably the agency will not mention your being an actor to the company itself. If an audition comes through which requires a bit of time off, be honest with your employer. Ask if you can have two or so hours off (an extended lunch break is the best phrase to use) and most of the time they will be absolutely fine with it, if you have been doing your job well. Also, offer to come in early or stay late to make up the work and apologise for having to take time off. Approach them *as soon as you know*.

★ If you are working for an employer that you can see will find it hard to accept the audition, then sadly, I have to advise you to lie. Tell them you have a doctor's appointment. Stay away that day and call in sick in the morning. But don't do this unless you really feel you have to. Usually honesty is the best way to go and most of my former employers have been really accommodating and nice about it. If they refuse to let you go to the audition and it's that important to you, quit the job and go to the audition. You will always get another temp job. I have had to do that once and my agency was very understanding. Remember that you are not the only actor surviving this way.

★ Fact: Most agencies will not care about you and you need to ring them regularly to get work. They may ask what seem like stupid questions. Although there are some very good agencies about, they will only take top-quality temps for banks, insurance companies (high-profile temping), etc. so it pays to work hard when you are there, make a good impression and have the right skills, attitude and demeanour.

★ *Never* let office colleagues know you're an actor! That's unless you have a good reason to do so, or have got to know the people quite well. People will ask the same annoying questions and offer 'helpful' advice such as 'Why don't you try *Les Miserables*?' Or 'I'm sure *EastEnders* would be helpful if you ring them up'. It's best to keep acting separate from the office.

★ Yes, working in an office really can be like the TV series *The Office*! Remember it's only temporary.

★ Promotional work can be tough and it's not regular work. You only get the odd day here and there. You can far more easily earn a decent amount from a day's office work and more on a regular basis. With promotions, you keep approaching people who usually don't want to be approached. This can get exasperating and you may also have abuse thrown at you, so try and take it in your stride. Not only this, but you are out in all weathers, rain or shine. However, on a good day being out in the fresh air can be enjoyable. Despite this, it's a pretty boring job, handing out leaflets.

★ Co-hosting social events (that is, events promotion) can be more fun than regular promotional work. However you also need to be a lot more qualified and, although possible, jobs can be hard to come by.

★ Part-time work as a masseur can be a good idea. It takes time to train and build up a clientele, however, and you need to spend money on qualifications and promoting your business, as it's very competitive. *The Stage* sometimes lists advertisements from companies looking for masseurs, so watch out for those. It's best to do this kind of work as part of a health club or through a company rather than as an individual advertising your services. Think of the phone calls you might receive otherwise!

★ Voice-overs (*see also* pages 113–115): Very good money if you do get a job but there will always be plenty of competition (nearly everyone in the business has a voice-over demo). It's a very, very competitive field. Worth a try, I think, but not everyone has the voice to do voice-overs and it's also who you know. Only consider this if you have (a) a very distinctive voice and/or (b) you can do many different accents convincingly on the spot. It's a unique talent.

★ Hairdressing/beauty therapist or nail technician: Here, a qualification is needed, but the hours can be good. If you make a name for yourself, you can even visit people at home. Like restaurant and bar work, you may receive extra cash in the form of tips.

★ Modelling work: To be a fashion model it's necessary to register with an appropriate agent who should *not* charge an upfront fee of any kind, although you may be charged for the initial test shoot. Once an agency is interested in you, they will arrange a test shoot to see how you photograph in different circumstances and also to start your portfolio so they can begin sending out pictures to clients. For an approved list of model agencies including glamour, children's, part modelling, etc., visit: www.albamodel.info/

Among the best-known – and extremely competitive – agencies in the UK for fashion modelling are: Select Model Management, Models 1, Storm Models, IMG Models and Premier Model Management (check out Google). For a list of named and shamed agencies to avoid, visit: www.albamodel.info/

Of course certain attributes are required for modelling: style, grace, good posture, professionalism, patience (there are long periods of waiting), being comfortable with your body (you may be shooting in difficult conditions and semi-dressed), handling high stress levels, resilience, good health and fitness plus the ability to cope with rejection. Whatever your age, these are essential. It's also beneficial to have a genuine love and appreciation of fashion.

Certain physical attributes are necessary for fashion modelling: clear skin, healthy hair and good teeth are the basics; also strong and distinctive or unusual-looking features, but the face must still be well proportioned. The Association of Model Agents (AMA) recommends female fashion models' measurements should be around 86-61-86cm (34-24-34in) and men should have a 97–102cm (38–40in) chest and a 76–81cm (30–32in) waist. For catwalk, the measurements are usually a 81–91cm (32–36in) bust, a waist measuring 56–66cm (22–26in) and 81–91cm (32–36in) hips for girls. The minimum height for girls is usually 1.73m (5ft 8in), although I know from experience that agencies usually prefer girls to be at least 1.75m–1.78m (5ft 9in–5ft 10in) as it makes them a lot more marketable. You do find a few models at 1.7m (5ft 7in), but they are the exception. Men should be between 1.78m (5ft 10) and 1.88m (6ft 2in), although 1.83m (6ft) seems to be the perfect average.

Girls are usually between the ages of 16 and 25, but this is a broad spec. I have met models who started at 14 and 15 (very possible), some even at 13 but they were mature for their age and had strict regulations with regard to hours. Really, most female models start before they are 20 – beginning a modelling career after the age of 20/21 is very rare, but it can happen. Boys are usually 16 to 26. It's common for men to start later and not usually before the ages of 16 or 18.

For further information and advice, contact The Association of Model Agents, 122 Brompton Road, London SW3 1JD, telephone 020 7584 6466.

★ Dresser: These are the people who dress the performers in shows, mainly musicals, where there are many quick changes. Jobs are usually advertised in *The Stage* or write off to theatres or drop off your CV with the stage doorkeeper. Usually the hourly pay is pretty good and you can get 'regular' temp work if part of a long-running show.

★ Corporate acting/role play: See pages 263–264 for specific section regarding this kind of work.

★ Tour guide: This is quite a good temping option as it pays well and you can choose your hours, as well as practise your people skills. Depending on where you work, you may have to train and also register with an appropriate tour guide association. Jobs are usually listed in *The Stage*; also try the most famous sightseeing points in your area for more information and any vacancies.

★ There are many other jobs you can do to pay the bills such as dog walking, house sitting, etc. but the ones described above are simply the most common ways actors keep themselves afloat in between jobs.

> ### TIP!
>
> Contact www.turns.net – this is an agency designed for actors looking for part-time/temp work when not performing and that send out regular emails offering different types of temping work.

Touring

> 'I have been on my own all my life except during those
> touring days.' – *Cyril Cusack*

Being 'on tour' as a performer is like entering into a completely separate world from your normal life – I often felt as if I was living a different life! Depending on the type of production you are in, touring means that you see a new town/theatre every week or month, and constantly have to adjust to new surroundings. Most play and musical theatre tours tend to be UK based, some are European or even world tours but these are rare. As some tours can go on for a year or even several years, it's easy to get lost in this kind of environment and to forget about the 'real' world out there.

Personally, I have found touring to be a very heightened experience. You are surrounded by the same, small number of people every day and are often together 24/7 as you don't know anyone else in the towns you are touring and you live in the same accommodation. Normal moral boundaries are often cast away as people get lonely away from home and their loved ones and some can end up behaving very out of character. The phrase 'it doesn't count on tour' is quite a common one!

Accommodation on tour ('digs')

Performers are usually responsible for finding their own accommodation on tour (called 'digs' within the profession), although TIE tours sometimes provide shared housing of some kind. Usually you will receive what is called a 'touring allowance' (extra money for accommodation/travel/sometimes food on a weekly basis), the exception here being TIE in most cases. In general, your touring allowance won't be a large sum of money, so make sure you budget accordingly.

> **TIP!**
>
> Your contract should state which part of your weekly fee is for your work and which part is for touring accommodation/expenses.

Types of digs

Several options are available, as follows:

★ Rooms in a family home: The cheapest digs are rooms as part of a house/flat, sharing with a family or couple. On tour, I have always stayed in these and have found them an extremely pleasant way to live. Not only do you save lots of money, but you also have a sort of connection, should you want to talk to someone. You're also in a home, rather than a cold hotel or hostel. Some digs' landlords are extremely kind and will cook you food for free, drive you to the theatre/train station and/or offer to show you round the town. A lot of people are proud of their towns and want guests to make the most of their stay. This is *not* part of the landlord's usual 'job' and they're doing you a favour. Other landlords may prefer to leave you to your own devices without interaction.

Usually digs' landlords are working in the industry themselves in some shape or form, or else they are extremely interested in it. Some have been in the 'digs' business for years. Digs accommodation means a room (double or single), sometimes your own bathroom but it's usually shared with other guests or family, and sometimes breakfast and/or coffee and tea, and so on are also included in the price. Landlords may do deals and discounts if you stay for a certain amount of time. Note: This kind of accommodation does not count as bed and breakfast.

★ Bed and breakfast/hotel: This tends to be more costly. However, you are left to your own devices. It can also be more luxurious and include features such as DVD/TV/Sky, hairdryers, etc. The choice really depends on your budget and what kind of accommodation you prefer. I have seen actors pay out a lot of money for smart hotels and get bad service and dull rooms, though.

★ Private flat/house: Some performers rent a house or flat together, much as a regular house/flatshare, or even an entire flat for themselves. Prices vary but it's usually more expensive than renting a room. It could be a good solution if you don't want to spend 24 hours a day with people involved in your production and prefer some time alone. It's popular with those household names on tour, who are often unable just to rent a room in a family home as they would not be left in peace.

TIP!

Digs in London tend to be a lot more expensive than in other parts of the country. For cheap solutions to staying in London, *see also* page 145.

How and when do you pay for your digs?
Hotels, bed and breakfast and full houses/flats usually demand a deposit or

credit card number up front and you pay the rest on the day of departure. When renting a room, most digs seem to be happy to be paid on the day you leave or throughout your stay (most seem to prefer cash, but a cheque is also OK). Some landlords ask for a non-returnable deposit (usually a cheque sent to them by mail) to make sure you turn up and they won't lose out financially if you decide to cancel your room. They may also want to see your passport so make sure you take it with you and keep it up to date. Make sure you take a copy of your passport and keep it in a separate place, too.

TIP!

> Book early! Good digs are always booked out and your fellow tour members may otherwise snatch the best accommodation. Your friends and contacts in the business may also know of good places.

Choosing accommodation

When arranging digs or other places to stay, certain considerations are important:

★ Proximity: Is the accommodation close to the theatre and transport links? Add about five minutes for all claimed walking distances! Remember that if it is not within walking distance you will have to pay extra for train/bus fares and may also spend time waiting for these to arrive if touring in smaller towns.

★ Parking: If you are touring with a car, is there any on- or off-street parking? Will you have to pay for this and are there any parking restrictions?

★ What type of equipment is provided? TV/DVD/stereo? TV in your room is not the norm, so it pays to ask. In some houses you may be allowed to use the family equipment located in the lounge or a separate TV room.

★ Pets: Are there any pets? Remember, pets can be noisy or out of control and may cause allergic reactions in some people. Check how clean the house is, too. I have usually enjoyed living with pets as they provide company. It's a personal choice, though.

★ Will you get your own bathroom and if so, does it have a bath and/or shower? If you are sharing, how many people will you be sharing with? Power showers are rarely found on tour so don't expect the highest quality bathrooms. I have been pleasantly surprised sometimes, though.

★ Some digs have a piano that you may be allowed to use. Ask if they mind you rehearsing some music (useful if touring in a musical). Some landlords enjoy this, others won't!

★ House rules: Ask if there are any specific house rules, such as when you need to be back home. In good digs you should be free to go about as you please and be provided with a key for the house/your room.

★ Can you lock your room? Some rooms are lockable and others not. Is there a safe you can use and who has access to it?

★ Are towels and bedding provided? In general, digs provide bedding but the ratio is about 50:50 when it comes to towels. Usually they will be happy to lend you one if you ask beforehand.

★ Are you allowed to use the kitchen or washing machine? Any other parts of the house like the lounge? It's useful to have access to kitchens in particular, not only to use the fridge, but also to cook – eating out daily can become expensive. If you are not allowed to use the washing machine in your digs, ask to use the one in the theatre. Check with the wardrobe person or assistant stage manager when you may use it as they have control of the laundry room for costumes.

★ Internet: Some digs let you to use their Internet for free or a small charge. Others may only offer this once you arrive and they decide they trust you. Some may have wireless Internet and you can take your laptop along and use the connection for free.

★ Garden: Some of you may like to have a garden. It's worth asking about this as it can be great to have some outdoor space in the summer.

★ Are you allowed to have guests, overnight or otherwise, in your room? Some landlords are fine with this as long as you let them know beforehand, others are not.

★ Is it a smoking or non-smoking house? Check when you phone to book a room, even if it says on the details – sometimes mistakes can be found on lists. Some places may allow smoking in your room and/or outside only, others prefer a smoke-free home. Note that the UK government ban took effect on 1 July 2007.

★ Children: Are there any kids? Again, this may be noisy if they have a small baby or you can hear the children getting up in the mornings for school – usually at a time when you will just have fallen asleep from completing the show and partying afterwards! A house with children will suit some people, but not others.

★ Bed: Single or double? Ask if this is important to you.

★ Are there other guests in the house? Ask if you will be the only one renting a room or if there are others.

★ Some digs may not be available over the Christmas/panto season. Others may charge more during this time or for bank holidays/weekends.

★ Heating is a very important factor. Make sure heating and all bills are included in your weekly rate (usually they will be) and that your room has central heating. You don't want to catch a cold and not be able to perform!

★ Check the price of your accommodation as it may differ from your list.

★ Phone your digs about two days before you are due to arrive just to check everything is running according to plan and to confirm your stay. Let your landlord know your approximate time of arrival and make sure someone is home to let you in.

Where can I find a list of digs?
For some productions the company/stage manager will send you a list by mail (or email) of all accommodation available in the towns you are travelling to. More often than not, though, you will have to request these lists yourself from the various theatres (free of charge). Visit their websites and email them (or phone). Some may also have links to digs' lists through their websites. Please note that the accommodation provided on these lists is almost always for cast/crew on tour with a professional production only.

Other places to look are *Contacts*, which has a section of recommended tour accommodation, as does the Equity website (members-only section). Also, visit the following websites: www.showdigs.co.uk, www.theatredigz.com/ and www.castingpeople.com/digs.htm. If you are having trouble finding digs, contact your company manager or the stage manager.

What to bring on tour

After lugging around a heavy suitcase for the first three weeks, climbing up steep backstage staircases and hobbling along platforms, I discovered 'less is definitely more' on tour. You can use the theatres' washing machines so don't worry about running out of clothes. Bring clothes you feel comfortable in, that can get dirty and that you can travel in. Trainers are a definite must. Really, you will only need one smart outfit to 'meet the cast' or similar dos at the theatre or should you all be invited to a good restaurant. High heels can be in the way as you will probably do a lot of walking and prefer comfortable shoes. One pair of heels should be sufficient. Guys: a good shirt and decent pair of trousers plus smart shoes is fine. Other items to include are hairdryers, shavers, laptops (especially if wireless), pen and paper, maps, iPods (handy when travelling), a good book or two perhaps, basic first aid medication, a needle and thread, Vocalzones (www.vocalzones.com, *see also* page 247), and a torch (useful when trying to sneak in late at night!).

On some tours you may be allowed to throw your luggage 'on the wagon' (the van transporting the set and props from venue to venue) free of charge. Be aware, though, that you may not see your bag until a few hours before the first performance in the new venue, depending on when you arrive there!

Commuting

Cars are usually cheaper than trains and can get you to a venue and back long after the trains have stopped running at night, meaning you can drive home and get an extra day/half day there and also save money on accommodation. They also guarantee you a lot more independence. Sometimes people will offer you a ride in their car if you contribute to the petrol, which can be a very good way to have a sociable journey and save money on both sides. It's eco-friendly, too.

Some performers prefer to travel by train even if they own a car – they don't want the risk of getting lost. Trains are usually fast (faster than cars), comfortable and efficient (if running on time). Make sure you don't cut it too fine, though: don't pick a train that comes in two hours before your first performance is due to start! Arrive at least four or five hours early in case there are delays and so you settle into your digs beforehand. Some digs will not allow you to arrive after a certain time. Make sure you book your tickets in advance. The earlier you do this, the more money you can save. Check out schedules and prices at: www.nationalrail.co.uk or telephone 08457 48 49 50.

> **TIP!**
>
> Performers age 25 and under can buy a Young Person's Railcard and this will save you a lot of money on train travel. Make sure you have your railcard with you at all times. Cards are also available for those aged 60 and over (Senior Railcards). For further details, visit www.youngpersons-railcard.co.uk/ and www.senior-railcard.co.uk/

Flights: Usually these are paid by the producer on top of your tour allowance, but check your contract. Usually someone from the production office will ring you and ask which flights you would like to take and provide you with tickets nearer the time. Always ask the company/stage manager if in doubt.

> **TIP!**
>
> In some cases you may be allowed to go by train or ferry instead (if you have a fear of flying, for example). It's best to ask early about this.

When can I go home?

If you are performing in the show you will usually be excused when it finishes on a Saturday night and not be requested at the next theatre venue until 6.00pm on the Monday (or whichever is the first day of performance). There may be exceptions if the director wants to rehearse you before a show but usually you will at least have the Sunday off. Many performers drive back to London (or their hometown) late Saturday night after the show and drive up to their new venue around lunchtime on the Monday. If you travel by train, things can be more complicated as most trains don't run that late and you will have to leave on Sunday morning instead.

The technical crew have to stay until after the 'get out' on a Saturday night ('get out' involves taking down the set, packing all set pieces, props and costumes, taking down all the lights and packing everything into the van). 'Get outs' last at least one-and-a-half hours, but usually up to three or four, especially for musicals. The technical crew is then requested at about 9.00am on a Monday morning at the next venue for the 'get in' (the opposite of 'get out', meaning unpacking the van, putting up the set, washing and preparing all costumes, dressing rooms, and so on), which usually takes the entire day. Due to this extra amount of work, most technical crew are unable to go home in between venues if shows finish on a Saturday and they have to open at the next venue the following Monday. If you are understudying/assistant stage manager you will also have to stay for 'get ins' and 'get outs' and the stage/company manager will excuse you once you have finished all your tasks.

'Meet the cast', 'friend of the theatre' and similar official dos

Touring shows often have a 'meet the cast' or 'friends of the theatre' party that happens whenever they open in a new town. These take place in the theatre after the evening performance. 'Friends' of the particular theatre hosting your show pay monthly subscriptions for the privilege of being able to have a drink and chat to you at this specially organised occasion. Sometimes these events involve food, often provided by the 'friends', so don't complain in a loud voice about the cake – the person standing next to you may have baked it!

Most actors do not enjoy being talked about and having to be themselves at these gatherings and try and hide away somewhere in the corner. Remember these people have paid to see you and it's part of your job as a performer to sign autographs, answer basic questions and promote the show in a good light. Some fans have waited for months to speak to the actors performing their favourite show or to meet their favourite soap star, so look approachable and friendly, even if you are bored.

It can happen that some 'friends' get too excited and also ask rather personal, strange or irrelevant questions. Try to be polite and diplomatic at all times without giving away anything you do not want to divulge. Usually the stage/company manager also keeps an eye out and will jump in to help those cast members bombarded with fans, who need a break or anyone who seems uncomfortable. Try and catch their attention and they will find an excuse for you to leave a situation if it becomes difficult. Sometimes mayors of the town, theatre managers or your producer/director may make a speech. Look attentive, even if you would rather be asleep in your digs at this point! Dress for these occasions: usually smart-casual, although some actors literally wear whatever they want.

Further help

Here are some final tips to help you make the most of your time on tour:

★ Libraries: These are very useful as often they provide free Internet usage. Some theatres also have green rooms with free Internet access for visiting companies. Most theatres also extend free gym membership to visiting companies, which can be handy. Ask at the stage door.

★ Sightseeing: At times a tour can be a bit of a holiday, so make the most of it! Don't spend all night drinking and then sleep all day until your performance. It may be fun and tempting at first, but you can miss out on some great stuff. You may also experience serious vocal problems if you spend half your time in a noisy pub or bar. Ask your landlord for sightseeing details.

★ Mobile phones: Make sure you are on a good contract that gives you as much free talk time as possible. In almost all accommodation, you will not have access to landlines.

★ Budget: Keep track of your accounts. It's so tempting to eat out every day, especially as food and drink can be so much cheaper outside London. It all adds up though, so keep an eye on finances and cook at home in your digs to save money sometimes. It's a good idea to eat as regularly and healthily as possible (from all food groups) to retain your strength and stamina.

★ Make sure your actual home is in good order, bills are paid and you have someone going round to check for post regularly if you are unable to go home weekly. Otherwise you may return home to the nasty shock of having had your phone line or gas turned off as you missed your payments!

★ Touring is a close-knit environment and people tend to gossip and talk more than usual. Remember this is a small industry and things will get back to relevant people, even if London and its community seems very far away on the Isle of Jersey. Be careful who you trust.

★ Be nice to your technical crew! Not only do they have control of the washing machine, are in charge of your props and costumes, etc., usually they have a lot more insider knowledge than the performers. It's a tougher job, too, as they have the longest hours of anyone.

Surviving London – the big bad city

'London is a roost for every bird.' – Benjamin Disraeli

Whether you are a student or a professional in the performing arts, moving to/living in London can seem daunting. Not only does the place seem too large for you to gain any perspective, it's also *very* expensive compared to most other cities and towns. How can someone constantly in and out of work survive here without going heavily into debt? And how do you find friends, if you are not attending drama school or a course? Here are some ideas to get you started.

First steps in London
★ Buy an *A–Z* (or similar)! You can also check out locations online at www.streetmap.co.uk and print off pages.

★ Get a tube map and train timetable for free at any London tube/train station. Familiarise yourself with the transport system as soon as possible. Generally, the London transport system is judged to be user-friendly, unlike Paris and Tokyo, for example, which are deemed tricky to get around. It's not difficult to find your way around the tube – there's lots of information to take in, that's all.

★ Londoners are generally not rude. They tend to be extremely rushed, though, as the pace of living is so fast (like any other major world city) that their stress tends to come across as being unfriendly. Also, Londoners are asked almost daily for help by those new to the city or tourists. It's OK to ask questions, if you need help, just ask!

★ Taxis are ridiculously expensive in London. Try to use the tube to get around, especially from the airport. An Oyster card (see www.sales.oystercard.com/) is the best way to get around, even though public transport prices are now reportedly the highest in the world. There are also plenty of buses but they tend to get stuck in traffic and/or are rarely on time so I am not such a big fan. I used to walk a lot when I was a student in London. I walked everywhere and some people I knew walked from zones one to three regularly!

TIP!

> A bike is also useful but make sure you can handle the traffic. Also, make sure you wear a crash helmet!

Making friends/finding someone to live with

Many non-Londoners worry about building up a social network. London may consist of several million people but where do you find those specific few with similar interests to yourself, if you are not part of a course? It's uncommon for actors to be able to afford to live by themselves in London. If you are in that position, lucky you! Most of you, however, will need to find someone (or several people) to share to be able to afford to live in London. It's extremely common for professionals from all walks of life to share property in London to save costs and not just a phenomenon found in the acting population. Finding people to share with is quite easy and there are many popular websites. In my opinion, the best one is ww.moveflat.co.uk, where it's *free* to advertise and respond! The site also includes a page of helpful hints and tips about choosing your house/flatmates and what to look out for. I have found a couple of people to share with myself through this site and people tend to respond very quickly.

Other websites (which may ask you to pay) are:

www.spareroom.co.uk
www.gumtree.co.uk (also free)
www1.flatmateclick.co.uk
www.uk.easyroommate.com
www.intolondon.com
www.flatshare.com
www.gayshare.co.uk (specifically for gay shared living)
www.loot.com

How do you find flatshares with actors, directors and others in the industry?
Check notice boards for advertised rooms at all London dance studios and at the Actors Centre (which can be a really good way to socialise as they also have a green room area for members). *See also* page 281. This is the best way to find people who share your interests and may also become friends. Advertise on/check the NCDT (National Council of Drama Training) online forum (www.ncdt.co.uk). Check out the UK screen notice board, too, which occasionally has ads (www.ukscreen.com/board/General/1).

To make friends, check out London's popular hangouts for performers. Apart from The Actors Centre and various dance studios as mentioned above, these are:

★ Bars and pubs close to theatre stage doors, where performers tend to go for a drink and chat after their performances. Particularly the Phoenix Bar underneath the Phoenix Theatre on Charing Cross Road, London WC2.

★ The Groucho Club in Dean Street, Soho is primarily a members-only club with many well-known actors as members. For more information, visit www.thegrouchoclub.com/theclub/ or contact via enquiries@thegrouchoclub.com or telephone 020 7439 4685.

★ Jerry's Wine Bar and Restaurant, 23–25 Homerton High Street, Hackney, London E9 6JP. Telephone: 020 8525 5666.

★ The Ivy, 1–5 West Street, London WC2H 9NQ, telephone: 020 7836 4751 or visit www.the-ivy.co.uk. It's opposite the theatre showing *The Mousetrap*, *very* exclusive and you will have to book ages in advance as it's a celebrity hotspot. The food is traditional English. If you are unsure, check their dress code in advance, too (and for The Wolseley, below).

★ The Wolseley, 160 Piccadilly, London W1J 9EB, telephone: 020 7499 6996 (or visit: www.thewolseley.com). This is an upmarket, but informal brasserie. Again, book early unless going for lunch. Many well-known theatre and film folk can be found here after shows and it's under the same management as The Ivy.

★ Joe Allens's, 13 Exeter Street, London WC2E 7DT, telephone: 020 7836 0651 (or visit: www.joeallenrestaurant.com/london/). A very popular hangout for many in the industry, particularly after performing or watching a show. There's a bar and restaurant with live piano show tunes. The food is so-so, but not too costly.

★ The Stockpot is an actor's favourite restaurant as it is dirt cheap (large, main meals for £4 at the time of writing). You can't book, you just have to queue, but it's fun. There are various branches throughout London: 273 King's Road, London SW3 5EN; 40 Panton Street, London SW1 4EA; 18 Old Compton Street, London W1D 4JL.

★ The Arts Theatre Club in Soho is a night club for performers, technical crew, musicians, etc., established in 1927. It hosts various regular events such as quiz nights, house parties, karaoke, comedy evenings and specific DJs. They also have a cheap drinks night every Tuesday. You need to be a member to have access to this club and three types of membership are available depending on the nights of the week you are allowed in, how many guests you are allowed to bring along and how much entry you have to pay. It's based at 50 Frith Street, London W1D 4SQ, telephone: 020 7287 9236. For further information, visit www.theartstheatreclub.com

★ Kudos is a theatre bar in the basement with musical theatre music only at 10 Adelaide Street, London WC2N 4HZ, telephone 020 7379 4573.

Other links
www.music-mate.com – find single music lovers.
www.actorpoint.com/date/index.html – online dating for single actors.

I don't know where to live in London!
This is a common concern. London has huge price discrepancies between areas. The best way to find out if an area suits you is to go and visit it. Walk round and check out the shops, etc. Make sure you go at different times during the day and evening to see if it is still safe to walk around. If you can,

ask people who live there already. Study a tube map or go to www.tfl.gov.uk/tfl/pdfdocs/colourmap.pdf for a basic idea of location. Now let me guide you through the basics:

Film-star salaries

The most expensive areas in London are Kensington and Chelsea (including Holland Park and Notting Hill), Victoria/Belgravia/Pimlico and Hampstead/St John's Wood. Basically all areas in Zone 1 will be highly priced. Some areas around King's Cross and Old Street can be more reasonable – you have to be lucky, though; also do your research. Marylebone and Regent's Park are also expensive. The City (E and EC postcodes in the east Zones 1–2) and central London (Green Park, Mayfair, Bond Street, anywhere near 'Theatreland') is also very pricey. Postcodes for these areas are: W, WC, SW1, 3, 5, 7, 10; W2, 8,11, 14; N1 and NW1.

Successful city earners

Places like Chiswick, Ravenscourt Park and Turnham Green in the south-west (District line) are also costly, as is Wimbledon (south-west and District line), Richmond in the same direction and Fulham/Fulham Broadway/Parsons Green. The south-west of London tends to be more expensive than other areas. Chiswick is popular with actors but they tend to be of the 'film fee earner' variety. Hammersmith is expensive, as is Belsize Park, Primrose Hill and areas close to Hampstead Heath. Ladbroke Grove, Westbourne Park and Paddington are also expensive and out of reach for most actors, as is Waterloo now – unless you manage to find a bargain.

Camden/Angel (N1, NW2) are fashionable hot spots as they are funky, quirky and very arty (Zone 1, Northern line), but again, expensive. Camden can sometimes be affordable depending on how many people you share with and where you live.

Swiss Cottage also tends to be just too steep with prices, although you do get some students living there, more towards the Chalk Farm side, especially in the surrounding council accommodation.

Warwick Road/Little Venice/Maida Vale (north-west) is a lovely area to live but normally too expensive for the budding actor (Zone 2, Bakerloo line) as is Islington/Highbury in Zone 2 on the Victoria line (north).

Young professionals

Many actors live in Crouch Hill/Crouch End (N12), which is very fashionable. However, it does not have a tube stop and is also not that cheap. Angel (N1) is fashionable but again expensive (Zone 1, Northern line).

Old Street in Zone 1 (the not-so posh part of Angel) can sometimes be affordable and is also young, artsy and trendy; equally, Kentish Town and Chalk Farm.

Shepherds Bush/White City on the Central line can be interesting as it is very central (west, Zone 2), but can be affordable if sharing with several people. White City is more affordable than Shepherds Bush, where prices soar.

London Bridge and Borough (south-east) on the Northern line are worth looking into, although prices are rising here too.

Brixton is also a popular arty area. It is generally expensive now, although you can find some good deals if sharing a larger property.

Wapping and any of the DLR stops near the City tend to still be reasonable if you are prepared to share with several people, although Canary Wharf is expensive.

Some areas in Surrey are worth a look. Surbiton, for example, is in Zone 6. It's reasonable and a regular direct train to Waterloo takes only 20 minutes. Twickenham can offer nice green, quiet living with reasonably good City connections.

Thespian 'hot spots'

Common areas where performers live, as it's cheaper but still quite central are: Finsbury Park, Finchley, Golders Green (Northern line) in Zones 2/3, Ealing (Zone 3, Central line, far west), Bethnal Green/Bow/Mile End (Zone 2, east), although prices are rising here.

Arsenal, Holloway Road, Mansion House and areas close by in Zone 2/3 on the Piccadilly line, although they are a bit rough around the edges. Southgate is also affordable.

Hackney is another popular hangout for actors. Although it does not have a tube, it's fast becoming fashionable.

Stratford is popular. Other cheap areas are Hounslow, Acton and Stoke Newington/Clapton as they are further east and don't have a tube station. Wembley and Willesden Green/Dollis Hill (Bakerloo and Jubilee lines) are also popular for students. Highgate is popular (Northern line, north) and Battersea (south-west), but again no tube. Vauxhall, Kennington and Oval are relatively cheap but still quite central being in Zones 2/3. Clapham can be good, although Clapham South tends to be expensive (as does Balham) and again, prices are rising. See if you can find former council accommodation near Clapham Junction to share. This is cheaper, but it's been done up by landlords interested in renting them. If it is in walking distance to Clapham train station you can get a train from there to either Waterloo or Victoria. The train journey is about seven minutes and trains go every few minutes. It's well worth investigating. Greenwich tends to be popular with lots of shopping facilities (south on the Jubilee line or DLR), about 40 minutes from the city centre by tube.

Students and those starting out
New Cross Gate and Lewisham, far-east London. Also anywhere out towards Essex in the far east (Hornchurch, Loughton, Leytonstone and areas near there on the Central line east), Wood Green/Turnpike Lane (north on the Piccadilly Line), Barnet (far north on Northern line), Harrow and Ruislip (far north-west on the Metropolitan line). Edgware (north) is very cheap, as is Walthamstow, and quite quick into the City via the reliable Victoria line. Tooting (south on the Northern line) can provide some good bargains. Streatham near Brixton is popular too for actors.

> **TIP!**
>
> If not a student, check your Council Tax band! Depending on which borough you live in, council tax varies enormously and it can make a huge difference when you choose somewhere to live. Check your council tax band here: www.direct.gov.uk/en/Diol1/DoItOnline/DG_4017252 or http://www.adviceguide.org.uk/index/life/tax/council_tax.htm to read about the definition of council tax and why it exists.

For more advice have a look at www.upmystreet.com, which shows you everything to find in a specific area of London (also by postcode), such as shops, doctors, transport, etc. Also very useful is *Where to live in London* by Sara McCowell (see page 275).

Fun and social stuff on the cheap
Despite the horrendous entrance prices for most London attractions and nightlife, there's also a surprising amount of free enjoyment to be had. Here are some examples:

★ Parks: Richmond and Holland Park are particularly beautiful. Kew Gardens is great; there is a small entrance fee, but they have an amazing tropical greenhouse.

★ Many museums and galleries in London are free. Some major ones are: The Houses of Parliament, The Museum of London, The British Museum, The Bank of England Museum, The Imperial War Museum, The British Library,

The Science Museum, The Victoria and Albert Museum, The National History Museum and the Theatre Museum! For more listings, visit: www.londonfreelist.com/

★ Covent Garden Piazza offers daily free street entertainment, including clowns, opera singers, jugglers and much more.

★ *Metro* newspaper is free every weekday morning and you can pick it up at any tube station – they do tend to go quickly, however. *London Lite* is one of the evening free papers.

★ The London Pass gives you free admission to over 60 venues (including cinemas), as well as free Internet access at the Global Café Soho, free public transport and money off some musicals! Also free ice skating, bowling, go-karting, roller blading, river cruises and guided tours. For more information, visit www.londonpass.com/

★ Go and see a television show, such as *Who Wants to Be a Millionaire* or *Ant and Dec Saturday Night Live* being recorded. The show's websites explain how to apply for free tickets and also: www.bbc.co.uk/whatson/tickets/

> ### TIP!
> Check out the London free list (www.londonfreelist.com/home). This is updated daily and includes everything from free bars and clubs to films, festivals, etc.

Cheap temporary accommodation
At various YMCAs and other youth hostels you can often get a shared room for about £12 per night or so. You can find temporary accommodation for this price in central London Zones 1 or 2. Visit:
www.yha.org.uk/Home/Home_Page/index.html
www.londonnet.co.uk/ln/guide/accomm/budget_hostels.html
http://roomsnet.com and www.londontoolkit.com/
www.laterooms.com

Discount theatre tickets
The National Theatre do free/cheap standing seats, as well as student discounts (*see also* page 279). Equity student and last-minute discounts also exist if you turn up at some theatres 30 minutes before the start of a performance. Try standing for free or cheap (about £10–15). I used to sneak

into all kinds of productions this way as a student!

TIP!

> If you have purchased a standing-only ticket, you can almost always move to a better seat after the first half if you see one that has become empty.

★ Try and see student shows at drama schools. These are usually cheaper and sometimes of extremely high quality, not to mention a way to make contacts in the bar afterwards.

★ Previews tend to be slightly cheaper than once the show has officially opened.

★ See fringe theatre that is cheap and sometimes 'profit share', which means audience members pay as much as they can afford or deem fit. The Bridewell Theatre (www.bridewelltheatre.co.uk) offers many productions of this kind. Also check out Soho Theatre (www.sohotheatre.com), The Finborough Theatre (www.finboroughtheatre.itgo.com) and The Unicorn Theatre (www.unicorntheatre.com). *The Stage* (www.thestage.co.uk) has all the listings.

★ www.lastminute.com often has deals for shows and also dinner/show deals. There are various other sites offering deals, but these tend to be the best I have found. Also, check out the Official London Theatre website for deals: www.officiallondontheatre.co.uk/offers.

★ Visit www.offwestend.com/ for a listing of fringe productions.

★ The Royal Shakespeare Company (www.rsc.org.uk/buyonline/955.aspx) do £5 tickets for all 16–25-year-olds.

★ Check out forums on www.dresscircle.co.uk and www.whatsonstage.com for people who are selling their own tickets at cost prices due to a change in their circumstances.

★ Become an usher and see shows for free/get paid to see them.

★ Go to the official half-price ticket booth from about 11.00am onwards (there's one in Canary Wharf and another in Leicester Square) to get reduced tickets on the day or in advance. Visit www.officiallondontheatre.co.uk/tkts.

★ Queue at the box office for returns the day you want to see a particular show. If you arrive early, often you will be able to get half-price tickets for front row or the first few rows for the big shows for £20–£25.

★ Check out www.swapmyticket.co.uk. This is a great site where you can swap theatre tickets. Also music, sports, travel, etc. It's well worth a visit if you are looking for something that is usually totally sold out or seats are hard to come by.

More useful links
www.officiallondontheatre.co.uk/tkts
www.1st4londontheatre.co.uk/

Eating out cheaply
Avoid obvious rip-off and tourist places. Also the usual fast food chains. Instead try these:

★ Food for Thought in London's Covent Garden (31 Neal Street, London WC2H 9PR, telephone 0871 332 8808). This is an amazing vegetarian restaurant/canteen that offers extremely healthy, delicious and cheap cuisine – you can easily fill yourself up for a fiver here. It's usually packed, though, as it's not very large, situated in the basement and you have to share tables with other people. There's no service charge as there are no waiters. They also have a takeaway option.

★ Check out Crazy Salads at 3 Fore St Avenue, London EC2Y 9DT, telephone 020 7719 1717 (and branches) for a range of cheap takeaway salads.

★ Wagamama (www.wagamama.com) is always a good bet. This is a chain with various restaurants all over London. They serve Japanese food (mainly noodles) and it's highly recommended.

★ Wetherspoons (www.jdwetherspoon.co.uk) and All Bar One (www.mbplc.com/allbarone) all serve good value food, if you like the pub-type atmosphere. Branches throughout London.

★ Masala Zone (www.realindianfood.com) is an Indian restaurant that has won many awards and serves inexpensive, healthy food. Branches in Soho, Earls Court and Islington.

★ Busaba Eathai at 22 Store Street, London WC1E 7DF (Goodge Street tube). Affordable Thai food.

★ Café Espana serves a selection of Spanish and Italian food and is based at 63 Old Compton Street, Soho, London W1V 5PN (Piccadilly Circus tube).

★ Canteen (what the name says really, various healthy food canteen style): 2 Crispin Place, Spitalfields, London E1 6DW (Liverpool Street tube).

★ Fish Central is a great fish place, where you can get a decent meal for £10 a head. It's based at 149–151 Central Street, London EC1V 8AP (Barbican tube).

★ Hummus Bros is a Greek eatery that's very reasonable with lunch for a fiver! It's at 88 Wardour Street, London W1F 0TJ (Oxford Circus tube).

★ Mildreds, 45 Lexington Street, London W1F 9AN, telephone 0871 223 8079. This is another vegetarian café (www.mildreds.co.uk/).

★ Chinatown in Soho has lots of really good deals, with big bowls of noodles for £3.50 and much, much more. It's an amazing area, packed with all kinds of shops, so have a wander.

Getting home at night

In London the tube stops running at 1.00am latest, so most people go for the night bus option as it's the cheapest. The night bus is fine so long as you are not using it alone and/or you don't have to walk home by yourself in the dark for long stretches once you reach your stop. As a precaution, ask a friend to wait with you for the bus and always sit downstairs close to the driver.

TIP!

Avoid unlicensed mini cabs – these are dangerous. If the company is registered and has been recommended to you by someone very reliable, that's fine. Try not to take a mini cab alone – there should be at least two of you, if not more. Note: registered mini cabs have a sticker on their windscreen or check Cabwise for a licensed cab: www.london.gov.uk/cabwise.

Black cabs are usually incredibly hard to find after about 10.00pm when the theatres finish. They are equally popular around 2.00–3.00am when all the clubs close. These are also very expensive and some don't go outside certain zones/areas after a certain time of night, so if you live in Zones 5 or 6 it may be impossible for you to find a black cab willing to take you home. If you are new to London, make sure you work out early all the ways to get home in your area.

More helpful links
Currency Converter (www.xe.com/ucc/)
London Weather (www.weatheronline.co.uk/ukweather.htm)
London Guide (www.tourstolondon.co.uk)
London Magical Tours (www.londonmagicaltours.com)
London Walks (www.walks.com/).

Info on other cities
★ Edinburgh (www.accom.ed.ac.uk/accom_info/useful/edinburgh/index.htm and www.edinburghguide.com)

★ Manchester (www.investinmanchester.com/lifestyle_livinginmanchester and www.mymanchester.org)

★ Dublin (www.visitdublin.com and www.dublinuncovered.net)

★ Cardiff (www.myvillage.com/cardiff)

Coping with nerves and stage fright

'We've out a man on the moon. If you miss a cue, no one will die.' – *Shelli Alderman*

Everyone gets nervous about performing and auditioning. Getting up in front of people and displaying emotion is one of the scariest things you can do, which is why so many people would rather eat spiders than perform! So don't feel bad about feeling anxious, what you are going through is perfectly normal. Even the most accomplished professionals suffer from nerves and sometimes more so than those starting out. Backstage at my first profession-al engagement I noticed one of the lead actors (with credits longer than my Amazon wishlist) was missing. Finally I tracked him down to where he was huddling in the corner of a toilet. I asked him what was wrong and if I could help. It turned out he simply couldn't face going on stage. He was shaking, sweating, and I was at a loss as to how to coax him back into the wings. My 'beginners' call (*see* glossary, page 297) came and I had to leave him and go on only to discover the same actor, who was terrified in a heap five minutes ago, proceeding to give an energy-filled, seemingly confident, convincing and entertaining performance!

Next day I wondered if any of the events would change, but they did not. The actor remained terrified the moment before the 'beginners' call. Sometimes newcomers have fewer problems with nerves as they simply have nothing to lose and no expectations to fulfil.

> ### TIP!
>
> I have discovered that the key in dealing with nerves is to find out how to turn them into positive energy. Adrenaline is good – you want to be a little anxious so that you are in a heightened state. Auditions and performances need that extra punch of energy, so be glad you are nervous. If you are not scared, something is lacking and you may give a performance that is too relaxed, underenergised and possibly even dull. You don't want to get rid of the butterflies in your stomach, just to make sure they don't take over you and your audition or inhibit you in any shape or form. See also below.

Some common problems connected with stage fright are:

★ Shaking/shivering, which can close up your voice and make you feel out of control.

★ Feeling you don't remember anything. A common expression is 'I can't even remember the first line!'

★ The sensation of feeling sick or as if you are going to be sick.

★ Feeling totally out of control and unable to focus.

★ Being paralysed or unable to move.

★ Having to rush to the toilet every few minutes or so.

★ Being terrified of going onstage/into the audition room and wanting to escape.

★ Sweating, clammy hands.

★ Fidgeting, not standing still.

How can you turn your negative feelings into positive energy for your audition?

★ First of all, rehearse. Know your lines backwards; also your stage movements and be familiar with any props you work with. Practice makes perfect and the more you go through something, the more it will settle in your mind so you can call upon it when needed. It's like the times tables – the more you memorise them, the more easily you can call them to mind, even in stressful situations. First aid medical professionals usually go through rigorous practice routines in the dark, in the rain, at night, and so on so they can recall emergency procedures under all circumstances. Sometimes an audition can seem like an 'emergency', especially if the panel spring something unexpected on you or you start to panic during a performance when someone forgets their lines and you have to improvise or save the scene.

The more practice you have as a professional, the less rehearsal time you may need. It depends on the individual. I know some performers who have been in the business for over 40 years who still rehearse everything from top to bottom for an audition. It's whatever makes you feel comfortable. Bear in mind that not rehearsing can make audition pieces seem too comfortable and your natural talent needs that extra rehearsal push to be in top form.

★ Find something to think or somewhere to think that makes you calmer, a place where you can escape for a few minutes before the audition/performance. Many people choose a tropical island with a beach in their minds, but really anything that helps you feel calmer and in control.

★ Don't worry about others. Others may prepare for their audition/performance in a different way to you. There's no right or wrong method – you do your thing and let them do theirs. Don't think about them. Think about yourself before an audition and a performance.

★ Don't feel you have to try out anything new for an audition or performance – that's what rehearsals are for! Do what you have been doing. In long-running shows a certain amount of improvement is usually unavoidable, but in general directors expect you to perform as rehearsed. This is also so other actors/technical crew are not put off their job.

★ Focus on your body and how it is working. Listen to your breathing and your heartbeat. Your body is your tool for telling a story and showing a character's journey. So be in tune physically. Sometimes deep breathing with your eyes closed while lying on the floor with your knees pointing to the ceiling can help.

★ Warm up. Do some humming and a general vocal warm-up, even if it's not a singing audition/performance. Knowing your voice is functioning well can give you confidence. Move around, jump about, shake your limbs, do anything physical that makes you feel positively energised and gets rid of any negative inhibitions.

★ Be aware that making a mistake is OK. It's not a crime, it happens! If you are in an audition, ask if you can start again. It will not count against you if you simply stop what you're doing and calmly ask the panel if you can start again from the beginning of your piece. During a performance can be trickier – even so, it's part of the life of a performer. Everyone forgets lines/moves all the time: it's just that many professionals are so good at hiding their mistakes that the audience doesn't notice. And even if they do, some audiences actually *enjoy* mistakes! It makes performers seem human and shows that we are not perfect either.

★ If it helps you, listen to music or read a book for distraction. Find a piece of music that relaxes you.

★ Stay away from alcohol, drugs and any other numbing substances before you audition/perform. Legend has it that a sip of strong whisky makes you more daring, but the truth is that (a) you get used to it, which is very dangerous and (b) it numbs the senses rather than heightens them – which is what you need to give a good performance.

★ Listen! When on stage, listen to anyone else who may be in the scene with you. Listen to your surroundings and the orchestra, if there is one. Listen, and you will feel and look involved.

★ Be prepared. Arrive early so you don't feel stressed. Drink, eat and sleep properly.

★ Keep to yourself, if you want to. This is not a time you have to be social. If you would rather sit in silence and not talk to anyone, do so. But if you enjoy talking and feel it distracts you, make sure you are not invading someone else's space by chatting to them too intensely.

Finally, the more you audition/perform, the more you will learn how to deal with your own specific nerves. It's not a case of getting rid of nerves, more of getting used to them and learning how to cope with them – it's like getting back on a horse if you have had a riding accident. If an audition or performance goes badly, do another one as soon as possible. You have nothing to lose!

Taxes and registering as self-employed

This can potentially be a hugely confusing and scary subject so I have tried to simplify it as much as possible – it took me literally months to get a grip on it.

Most performers register as what is known as being 'self-employed'. This means you are not employed with an organisation that pays you a regular amount of money every month or so but instead you work for yourself. Of course there are some acting jobs (for example, a regular contract for a television soap or performing in a West End musical for three years running) that qualify for an actor not to be classed as self-employed. However, most of the time and for most of us, work is sporadic, of short duration and you will work for many different employers throughout a tax year. Therefore, most actors, even those employed in longer contracts, register as self-employed. You can remain self-employed for as long as you like. If you decide to be permanently employed long term at a company your status will change, however. Even if you do not work in acting for more than four weeks a year, for example, your status remains as self-employed, if you wish it to do so.

To work as a professional performer, you need to register as self-employed (also known as Schedule D). There are several ways to do this:

★ Call 08459 15 45 15 (the helpline for the newly self-employed).

★ Fill out a form found online: www.hmrc.gov.uk/forms/cwf1.pdf. Print and post this or give the details on the form to someone in person when calling the helpline above.

★ Register online at www.hmrc.gov.uk/startingup/register.htm. This means you will receive all your correspondence here and can also download appropriate forms from the Inland Revenue website.

The day you start working for yourself is when your student status ends, so the day your degree officially finishes (ask your college, if uncertain) is when you should register as self-employed. I would advise seeking help regarding your own case before registering as self-employed and this is best from Equity, if you are a member. If you are not attending drama school, register as self-employed the moment you start acting-related work.

With every job, not only will a percentage of your earnings be deducted for taxes but you also have to pay your Class 2 National Insurance (NI) Contributions at £2.20 a week as of 2007/2008. Class 2 Contributions count towards certain benefits such as the State Pension, Maternity Leave and Bereavement Benefit. When completing the self-employed registration form, turn to a section 'How to pay your Class 2 NI contributions'. Tick the box beside 'Please send me more information about SEE' (small earnings exceptions). Class 2 NI contributions are not payable if your earnings from self-employment are below £5,225 (for 2007/2008, www.hmrc.gov.uk/rates/it.htm). Register for Class 2 NI contributions when you register as self-employed as detailed above.

> **TIP!**
>
> Registering as self-employed may limit you to receive certain job seekers allowance benefits. For more help on this subject, check out: www.direct.gov.uk/MoneyTaxAndBenefits/ or the Inland Revenue website: www.hmrc.gov.uk. Remember you are also eligible to seek advice in person from your local council for free. For local council contact details, visit
> www.direct.gov.uk/Dl1/Directories/LocalCouncils/fs/en

National Insurance numbers

To register as self-employed you will also need a National Insurance number/card to quote when you register. All UK nationals will have received a National Insurance number and card on their 16th birthday. If you are not from the UK you will need to apply for one (see pages 175–176).

Filling out tax forms

Once you have registered as self-employed and have a NI number, you are in the system and will be sent an annual set of forms by the Inland Revenue to declare your tax. This form usually arrives in April of each year and you will have until 31st January of the next year to send it back (the exact deadline will be marked on your form). If you are registered online, you will be sent a

'Notice to Complete a Tax Return' (SA316).

Basically, the Inland Revenue wants to know:

★ What work you have had in the year (performing or other) and how much you have earned.

★ If you have already paid tax on it (and if so, how much?).

★ If you want to claim back any tax on spending related to your job.

You will also be asked to declare any interest you earned that year from all your bank accounts. (Just call your bank and ask them to send you a statement of interest for all your accounts for tax purposes. Most banks do this automatically each year, however.) Phone the self-assessment supply helpline on 0845 9000 404 to ask for specific forms, or download them if you are registered online.

TIP!

You cannot use forms from the year before, you need forms with the appropriate year (e.g. 2007/2008) marked on them. Forms are usually available as soon as you receive your tax return forms from the Inland Revenue in April.

Most of the time, you need two types of form:

★ Forms for self-employed jobs (anything to do with performing or where you are not taxed at source).

★ Forms for your temping work and any other non-performance jobs like office temping, bar work, ushering, etc.

Usually two or three forms of each type are included in the initial envelope they send you. However that is usually nowhere near enough as you need to fill out a separate form for *each* employer for whom you have worked that year. So, if you did a television appearance in *Holby City*, temped at an accountancy firm for a week through an office agency, then got a bar job for four weeks, spent two weeks ushering at the National and went on tour with a play for four months then that's already five forms! Phone the number listed above and they will send you more forms through the post or print them off online. Details will be available on your personalised website if you are registered online.

If you are temping make sure you are put on PAYE (Pay As You Earn) by your employer, which means your tax is automatically deducted each week from your pay. You will not have to worry about putting aside money from those jobs to pay your tax bill at the end of the year as the appropriate tax gets deducted automatically from each payslip. Office jobs usually have this pay system, but if you are unsure check with your employer when you first start working. Make sure you give them any required paperwork, such as a P45 (when you leave a job it shows the tax you have already paid and this should be passed on to your new employer) or P60 (see below). Even though your tax is already deducted automatically through PAYE, you still need to put down details of that particular job on your tax forms. On the appropriate form for temping work (see also above), there will be a box to fill in the total you have earned, as well as a box to add in the total tax already paid on those earnings. You can find these two figures on your payslips, so simply copy the information from there.

TIP!

You are filling out your forms according to the number of employers you have had that year and not the number of jobs. So, if you are getting all your temp work through one agency, you only need one form, even if you had 15 different office jobs throughout the year. As long as they all go through the same agency, then you can add up your total earnings and put them on one form rather than 15. This is why it pays to keep one temping agency, rather than to keep skipping from one to the next.

Office temp agencies will send you what is called a P60 at the end of each tax year, stating exactly how much you earned through them that year, and how much tax has been deducted. That way you don't have to copy every single payslip for that employer but can copy the total sums from the P60, making your life a little easier. Acting agents will also send you payslips of your performing work, stating how much you were paid. Remember that in this case, most of the time tax will not have been deducted. If in doubt, call your agent.

Sometimes you will have been charged emergency tax (40% of your earnings) on temp work if you did not hand in a P45 in time before your job started or your self-employed status has not yet come through. On your tax forms you'll find a box to tick if you have paid too much tax and want to claim it back. Also tick this if you are not sure whether you have been charged emergency tax.

If you need to claim back emergency tax, call 0845 077 6543 for the relevant forms and/or have a look at:
www.direct.gov.uk/MoneyTaxAndBenefits/Taxes/ReclaimingTax/Reclaiming TaxArticles/fs/en?CONTENT_ID=10015058&chk=HExClP

With performance-related work, unfortunately it is usually not possible to have your tax automatically deducted from weekly or monthly pay. You will either get paid weekly or receive a one-off payment and it will state in your contract that you are responsible for your own tax. This means that if you have lots of acting jobs throughout the year, you will probably not have paid any tax on them at all yet. It's important to remember this!

> **TIP!**
>
> Set aside money, about 25% of your untaxed earnings, in a separate bank account with a good rate of interest to pay for your outstanding tax or you may get a shock at the end of the year!

For help filling out your tax forms, ring the following helpline: 08459 000 444

How much tax do I have to pay?

The amount of tax you have to pay depends on your taxable income. This is your total gross income minus your tax-free personal allowance and any tax-deductable allowances and expenses (or proportion of expenses); there are also certain types of income that are exempt from tax, such as the interest on ISA accounts. Details change from year to year and you should check the government website for your own particular case: www.direct.gov.uk/en/MoneyTaxandBenefits/

Paying tax/claiming expenses

Once your completed tax forms reach the Inland Revenue, they will calculate how much tax you owe them and send you a bill. There is a deadline for this, usually stated on your form, and if you don't send forms back by a certain date you will have to calculate the amount of tax you owe yourself. Trust me, this can take ages, so send in your forms *before* the mentioned deadline (usually 30 September)!

Calculate your tax with the aid of computer software from: www.taxcalc.com. I have no personal experience of this, but friends tell me it has been very useful to them.

You will usually receive a letter of confirmation a few weeks after sending in your forms, stating the amount of tax you still owe and how to pay it (or stating that you will be paid back the tax you have overpaid). If you do not pay your tax on time (usually 31 July), you will have to pay interest and perhaps a penalty fee (surcharge). You can sometimes make an arrangement to pay, but you cannot do this every time, so make sure you set money aside for tax.

TIP!

For those of you graduating from drama school: If you complete your course in the summer/autumn of 2008, for example, and start working then, you will be sent your first tax form from start date in 2008 till April 2009 in April 2009. You will then have until 31 January 2010 to complete them (30 September 2009 if you want the Inland Revenue to calculate how much tax you owe) and until 31 July 2010 to pay your tax bill.

Being self-employed you can claim back expenses connected to your 'business'. There will be a part in your tax declaration form asking whether you would like to claim back expenses and how much. Expenses you can claim back as listed by Equity are as follows:

★ Agent/manager commission fees.

★ Secretarial services, travelling and subsistence on tour.

★ Make-up and hairdressing, costume and props.

★ Laundry and cleaning of costumes; also renewal, replacement and repair of costume and props.

★ Travelling and expenses while attending interviews.

★ Postage for business letters/fan mail and business stationary.

★ Tips for stage-door keepers, dressers and make-up artists.

★ Tuition and coaching for singing/dance/speech, etc.

★ Professional publications like *PCR*, *The Stage*, *The Radio Times*, etc.

★ Equity subscriptions, accountant's fees, your photo sessions and repros.

★ *Spotlight* and other agency books.

★ Maintenance of instruments and instrument insurance.

★ Theatre and cinema tickets.

★ CDs and DVDs.

★ Scripts and sheet music.

★ Legal charges regarding debt recovery in contract disputes.

Other acceptable expenses may be physiotherapy, cosmetic dentistry, chiropody (if a dancer), hire of electronic goods such as a telephone, television (and a percentage of your TV licence), use of a room in your house as an office. Check with the Equity helpline on 020 7670 0223, Tuesdays and Thursdays from 10.00am–1.00pm and 2.00–4.00pm if you are unsure whether your expense qualifies.

Important! Being self-employed you will have to keep all receipts for which you wish to claim back tax for *five* years. Photocopies are not enough: you need actual receipts. Also, make sure you keep all payslips, correspondence with the Inland Revenue and other related paperwork. The Inland Revenue has the right to contact you at any time and ask to look into your paperwork.

Accountants

Filling out tax declaration forms can seem a complicated nightmare to many people – it took me a whole weekend to figure it out. If you are not comfortable doing this, you can hire an accountant (see *Contacts* for listings or visit Equity online: www.equity.org.uk/members/start_mo.htm) to deal with this. An accountant cost you at least £150 a year, though, and it can save you money if you learn to do it yourself. Again, you can get free help and advice from your local council.

Important tax dates

Here is a quick guide through the tax year:

April: Your tax return arrives asking you to declare your earning from May the year before until April of the following year.

30 September: This is the date to send in your tax return if you want the Inland Revenue to calculate how much tax you owe/have reimbursed.

31 January: The final date to send in your tax return (having calculated how much tax you owe/are owed if you wish to do so).

31 July: The final date to pay tax owed from the last bill sent to you by the Inland Revenue.

Setting up a system for tax
It really helps to know where everything is and to keep it in date order, especially when the time comes to declare your annual taxes. Here are my general recommendations for anyone who is self-employed:

★ File all your bank statements and any letters the bank sends you. Also, annual statements of how much interest your account(s) made over that year.

★ Again, keep a folder of all your pay slips. Separate temp work from acting-related jobs. This includes any correspondence with your agent.

★ File all correspondence with the Inland Revenue, including NI details.

★ Keep a folder of receipts of expenses you wish to claim back. Write on the back what they were for (tap shoes, agent's commission, etc.).

> **TIP!**
>
> You can get *free* tax and general advice on your finances (benefits, housing debt, etc.) if you are a member of the Actor's Centre. They offer half-hour one to one sessions hosted by professional accountants/auditors specialising in entertainment tax situations. Sessions take place on one day every two months and you must book in advance and pay a £10 fee if you fail to turn up to your appointment.

The Inland Revenue website also provides helpful tips on this subject: www.businesslink.gov.uk/
    For more details on self-employment for performers, check the Inland Revenue website or Equity (members only) on www.equity.org.uk/

members/welfare/taxandni.pdf. You can also contact Equity as a member at info@equity.org.uk for written guides on the Jobseeker's Allowance and other briefings. Most drama schools hold tax workshops in the final year/term, so make sure you ask relevant questions there. *The Stage* also has a helpful guide you can read for free: www.thestage.co.uk/connect/howto/freelancetax.php

'An actor is something less than a man, while an actress is something more than a woman.' – *Richard Burton*

Disabled peformers

Performers with disabilities have a place in the industry. The type and amount of roles you can take on may be more limited, though, depending on your impairment. Due to an announcement made by the Broadcasting and Creative Industries Disability Network (BCIDN) in 2002/03, the percentage of disabled individuals employed as professional performers is bound to change dramatically for the better. For more information, visit www.employers-forum.co.uk/www/bcidn/overview/index.html.

Can I still go to drama school?

Check with specific schools but yes, generally, drama schools are very open to the disabled – this is part of the Equal Opportunities regulation. Find out whether wheelchair access is available for your audition and if you will be able to get around the school easily. As long as you are physically able to take part in the course and all classes, it should not be a problem. With some disabilities, you may be limited when applying to musical theatre courses as these require a strong physical commitment and proof from your GP that you will be able to handle the course. Again, check with each school as they all have different policies, some maybe more accommodating than others.

TIP!

ALRA (Academy of Live and Recorded Arts) in London now offer a free 10-week evening actor training course for deaf actors age 18+. See www.alra.co.uk/v2/courses/short%20courses/PATFDA.html for details.

Agents/casting directors

Let them know about your disability in advance. When invited for interview, ask about wheelchair access and if you will be able to get to their office without any problems. Once signed with an agent, it should be their job to make potential employers aware of your impairment.

Check out www.visablepeople.com, an agency specialising in individuals with physical disabilities.

TIP!

When preparing your professional application, on top of the usual photo, add a full-length shot of you and your disability, including any guide dog. That way, the agent/casting director has a clear idea of your disability and how it affects you, as well as how you as an individual would suit the character/production.

More useful links

★ Equity has a disabled register: www.spotlightcd.com.

★ Channel 4 provides a database which includes disabled actors: www.channel4.com/fourall.

★ Check out the National Disability Arts Forum (NDAF), which distributes *Etcetera*, a weekly news bulletin advertising jobs for disabled performers. www.ndaf.org.

★ Graea Theatre Company (www.graeae.org) is the UK's national theatre of disabled performers and they also have a mailing list.

★ Contact Broadcasting and Creative Industries Disability Network (BCIDN) by emailing stevens@employers-forum.co.uk or visit their website www.employers-forum.com. You can also telephone 020 7403 3020.

And also have a look at: www.employers-forum.co.uk/ www/guests/bdn/casting.pdf#search=%22impaired%20actor%22

TIP!

Scene Change (www.graeae.org/content.asp?id=95) is a workshop programme for actors aged 16–25, wishing to become professionals, who have physical or sensory impairment. In association with Mountview/Arts Ed and led by Graeae Theatre Company. Auditions/taster workshops take place in Newcastle, London, Manchester, Plymouth, Nottingham and Birmingham.

Size, height and other concerns

'At bottom every man knows well enough that he is a unique being, only once on this earth; and by no extraordinary chance will such a marvellously picturesque piece of diversity in unity as he is, ever be put together a second time.'
– Friedrich Nietzsche

Consciously or not, many of you may hold some insecurity about your looks. Who doesn't, in this looks-conscious, size-zero obsessed industry, where it seems like one can never be slim or attractive enough? Does how you look matter in this industry? Unfortunately, it really does and there is definitely a general pressure on women to stay slim. It's not by coincidence that your photo is the first thing most casting directors and agents look at when considering you. Whether you need to be a size 8 or built like a body builder to succeed depends on what part you are auditioning for, and what your casting type is. What also matters is your individual look as a performer. It is sometimes helpful to look unique and different, rather than conventionally beautiful although admittedly, looking like a supermodel can certainly be a plus. The looks factor can be equally or more important than actual skill and talent as a performer depending on what the casting is for. A lot of it comes down to the vision of those casting – for example, if the director envisages a blonde Cinderella, then a stunning brunette with a gorgeous voice may have no chance!

Another thing to consider is the expectation of the audience. Most of the time people go to the theatre or watch a film and expect to see a certain type of look for a certain part. In terms of MT, especially, audiences expect leggy chorus girls (à la *The Producers*) and pretty, slim and good-looking leads if the character calls for it (Curly in *Oklahoma!*, Juliet in *Romeo and Juliet*, and so on). It is up to the producer/director whether they want to challenge audiences' perceptions and as a performer you are in their hands.

Some auditions state size and height limits in their casting breakdowns.

For example, I have noticed that pantomimes tend to be quite strict and ask for females applying for ingénue leads to be between 1.6 and 1.7m (5ft 3in and 5ft 7in) and a size 8–12, while males applying for the lead tend to be 1.75m (5ft 9in) and above. Please note that these are general statistics from my personal experience and they may vary. However, I have to admit that in this case the exception proves the rule. It also depends on what production you are auditioning for. For a show like *Jerry Springer*, for example, size and height are really not that relevant for casting. Television dramas and soaps often prefer 'real life' casting where size and shape can be more varied.

Your size does state which kind of castings you are suitable for. I wish I could say that it wasn't so, but I have had my own experiences of this. I am nearly 1.8m (6ft) tall and was a size 10–12, but I was told that it may be wise to drop a few pounds to a size 8 to appear 'less large' at castings as I apparently come across as 'quite heavy'. Whether or not this is healthy or something to pursue is up to the individual. I have also had feedback that I am simply too tall (or taller than the leading man I would be playing opposite) and have therefore not been considered further. Friends and acquaintances of a size 10 or 12 have been told they need to lose weight to suit a part and it is a common theme one hears while chatting to fellow actors at auditions. Girls are often told frankly by industry professionals that they need to watch their weight, even if in medical terms they are merely 'healthy'. On the other hand, you may not have a problem and they may cast around size and height issues if an actor is that important to the production.

> ### TIP!
>
> Don't beat yourself up about the way you look. You are you! It's important to look and stay healthy. You want to appear fit and agile. Eating disorders only kill your stamina as a performer. Everyone has a body weight they suit best and in the end you cannot change your gene pool, however hard you diet. Trust me, I've tried!
>
> For drama school courses your size/weight/height will not be relevant as to whether or not you are offered a place. If you are applying to dance schools or very dance-orientated MT courses then your size may well be of importance and some dance schools weigh you on your audition day.

It really depends on the individual and what seems to be the key is being a matching package. If you have a sweet, ingénue-type face, for example, but are a larger build, you may find it hard to get work because in the eyes of those casting you are too large for most ingénue castings. However, your face may not fit character parts. And if you are 1.5m (5ft 1in) tall you may be typecast for child parts. If you are a leading man type actor but 1.67m (5ft 6in) tall, you may be too short for many roles in comparison to the rest of the ensemble. Meanwhile if you are a tall female, you may be simply too tall for many roles and stick out of the chorus.

Everyone will have something to deal with, but if you have the talent, skill and determination, then issues like size and height can be overcome. You just need to find your niche. In the dance world size matters very strongly and you would be hard-pressed to find a dancer above a size 10, depending on the type of dance.

Non-whites

Colour-blind casting has always been a sensitive issue. Officially, according to the 2001 UK Census about 92 per cent of the British population is white, which is reflected in the casting of theatre and screen productions. If you go to China, you will see mainly Chinese actors in the theatre or on the screen, while in the UK you will see mainly white actors on the screen. This is not a case of racism, more reflecting society in art. That said, there have been many examples of very successful all-black or all-Indian productions. Colour-blind casting is becoming more and more popular (*Billy Elliott*, for example) and if you have what it takes, your ethnicity should not stand in the way of success.

Parental problems

'Parents have to understand: if your kid isn't you, don't blame the kid!' – *Chastity Bono*

This is a topic I have often been consulted about and have lots of personal experience with. You may have made up your mind you want to try your luck at the performing game but there's one slight problem: either your parents don't know about this and you are worried how they will react, or they do know and are not supporting your decision. What I could never quite understood as a teenager was why parents could be so against their children choosing performing as a career when they could see how good their kids were and how much they enjoyed it. Most of the time there's one very simple reason for this: your parents are worried that this choice is going to have some sort of negative effect on you and not make you happy. I know that to you this makes no sense and why should they be worried? You love it, you work hard for it, you are told you are good at it, so shouldn't they be supportive?

The truth is most parents know nothing about the industry and how it works, even if they won't admit it themselves. Due to the rather negative publicity this industry can get, they have usually heard only the bad side and some of the sob stories, governed by the media and the few public interviews given by very famous performers. It's human nature to be wary of something you know little or nothing about, especially when it concerns a child who might be stepping into untested waters. That's unless your parents are in the industry themselves and even then they may not be supportive because they themselves have witnessed and/or experienced how tough it can be, how disappointing and how mentally challenging it all was for them. Also, don't forget that this industry comes with a whole bunch of clichés, which to be fair usually have some truth in them. Here are some of the reactions you may come up against:

'There are too many people – you'll never make it as the competition is too high!'
This is a fair point. There are a lot of people out there trying for a job. However, this is also true for many other careers. Bankers, lawyers, doctors, these professions were once considered the pinnacle of the career world with guaranteed work for life after completing university. This is no longer the case and the competition in these fields can be almost as fierce as in the performing world. Be prepared, though: you may work hard for years and never achieve being employed and paid as a performer.

'We think you should get a "proper" job'
A 'proper' job in this case usually means a full-time contract with a regular income, pension scheme and other benefits. You cannot blame your parents for wishing you to have security. However, these days job security is extremely hard to find in most careers and has become a bit of a passé phrase. Many high profile jobs have a high changeover rate. People lose their jobs all the time due to 're-structuring' or companies being bought up by larger organisations. Most graduates from universities have problems finding employment in their chosen field and are forced to look elsewhere. There are of course still some jobs that still promise a certain amount of security, such as government departments and teaching.

'I want you to go to university first'
If you are academically inclined, your parents have a fair point here. It can be beneficial to have a university degree in another subject under your belt and then complete a postgraduate (or three-year course, if you can afford it) in performing. You can still take lessons and practise your performance skills

while at university. Consider carefully. Looking back, the ideal option for myself would have been to attend university and then follow up with three years at drama school. I think I would have benefited more from this set-up, which is why I urge others to have a think about it.

'People will want sexual and other favours from you in order to give you a job'

This goes back to the clichéd old Hollywood movies and generally, it's not true in this country. Hollywood may be a different ballgame, however. I'm not saying it never happens here and sure, people do get hired for a part because someone fancies them but you are not a prostitute. In general, people won't expect you to offer sexual favours in return for a job. That said, once again this attitude can also be found in many other professions. It's just that the performing industry has always had a much more public reputation for this.

> ### TIP!
>
> You always have a choice whether you commit to nude/topless work. You will *not* be seen as an inflexible performer if you choose to keep your clothes on. Sex scenes themselves vary from film to film and director to director. Sometimes they will close off the set, sometimes not. Some directors are fine with actors wearing underwear, others are not – it all depends on the individual circumstances. Some drama schools offer film technique classes that include kissing scenes and similar, although not full-on sex scenes!

'You don't know anyone in this business'

True, without connections this industry can be tough, a lot tougher than if you have someone to help you. That's not to say that you cannot get to know people and create a your own network. How successful you are depends entirely on you as an individual and your networking skills. Drama school can be very useful in the networking department.

'You didn't start training when you were little and it's too late now'

Many parents think that if you don't perform from age three onwards, you won't succeed. For acting, this is certainly not the case. You can begin at 50 and have success (*see also* pages 185–186). With singing, I know many people who started training at 18–21 or so, who have become working professionals. It can actually be dangerous to train the voice too early. If you want to be a professional dancer, then yes, you have to start very young. For musical theatre, however, some people don't start until they attend drama school, while others never, ever take regular lessons. While I would not recommend this (competition is now too high), there are examples throughout the business. It's beneficial to start training and performing from an early age but not mandatory.

'It's too expensive! We can't afford to pay for your training and it's a waste of money as there's no guarantee you'll make it'
But there are scholarships and grants available (*see* pages 42–45) just as for any other career path. Do the research yourself; don't expect your parents to. There's no guarantee, true, but then there are few guarantees for any career these days.

'Most actors end up poor and starving in the streets or as pole/lap dancers'
Many actors *will* end up not knowing how to pay their bills, moving back home, giving it all up due to lack of money and taking on low-paid or eccentric (escort, table dancer, etc.) jobs. That's a fact. Most of this problem comes from poor preparation and lack of planning. If you are open to learning and aware you may need a different job for the times when you can't get work, make sure you achieve good grades in your exams to avoid this. It's your choice. *See also* pages 122–128 for other options. Be your own business as well as a creative being. While you can't prepare for your performing career (so much is down to luck and being in the right place at the right time), you *can* have a general plan about how you want to lead your life. Be aware that you may have to dabble in two careers at the same time in case acting work is scarce.

'OK, but if you don't make it by a certain age, we will think it was all a waste of time'
Unfortunately it's impossible for you to give your parents a date when you will have 'made it'. Some people make it very young and then their career fades, others don't become successful until much later on in life. There are countless stories of people who auditioned for years with no success and then suddenly got a break. Again, there are no rules. It's up to you how long you want to keep trying. Some people move away from performing when they can't find work and then come back to it years later and are suddenly in demand. This business really is that vague.

'As a performer, you won't be able to have a family'
I know many performers who have a successful family life. Performing is

actually a useful job for this, especially if you are in a regular play/show/musical as it means you have the whole day until about 5.00pm or 6.00pm free to spend with your child/children – unless there are rehearsals or matinees, of course. You can spend time with your kid(s), do the school run and once they are ready for their supper/bedtime then you can work while they are asleep. Of course, it's useful if your partner has a job with opposite hours to yours so you don't have to spend vast sums on childcare. It helps if one of you does a job (such as a lead in a musical) while the other stays at home and takes care of the child and/or works from home or does the occasional job to still be there for the children.

Problems can arise when you both perform full-time for long periods and it helps to have grandparents, or other relatives around. It seems to me that in successful relationships there's one main performer and the other supports or performs a little, or the couple take turns or else the other partner does work unrelated to show business at opposite hours to the performer.

'People are bitchy and unpleasant in this industry, you won't have any friends'

Yes, some people may be so, but is it really so much better in other fields? The performing world is possibly more so than most as people can be highly strung and emotionally charged due to the make-up of a performer. Some people are unable to handle this cut-throat business. However, most realise this relatively soon and leave to pursue something else or abort their training.

'It is very low paid and you will never be able to buy property, save for a pension, get health insurance or afford any luxuries'

True, this job can be very low paid. If you are prepared to be on the lower scale of the earning line and work infrequently, fine. Not everyone needs money to be happy. Again, you may be prepared for this, but your parents may not and they may want something different for you. For both of you, have something else going on the side that they know will guarantee you a decent and/or regular income, should the performing not work out.

'You are too fat/thin/unattractive for this business'

Many parents are of the impression that you have to look like a model to be a successful performer and they think they are being cruel to be kind when they say this. Although looks can, of course, help and will open doors, there are also performers who are successful and are not what the media tells us we should be like. There are lead/romantic lead actors and there are character actors. You do not necessarily have to be a size zero to succeed, although admittedly the weight issue is a prominent one, especially for females (*see also* pages 163–165). If you feel you need to work on your self-esteem, find a good counsellor.

'Your mum/dad/aunt/uncle/sister/brother didn't make it, so why should you?'

Some parents are wary because someone else in their family has already tried the performing route but it didn't happen for them. The thing is that everyone is different. So much is dependent on luck and other factors out of your control. Your relative might have been a stunning performer, but just unlucky or not had the right contacts. You may actually be less talented but meet the right people and work regularly.

'You are too intelligent to be a performer'

Another common misconception is that most actors and performers are not very bright. It seems that intelligence is often confused with academic talent. Yes, many performers are not academically minded as their brains work in different ways. This does not mean they are not intelligent. Many entrepreneurs never went to university and are now millionaires. You can be intelligent in different ways, including life intelligence. I have met many highly qualified professors who were extremely knowledgeable in their one field of study. People can be as narrow-minded in law or business as performers. You will meet bright people and those less so in most fields of work.

Most good performers are open and broad-minded people. They have to be. Incidentally, some of the most successful actors and performers around are also very academic. Take Stephen Fry and Emma Thompson. Both went to Cambridge, while Barbra Streisand finished fourth in her high school year out of thousands and completed high school a year early at 16 years of age. Peter Ustinov spoke seven languages and Sharon Stone has an IQ that would guarantee her a place in MENSA. It's best not to generalise.

'All male performers and actors are gay'

Sadly, some of you may have to deal with this issue, which is another gross generalisation, but a belief held by surprisingly number of people. Yes, many creative people *are* homosexuals. It's by no means true, though, that *all* male performers are so inclined. Homosexuality is often associated with musical theatre and dance. While I cannot say this is untrue, what I can say is that (a) there is nothing wrong with that, and (b) just because you are surrounded by gay men does not mean you will be 'turned gay'. The same applies for women.

> **TIP!**
>
> If you are experiencing this kind of prejudice at home and feel rejected by your parents, I suggest you find a good counsellor to help you, as it is a sensitive subject.

'You didn't get into drama school first time round and you haven't worked even though you've had lots of auditions. You're not good enough, so give up the dream!'

If you're not offered a place at drama school first time round this does *not* necessarily mean you don't have the talent to succeed. There may be many good reasons why you were rejected (*see also* page 28). Professional auditions are a funny thing. I know of people who have been seen by the same casting director for years and years, and never got a job. All of a sudden, that same casting director offers them a big part or a lead. How does this happen? The truth is that some casting directors may see you again and again for different jobs over the years because they think you are great but sadly each time someone more suitable comes along and they have so many people to choose from. You may also lose out due to other factors, such as height, and these factors may be beyond casting directors' control.

Usually, the main thing parents don't understand is that it's not a case of wanting to perform – you *have* to perform. The arts are not a job, they are a certain lifestyle. I always say you don't choose performing, it chooses you, and as a rule, only people in the industry really understand how you feel, and that's OK. Not all parents will be able to relate to this. It doesn't mean they don't love you – or don't want you to be happy. In the end, most parents only want the best for their children. Yes, in some cases there is jealousy involved – your parents (or another family member) may be envious because they secretly wanted to follow the same path but perhaps no-one ever gave them the chance or they were too scared to pursue their goal. Hence, there may be some resentment present, even if subconsciously. It does happen. Some parents may provide financial but not emotional support. If this applies in your case, it's is hard to deal with, but try and find emotional support elsewhere.

So, how can you convince your parents that you are serious and willing to approach this career choice in a mature fashion and that it's not just a whim or a desire to be famous for the sake of it? Here are some suggestions:

★ Explain to your parents that you believe nothing else will make you truly happy.

★ Say to them that although you see you have many talents and skills, this is the one you believe you are best at.

★ Offer to work part-time or during the summer to pay for items such as dancewear, plays and theatre tickets or some lessons.

★ Say that you will give up your pocket money to pay for lessons instead.

★ Do your research so they can see you are not going into this profession blindly. Be intelligent about it.

★ Offer to help out at home with extra chores if they support you financially.

★ Research funding and present them with schemes showing how you can get a scholarship to save money.

★ Be mature. Don't have a crying and/or screaming fit! Stay calm. If your parents see you are approaching this rationally, it will calm them down and give them confidence in you and your decisions.

★ If still at school, say that you will definitely make GCSEs and A levels your priority and study to the best of your academic ability.

★ Find a professional in the industry to speak to your parents about what it entails; also to discuss your chances of making it.

★ Inform your parents about the industry. Explain to them what it is about. Get them clued up!

★ Take them along to drama school open days (and yes, I *know* you may not want your parents there. I didn't want my mother when she came along!), summer schools, and so on so they get a feel for your chosen environment. This also gives them a chance to talk to tutors about any concerns or questions they may have. Involve them in your decision.

If all of the above fails, it's your life! Once you are financially independent, it will be up to you to decide how you want to live it. If you want to choose this career then do it with a full idea of what you are getting yourself into. Maybe your parents will come round, maybe they won't, but at least you will have tried.

Non-UK performers

'Being a foreigner is not a disease.' – *Alden Nowlan*

As a foreigner coming to the UK to study or work, all the usual insecurities about training and working are heightened as you are often going through the process in a foreign language and are used to different attitudes and customs in your home country. Often you have to cope with a whole set of issues that most native UK students will be unable to relate to.

English is not my native language and I have an accent, will this hold me back?
Yes, a foreign accent can hinder you getting work, unless it is very, very faint or you make it your trademark (for example, become a voice-over artist with a Norwegian accent). Most foreign drama school students I know went back to their home country, mainly because their accent got in the way of them finding work/representation. Of course there are always exceptions, but the number of non-native speakers working in the UK is few and far between. Many drama schools now have special voice classes in the evenings for foreign students to improve their RP (received pronunciation, 'neutral' UK) accent. This supports my theory that without a native sounding RP accent, it's tough getting work or an agent. Is it possible to rid yourself of your accent during your time at drama school and/or with intensive tuition? In my experience, no, this isn't possible although you can certainly improve your accent. Unless you learn English as a very young child and/or are bilingual (like myself), most of the time, you will not be able to get rid of your accent.

> **TIP!**
>
> Agents may see your accent as a problem. This will vary from individual to individual and also depends on your talent and skills. To my knowledge, there are no specific agents that concentrate solely on representing foreigners and you will have to apply as you would without an accent.

If English is not your first language you will need to prove that the standard of your written and oral command of the language is high enough for drama school entry in the UK. A minimum IELTS (International English Language Testing System) score of 6.5 or TOEFL (Test of English as a Foreign Language) 500–550 (220 for Computer Based Testing) is requested for entry to most college courses. A Cambridge Certificate of Proficiency in English (CCPE) at grade C or above is also normally acceptable. Contact individual schools for regulations regarding other English language qualifications.

Americans in the UK

With regard to getting work in the UK, American accents do not seem to pose a problem. I know quite a few people who have successful careers and have even been cast in typically English roles if their RP accent is convincing. An American accent can be useful, particularly for musical theatre.

Important! You will *not* be allowed to stay in the UK once your student visa runs out. It's illegal to stay on without a visa. Getting a work visa is extremely difficult (for details, check with your country's embassy) and people can have problems finding representation because agents do not want to take them on if they do not have a full working visa. In some rare cases you may be offered help getting a work visa after a successful audition, but this is not typical.

> ### TIP!
>
> American students do *not* get automatic American Equity status, should they return to the USA with a performing-related UK degree. They will have to earn their Equity by working professionally once they are back home which can be a major issue as many shows in the US have 'Equity member only' auditions first before seeing anyone else. By the time they get round to non-Equity members, shows have sometimes been cast or they may have run out of time. Some drama schools have contacts in New York and organise showcases for Americans there after graduation in the UK to open doors and introduce them to representation. Check with your chosen school.

Americans coming over to fulfil a contract in the UK for a West End musical, for example, are usually not allowed to exceed a working visa of six months. After that time, the role must be re-cast with local talent. There is a trade agreement between UK and American Equity, where a certain number of American and EU nationals are 'traded' each year. In brief, if five American citizens perform in the UK this year, equally five UK nationals will be allowed to work in America for the same amount of time. To give an example: Idina Menzel was permitted to star in *Wicked* in the West End for six months, while a British national worked in the US for the same length of time.

Australians/New Zealanders/South Africans in the UK

Australian and New Zealand are part of the British Commonwealth so getting a visa should be more straightforward. In the case of South Africa, there are 'relatives visas'. For more information, visit www.workingintheuk.gov.uk and www.rsgaustralia.co.uk/visas.html.

Finally, remember that as a non-EU national you will pay 'foreign' drama school fees, which are considerably higher than the EU fees.

Auditioning for drama school while living outside the UK

Some schools accept a video audition for either the first audition round or even the entire process. Certain schools also audition in the US in cities like New York and Chicago, so American students don't have to travel all the way to Europe to audition. Check individual schools' websites for more details.

Funding for foreign students

As an EU national, you can apply for the dance and drama award scheme (www.dfes.gov.uk/financialhelp/dancedrama/index.cfm) in the UK. From experience, however, I have found it is best for foreign students to look for funding in their home country as the UK schemes are mostly for UK nationals. If you are from outside the EU, funding from a UK sponsor is pretty much impossible. Contact your chosen school for more details and if you are from a country that is part of the Commonwealth and wish to do a postgraduate course, contact:

The Scholarship Guide for Commonwealth Postgraduate Students,
Association of Commonwealth Universities,
John Foster House,
36 Gordon Square,
London WC1H OPF
Telephone 020 7380 6700
www.acu.ac.uk

Working part time as a foreign student

As an EU student there are no barriers. Anyone from outside the EU is allowed to work part time in the UK but this is limited to 20 hours per week. For more details, visit www.ukstudentlife.com/Work/Rules.htm. Remember that as a student you do not have to pay tax on your earnings. For further information, visit www.hmrc.gov.uk/students.

More useful websites:
www.dfes.gov.uk/international-students/vaetuk.shtml
www.dfes.gov.uk/gfees

National Insurance (NI) numbers for non-UK nationals

To work in the UK you need a National Insurance number (*see also* page 154). As a foreigner, you need to apply for one by calling 0845 600 0643 (8.00am–8.00pm, Monday to Friday). You can only apply for an NI number if you are in full time work as you need a letter from your employer to prove this. It's a good idea therefore to try and get some part-time work in the holidays or while you are at drama school as sometimes it's possible to apply for an NI this way, depending on the job, and you can resolve this before you graduate. Alternatively, I suggest you get *any* kind of job within reason once you graduate to apply for one of these numbers as soon as possible, otherwise you will have to pay emergency tax on your temporary NI number (the numbers are made up from your birth date). Emergency tax is about 40 per cent of your earnings, so *nearly double* the tax you would normally pay if you were earning not more than £40,000 per annum. You can claim this emergency tax back at the end of the year, but it's a complicated procedure and best avoided. If you need to claim back emergency tax, call 0845 077 6543 for the relevant forms and/or also have a look at: www.direct.gov.uk/MoneyTaxAndBenefits/Taxes/ReclaimingTax/

Once you have applied for a NI number by phone, you will then be asked to attend an interview where you will asked questions about your identity and why you need the number. Don't worry: the Inland Revenue just wants to establish you are not a criminal or a refugee. You will be sent a batch of forms (or given these at interview) to fill out, such as your address history. In addition to this, you will have to bring your passport, driver's licence, possibly a rental agreement, proof of where you live, a letter from your college (including course details) and a student card if you request a NI number while still at drama school. If you have graduated, you will need to produce a letter from your employer to prove you have work. After the interview you will be sent a letter stating your NI number and finally a card with your name and NI number.

This process can take time, so get started as soon as possible. For more details, see www.dwp.gov.uk/lifeevent/benefits/ni_number.asp

> **TIP!**
>
> Most drama schools hold tax workshops in the final year/term so make sure you ask relevant questions there.

Specialist courses for foreigners and/or non-native English speakers

★ Bristol Old Vic (www.oldvic.ac.uk/1yr_acting_overseas.html) offers a specialist one-year, full-time course for students from abroad.

★ Rose Bruford
(www.bruford.ac.uk/courses_fulltime_t.aspx?BackTo=courses_fulltime.aspx&C
ourseID=18) offers a one-year foundation course designed for overseas students.

★ Central School of Speech and Drama
(www.cssd.ac.uk/pages/Spoken_English.html) offers a two-week summer
course specifically designed for non-native English speakers.

★ RADA (www.rada.org/sum/inex.html) has a four-week course for professional Japanese actors to study classical Western acting, including rehearsals of
texts in Japanese translation.

Gap-year advice

'Who forces time is pushed back by time; who yields to time
finds time on his side.' – *The Talmud*

Taking a gap year is becoming more and more common and should not be
regarded as failure. Personally, I wish I'd taken one! People take gap years for
various reasons, whether it is to save money for drama school, mature and
gather some life and work experience before drama school or simply because
they are unsure about what they want to do. If, ultimately, you want to be a
performer or train at drama school but feel or have been advised you are as
yet too young, or perhaps you have been rejected first time around, there are
still various options to consider. There's no need to panic or feel lost and
there's *plenty* to do and experience. Here are some ideas:

★ Year Out Company (www.yearoutdrama.com/): This is a theatre
company/course based in Stratford-upon-Avon that's specifically designed for
people wishing to attend drama school at a later stage.

★ Foundation courses: Various schools offer these, including East 15,
Mountview and Oxford. *See also* pages 199–200 for a list of schools offering
full-time foundation courses, including the ones listed here.

★ Work: Yes, go out and get a job! You could even move away from home to
do so and build up some savings while you wait to go to drama school. Many
people take this option so they can afford drama school – even if you receive
funding, you will still have to pay living costs, including accommodation. You

don't want to be £20,000 in debt when you graduate, if you can help it! Inevitably, you will end up with some debt but there are student loans available that you can pay back once you leave college and start work (your college and Local Education Authority can provide details).

★ Travel: Earn some money and then spend it travelling. Go backpacking, build schools in India, do charity work in Africa! You could get a placement somewhere, sell boogie boards in Australia or simply earn your money around the world.

★ Teach English in a foreign country, Explore the world, gain work experience and earn money while doing so. Or go and learn a foreign language yourself.

★ Volunteering: Help the community! Old people, children, schools or the environment, the choice is endless. Visit www.gap-year.com/

★ Put on a production at one of the UK fringe festivals (*see also* page 294, *Contacts* and *The Actors Yearbook* for a list of festivals in the UK).

★ Get work experience in a theatre-related environment. This could be helping out for free at your local theatre, at a West End theatre, London's Globe Theatre, in a performance-related shop such as Dresscircle (*see also* page 279), even at TV studios. The BBC has some great work placements: www.bbc.co.uk/jobs/workexperience/

★ For theatre work experience, write to the various production companies (or check their websites) and write off to the theatres directly or visit them. The Theatre Royal Newcastle offers work placements each year: www.theatreroyal.co.uk/education_community/work_placement.html

As do the following theatres:
www.wycombeswan.co.uk/
www.tightfittheatre.co.uk/
www.queens-theatre.co.uk/
www.sheffieldtheatres.co.uk/
www.jghonline.co.uk/orangetree/
www.stevenage-leisure.co.uk/
www.cornwall.gov.uk/media/
www.yvonne-arnaud.co.uk/jobs.asp
www.wyverntheatre.org.uk/

www.royalexchange.co.uk/
www.youngvic.org/get-involved/
www.nationaltheatre.org.uk/
www.arctheatre.org.uk/
www.theambassadors.com/richmond/
www.guildford.gov.uk/GuildfordWeb/Leisure/ElectricTheatre/Employment/
www.halfmoon.org.uk/
www.warwickartscentre.co.uk/

Go to the theatres, drop off your CV and talk to people. Offering your services for free should usually get you some interest – there are never enough paid people around to do the work! For more listings of theatres and similar venues that provide work experience, check out *Contacts* and *The Actors Yearbook*.

★ Become a drama counsellor at Camp America:
www.gapyear.com/placements/gyc1711_drama_counsellor.html

Further acting placements, which sound very interesting, can be found at:
www.gapyear.com/placements/gyc_acting.html
www.gapyear.com/placements/gyc_drama.html

For dance placements, visit: www.gapyear.com/placements/gyc_contemporary_dance.html

And for all other types of placement:
www.gapyear.com/placements/index.html

★ Try a course that's not related to performing. This will give you a different insight into life because being a good performer is not just about thinking about acting 24/7. It may also make you a more rounded person. It's OK to also have other interests and pursue them! You will also have a trade of some sorts to pay your bills when your are out of acting work. Only a very small percentage of all Equity members work constantly. Most actors have other jobs and businesses to keep them afloat while auditioning for performing work.

★ Become an usher at a West End theatre or your local theatre (age 16-plus usually). Make money, see lots of productions, get to know performers and crew and make connections.

★ Do some TIE (Theatre in Education) jobs, which are often advertised in *PCR* and *The Stage*. This is a great way to learn about putting on a whole production and being responsible for everything, not just the performing side.

★ Take dance, drama and singing exams to further your skills. *See also* page 294 for links to the relevant pages.

★ Attend a part-time course and/or summer school. *See also* pages 187–189 for details of where to find a suitable part-time course in your area.

Whatever you choose to do, make sure you keep performing regularly in amateur or youth theatre. Keep watching productions, reading, listening and learning! If you wish to do MT, keep up your singing and dance training.

> **TIP!**
>
> If you want to go travelling or do a placement abroad, try to restrict this to just a few months so you still have time to prepare for your drama school auditions.

For more information, take a look at The Gap Year Guidebook: www.gap-year.com/browse.asp?catID=1001&sNode=1001&Exp=Y#1001

Performing opportunities for teenagers

'As a teenager you are at the last stage in your life when you will be happy to hear that the phone is for you.'
– *Fran Lebowitz*

So many teenagers I know are dying to get an agent and work professionally. Ever since the *Harry Potter* phenomenon, more and more young people want to be involved in the movie versions of the bespectacled magician, as well as other screen and stage projects. The reality about securing professional work as a teenager is rather bleak. As if being a teenager wasn't hard enough, this particular age also heavily reduces the amount of professional performance work opportunities. There's a simple reason for this: teenagers, particularly below the age of 16, prove difficult to hire for performance-related work because of all the legal issues connected to their age. They are too old to play children's parts; however if they are below 16 years old they will still need a guardian or police-checked chaperone to accompany them to every rehearsal, shooting, performance, and so on, just like a younger child. They also need a Children's Performance Licence. These have to be paid for and there are strict rules that need to be followed backstage and on the set, and possibly private school tutors to worry about, too. Contact Equity for more details about this. Teenagers are also only allowed to work certain hours a week and with full-time running shows, they are usually not allowed more than three or four performances a week, hence there may be two (or even three) sets of children cast.

It is therefore much easier for producers to hire actors who are18-plus, who simply look much younger but are professional actors with the required discipline and experience. They can work the full hours without a guardian and without other complicated rules connected to hiring children for professional performance work. Also, due to the fact that most teenagers are busy concentrating on GCSEs and A levels most of their focus often lies in this department, as it should. Of course there are always exceptions, like the young actors in *Harry Potter* or *Billy Elliott the musical*.

But I still want to perform, so what can I do?

At this point, I believe it's best to concentrate on your education and keep performing as a hobby. You want to get good grades so all options are open to you. Yes, school may seem like a chore, but it's really important to focus on your classes. You only have this time once in your life, so enjoy it! There's plenty of time. By all means go to dance, singing and other lessons or attend organisations like Stagecoach (www.stagecoach.co.uk) and Theatretrain (www.theatretrain.co.uk), which have specialist part-time courses for children and teenagers all over the UK. Try amateur and youth theatre (*see also* pages 290–292), even school theatre. Guildford Conservatoire offers a great weekend school for young performers as do various other schools. Surf the Internet for details. There are even young people's performance holidays: www.mysummercamps.com/camps/Arts_Camps/Theater/index.html, http://www.teen-summer-camps.com/ArtsMusicalTheater.htm,

You can do music and dance exams if you wish, and if you are 16 and above, try ushering part time at your local theatre. Pantomimes often look for local children and young adults to take part in the show, so keep an eye out for this as dance schools are usually involved. There are many different options. You don't have to be in the West End at 14 to have a lasting career! Many child and teenage performers burn out by the time they become adults. They may have vocal problems or become tired of performing and having to deal with so much pressure at a young age so they choose a different career. Others become successful adult performers. I would say the ratio is about 50:50.

If you do wish to find professional performing work, try open calls and write off to agents listed in *Contacts* that specifically look to represent young adults.

Attending a stage school

Stage schools like Sylvia Young (for contact details, *see also* page 183) are designed for children who wish to combine school work with acting/singing/dance classes and performing. There are various opinions on this kind of training and here are a few of the pros and cons:

Pros:

★ You can enjoy daily and regular lessons by consummate professionals.

★ Often you are represented by the in-house agency of that particular school, who will submit you for professional performance work, such as West End musicals, films, plays, commercials, etc.

★ This kind of training may benefit you when applying for drama school or you may be able to go straight into the profession.

★ You can make extensive contacts as you will be auditioning professionally quite regularly.

★ Stage school may build your self-confidence.

Cons:

★ It can be costly: Scholarships are available, but are limited.

★ You may have to board away from home, as these schools are usually located in and around London.

★ Your school work may suffer due to you having to focus so much energy on your performance classes and outside performances, especially if you are not academically minded.

★ It can be very hard work if you are actually working as that means you have school, your performance classes *and* performing/rehearsing for professional productions to worry about.

★ Stage school life may be too tough for many kids as it demands extreme discipline and independence. They grow up fast and behave like little adults, rather than children because for film/television/theatre producers, time equals money.

★ You could damage your voice. This is a tricky subject – if taught properly, your voice should be very strong, having been trained from such a young age. However, overuse of the voice from the amount of lessons, an over-ambitious/inexperienced teacher or having to perform, audition and do lessons may simply be too much for some young voices. Usually tutors should be able to gauge when enough is enough, however this is not always put into practice.

★ Stage school may focus you too soon into one career area and narrow your view of your other abilities. It could prevent you from enjoying other activities, which may help you to become a more rounded person.

TIP!

You do *not* need to go to one of these schools to have a long-lasting career in performing. Most performers in the profession have not attended one of these institutions and instead left professional performing until they were adults. In the ballet world, this kind of rigorous training from a young age may be required to be successful.

Below are the major schools offering training for those under 16, but there are also others:

★ Sylvia Young (www.sylviayoungtheatreschool.co.uk/) also do a Saturday and summer school and are located in London.

★ Redroofs (www.redroofs.co.uk/) located in Maidenhead, Berkshire.

★ Laines (www.laine-theatre-arts.co.uk/) in Epsom, Surrey.

★ The Hammond School (www.thehammondschool.co.uk/) focuses on dance and is located in Chester, Surrey.

★ The Brit School (www.brit.croydon.sch.uk/) is an independent, state-funded city college in Croydon, Surrey.

★ Pattison College (www.pattisons.co.uk/) in Coventry, West Midlands.

★ Ravenscourt Theatre School (www.ravenscourt.net/) in London.

★ Stonelands (www.stonelandsschool.co.uk/home.htm) in Sussex.

★ Arts Ed (www.aes-tring.com/index2.asp) in Tring, Hertfordshire.

★ Italia Conti (www.italiaconti.com/fullcourse5.html) in London.

★ London Studio Centre (www.london-studio-centre.co.uk/theatre_dance_course.html) in London.

★ The Academy of Performing Arts in Hove, Sussex (telephone 01273 383 999).

★ McKee School of Education, Dance & Drama in Liverpool (telephone 0151 724 1316).

★ Barbara Speake Stage School in London (telephone 020 8743 1306).

★ BLA (British Learning Association) Academy of Performing Arts in London (telephone 020 8850 9888).

★ Bright Sparkes Theatre School in London (telephone 020 8769 3500).

★ Sheila Bruce Community Arts in Hartlepool, Cleveland (telephone 01429 264 976).

★ Theatretrain in Sidcup and Dartford, Kent (telephone 01732 840 856).

★ Elliott Clarke School in Liverpool (telephone 0151 709 3323).

★ Greenwich Musical Theatre Academy in London (www.greenwichtheatre.org.uk/gmta.html).

Part-time courses for teenagers and children offered by NCDT (National Council of Drama Training) accredited drama schools:

★ Bristol Old Vic (www.oldvic.ac.uk/activ8.html).

★ Birmingham School of Speech and Drama (www.bssd.ac.uk/Courses/Young%5Fpeople).

★ East 15 (www.east15.ac.uk/courses/workshops.shtml).

★ Guildford Conservatoire
(www.conservatoire.org/content.asp?CategoryID=39).

★ Guildhall School of Music and Drama (www.gsmd.ac.uk/juniors/).

★ Italia Conti (www.italiaconti.com/shortcourse.html).

★ Mountview Academy
(www.mountview.ac.uk/community_courses_level2.asp?level2_ID=315).

★ Rose Bruford (www.bruford.ac.uk/courses_childrens.aspx).

★ RADA (www.rada.org/workshop/youth.html).

★ Royal Scottish Academy (RSA) (www.rsamd.ac.uk/drama/ywd.htm and www.rsamd.ac.uk/music/jam.htm).

★ Royal Welsh College (RWC): www.rwcmd.ac.uk/jmas/index.asp

★ Laines (www.laine-theatre-arts.co.uk/Junior_Squad.htm).

Also, have a look at the 24-hour Plays Scheme hosted by the Old Vic Theatre in London for young people aged 16 to 25: www.oldvictheatre.com/starbucksnewvoices.php.

Am I too old?

'For an actress to be a success she must have the face of Venus, the brains of Minerva, the grace of Terpsichore, the memory of Macaulay, the figure of Juno, and the hide of a rhinoceros.' – *Ethel Barrymore*

I believe that one is never too old to act or perform for a living. There are several examples of actors who started out at a later stage in life and gained success. Sometimes life experience and having worked in other professions can benefit your acting career. You may be limited in terms of full-time training options, though, as some drama schools exercise age cut-off dates (usually between the ages of 30 and 40). You may also think drama school not that suitable, as most students will be a lot younger than you. That said, I remember we had some mature students in their forties at my school, who integrated perfectly and enjoyed their training and the social side despite a recognisable age difference compared to their fellow students. It really depends on the person.

If drama school is not for you or you have family to consider, you could always go for the evening or part-time course option and practise with amateur groups. There are also specific schools for mature students who need to work during the day and do evening and weekend classes only. An example of this is The Poor School (www.thepoorschool.com) in London. Drama schools are usually supportive but will expect you to commit fully to a course and attend all lessons and rehearsals. This is something to consider if you have children and need to be home for them at a certain time. Often drama school days go beyond the original timetable and you may easily find yourself rehearsing until 11.00pm instead of the originally announced time of 8.00pm, which could cause problems if you have other commitments.

Really, there are no rules to follow and no definite age when one must stop trying. There can be various 'age gaps' in the market – some actresses, for example, decide to take a break and have a family at a certain time. This may form a niche for some aspirants just starting out. For musical theatre, however, it's good to train young. It is generally a young business and most MT courses have a definite cut-off age (generally from 18–30). However, this can vary from person to person. As long as you can keep up with the physical side of things, have the natural talent required and the drama school you wish to attend believes you have potential and a chance to be considered for professional musical theatre work, why not give it a try?

It's important to bear in mind, though, that if you are starting out at a later age then you will be competing with actors in your playing age range who will already have a lot of professional experience. Whether a casting director wants to go with a new face or cast someone they know with a proven track record depends on the situation and the person.

TIP!

You do *not* need to put your real age and birth date on your CV if you prefer not to! It's perfectly fine to put your playing age (e.g. 16–25). Your playing age is the age that you can be cast physically as yourself without special make-up or costume. You may be 30 on paper, but your *playing age* can be 20–30, rather than 30–40, especially if you keep yourself fit, follow a healthy lifestyle and have the right attitude. When determining your playing age, always ask advice from several industry professionals who are not too close to you so they can stay relatively neutral.

Courses and Resources

'The only place where success comes before work is in a dictionary.'
– *Vidal Sassoon*

Summer courses

An extremely good way to gain insight into drama school life, including schools and staff, is by taking a summer course. Many summer school staff members also teach on the full-time courses. I have found this experience to be extremely helpful and built up my confidence as I was encouraged to audition for a full-time course after being observed for two weeks on the summer course. It also gave me a good insight into how the school worked and what they expected of full-time students. Summer courses can be expensive and are usually not eligible for funding. Some schools offer free courses for certain age groups (*see also* pages 339–345 for the summer school listing). There's no official ranking as to which course is best and different courses suit different people.

> **TIP!**
>
> Have a look at drama school websites as most of them offer evening, weekend or other part-time courses for adults.

Part-time and evening courses

If you decide not to go to drama school, there are other options also in preparation for drama school. Further places to look at for part-time courses are:

★ The City Lit (www.citylit.ac.uk) is based in central London. Telephone 020 7831 7831. This college also offers a full-time one-year foundation course and a theatre company you can join by audition.

★ Goldsmiths College (www.goldsmiths.ac.uk) is based in south London (near New Cross). Telephone 020 7919 7200.

★ Liverpool Theatre School and College (www.liverpooltheatreschoolandcollege.co.uk/courses.html). Telephone 0151 728 7800.

★ Morley College (www.morleycollege.ac.uk) is in Waterloo, London. Telephone 020 7928 8501.

★ Act up (www.act-up.co.uk): funded part-time acting courses for adults 18-plus, professionals and those wishing to turn professional. They are based in London but also offer funded courses in Nottingham and Manchester. Telephone 020 7924 7701 or email: info@act-up.co.uk.

★ London Academy of Radio, Film & TV
American Building
79a Tottenham Court Road
London W1T 4TD
www.media-courses.com
Telephone 020 8408 7158
email: help@londonacademy.co.uk

★ FT2 (Film and Television Freelance Training)
4th Floor, Warwick House
9 Warwick Street,
London W1R 5RA
www.ft2.org.uk
Telephone 020 7734 5141

★ National Short Course Training Programme
The National Film and Television School
Beaconsfield
Bucks. HP9 1LE
www.nftsfilm-tv.ac.uk
Telephone 014946 71234
email: admin@nftsfilm-tv.ac.uk

★ Lists of more courses can be found on:
www.floodlight.co.uk/pls/courses/fl_home.pg_home

www.ukperformingarts.co.uk/.

Also, have a look at *The Actors Yearbook* for a list of courses and adult colleges in your area and contact your Local Education Authority for details of any other part-time courses in your area.

Studying and working in the USA

'Hollywood is a place where they'll pay you a thousand dollars for a kiss and fifty cents for your soul.' – *Marilyn Monroe*

We hear many stories of actors who made it in Hollywood or who got a big break in America when the UK market would not give them a chance. But what does re-locating to the USA really involve?

Studying in the USA

To gain entry to American universities or colleges you will need to complete SATs. The SAT (pronounced 'S-A-T') Reasoning Test, formerly called the Scholastic Aptitude Test and Scholastic Assessment Test, is a type of is a type of standardised test frequently used by colleges and universities in the United States to aid in the selection of incoming students. In the USA the SAT is administered by the private College Board and is developed, published and scored by the Educational Testing Service.

To register online for taking your SAT test:
www.collegeboard.com/student/testing/sat/reg.html

To practise for your SAT test: www.testprepreview.com/sat_practice.htm

---

TIP!

Due to the difference in education systems and the fact that you must take SAT tests to be offered a place at a US college/university, your general school grades *are* important and *will* matter!

Check with individual schools for specific audition requirements. Most of the time they will expect you to attend an audition in the US, but some will accept a video audition.

TIP!

The following are two Internet boards where performance students and those aspiring discuss US-based courses and schools: www.broadwayworld.com/board/index.cfm?boardname=student and http://talk.collegeconfidential.com/forumdisplay.php?f=501

As in the UK, there is no official ranking system for US performance courses. The following is a list of all main universities/colleges offering acting musical theatre courses. Schools offering MT courses are marked as such:

★ Alabama
Birmingham-Southern College
University of Alabama
University of South Alabama

★ Arizona
Arizona State University
University of Arizona (MT)

★ Arkansas
Ouachita Baptist University

★ California
California State University, Chico
California State University, Fullerton (MT)
Notre Dame de Namur University
University of California – Irving
University of California – Los Angeles
University of Southern California

★ Colorado
Metropolitan State College of Denver
University of Colorado
University of Northern Colorado

★ Connecticut
Hartford Conservatory
University of Hartford – The Hartt School (MT)

★ District of Columbia
American University
Catholic University
Howard University

★ Florida
Florida State University
New World School of the Arts
Palm Beach Atlantic University
University of Central Florida
University of Florida
University of Miami (MT)
University of West Florida

★ Georgia
Brenau University
Shorter College
Valdosta University
Young Harris College

★ Illinois
Columbia College
Illinois State University
Illinois Wesleyan University
Millikin University
North Central College
Northwestern University (MT)
Roosevelt University (MT)
Western Illinois University

★ Indiana
Ball State University
Indiana University
Vincennes University

★ Iowa
Drake University

★ Kansas
Friends University
University of Kansas
Wichita State University

★ Kentucky
Northern Kentucky University
Western Kentucky University

★ Louisiana
Tulane University

★ Maine
University of Southern Maine

★ Massachusetts
Boston Conservatory
Dean College
Emerson College (MT)
Northeastern University

★ Michigan
Central Michigan University
Oakland University
University of Michigan (MT)
Western Michigan University

★ Minnesota
University of Minnesota-Duluth

★ Mississippi
University of Mississippi

★ Missouri
Avila University
Missouri Valley College
Southwest Missouri State
University of Missouri, Kansas City
Webster University (MT)

★ Nebraska
University of Nebraska
University of Nebraska at Kearney

★ Nevada
University of Nevada, Las Vegas

★ New Hampshire
Plymouth State University
University of New Hampshire

★ New Jersey
Montclair State University
Westminster Choir College

★ New Mexico
College of Santa Fe (MT)

★ New York
American Musical and Dramatic Academy
Circle in the Square Theatre School
Ithaca College (MT)
Marymount Manhattan (MT)
Nazareth College
New York University: Tisch School of the Arts (MT)
New York University: Steinhardt School of Education (MT)
Russell Sage College with NYSTI (New York State Theatre Institute)
SUNY (State University of New York), Buffalo
SUNY, Cortland
SUNY, Fredonia
SUNY, Geneseo
SUNY, New Paltz
Syracuse University (MT)
Wagner College

★ North Carolina
Catawba College
East Carolina University
Elon University (MT)
Lees-McCrae College

Mars Hill College
Meredith College
University of North Carolina at Pembroke
Western Carolina University

★ Ohio
Ashland University
Baldwin-Wallace College (MT)
Kent State University
Marietta College
Ohio Northern University
Otterbein College (MT)
University of Akron
University of Cincinnati – College Conservatory of Music (MT)
Wright State University
Youngstown State University

★ Oklahoma
Oklahoma City University (MT)
University of Central Oklahoma
University of Oklahoma (MT)
University of Tulsa

★ Oregon
Southern Oregon University

★ Pennsylvania
Carnegie-Mellon University
Muhlenberg College
Pennsylvania State University (MT)
Point Park University (MT)
Seton Hill University
Susquehanna University
University of the Arts (MT)
West Chester University
Wilkes University

★ Rhode Island
Rhode Island College

★ South Carolina
Coastal Carolina University
Coker College

★ Tennessee
Belmont University

★ Texas
Abilene Christian University
KD Studio
Sam Houston State University (MT)
Texas Christian University
Texas State University-San Marcos
University of Texas at Arlington
West Texas

★ Utah
Brigham Young University
Weber State University

★ Virginia
James Madison University

★ Washington
University of Puget Sound

★ West Virginia
West Virginia Wesleyan College

★ Wisconsin
Carthage College
University of Wisconsin – Green Bay
University of Wisconsin – Stevens Point
Viterbo University

★ Wycoming
Casper College

TIP!

MT is also offered at Carnegie Mellon University in New York and Shenandoah Conservatory in Winchester, Virginia.

Colleges offering graduate (meaning postgraduate) MT degrees
★ Arizona State University
★ Boston Conservatory
★ Oklahoma City University
★ San Diego State University
★ University of Central Florida
★ University of Nevada, Las Vegas

The advantages of studying performance in the US as an EU citizen

★The United States programmes, particularly musical theatre, have an international reputation for excellence.

★International contacts can be very useful for the future.

★The experience will broaden your view of the world and promote independence.

★You may be able to acquire professional work from auditions you take part in during your studies there and perhaps secure a green card this way. This is a rare case scenario, though, so do not depend on it.

And the disadvantages

★You will usually need to leave the country as soon as your student visa runs out.

★Possibilities for part-time work are restricted but you are usually permitted to complete on campus part-time work if you apply for a specific type of visa (J1 visa). Check with colleges individually.

★ Unlike UK course, most US undergraduate courses are four and three years in length. In some cases, it's possible to complete your degree in three years if you take classes during your holidays, particularly the summer break. Again, check with schools direct.

★ Upon returning to the UK, you will have no contacts there and agents will not have seen you perform on final term/year productions or a showcase.

★ You will not automatically be eligible for UK Equity status.

★ Courses are very expensive (more so than in the UK) and you are usually not eligible for any funding and, of course, you will not be able to live at home to save money. Contact individual schools to see what's on offer for various routes to financial aid in the UK. You may be able to get loans from certain banks like Citibank.

Also visit:
www.useduguides.com/europe/index.html?area=europe&source=googleeuro

TIP!

Here is a website offering various publications for free (download in PDF format) for foreigners wishing to study in the United States: www.educationusa.state.gov/
For visa queries and other information, check out: www.getvisas.co.uk/

I want to try and make it in America, is this possible?
Working professionally in the US without a Work Permit (green card) is illegal. Ways to acquire a green card are few, as follows:

★ Join the green card lottery at age 18-plus: www.official-green-card.org/

★ If you have any relatives who are US citizens (or were born there) or you marry a US citizen, you can get a green card. For more details: www.soyouwanna.com/site/syws/greencard/

★ You may be able to get part-time work on a student visa but check before you go. There are people who have managed to secure work in the US on this kind of visa, however it is rare and since September 11 the rules and restrictions have tightened considerably.

★ Sometimes performers come to the US in UK touring productions and attract the interest of an American agent who will try and help them arrange a work permit.

TIP!

You will not be eligible to join US leading casting directories without a green card.

If you do decide to try your luck
★ Make sure you have a place to stay.

★ Remember that the sheer number of aspiring performers is even higher than in the UK, simply due to the size of the country. There are even more people around going for the same auditions.

★ I recommend going to the US with a CV consisting of good professional UK credits, a show reel/demo CD/voice-over CD of UK work. It's best to go with some sort of history, or even better, a UK agent who can recommend you or offer US contacts you can approach.

★ Network! Make sure you know some people or have some contacts to look up before you go.

★ Do your research first. Depending on whether you are going to LA or NYC make sure you know how to contact casting people, agents, find places to train in singing, dance, etc. and you have a good idea of how the audition process works. It's important to know, for example, that US Equity is much stricter than their UK counterpart and most auditions on Broadway are 'Equity member priority' or 'agent only'. As a UK citizen you are not automatically be eligible for US Equity, so you may end up not getting seen at all.

★ Give yourself a year there and if you have made no progress at all by that time, return home.

★ Make sure you have saved up enough money before you go. You will *not* be able to work in the US on a holiday visa!

★ The main US casting directories are: www.academyplayers.org and www.breakdownservices.com

★ Get some American photographs done as requirements differ from the UK. The US tends to go for glamour, while the UK prefers naturalism/realism. Note that American CVs are constructed differently to those in the UK; LA requires colour photographs.

★ Be aware that LA is extremely looks- and body-conscious.

Foundation courses

These courses have become more and more popular as an alternative to, or preparation for, full-time drama school. There are full-time and part-time variations and they are generally meant for students who are not yet ready to attend full-time drama school due to age, lack of experience or general lack of focus and direction.

A full-time foundation course may be too intense for some students – it is often a simplified version of the first year at drama school. Part-time courses are useful as you can pursue work, other studies and/or amateur dramatics at the same time.

> **TIP!**
>
> You do not have to attend a foundation course to be ready for full-time training and there are other less expensive options such as amateur and youth theatre. Students have gained places at drama school before foundation courses ever existed – they are not mandatory! Foundation courses may be beneficial for those who are still very young and/or have had very little acting and performance experience. They can also further self-discipline and organisation skills for those students who need more practice in these areas to cope with the demands and pressures of drama school.

Musical theatre foundation courses

These can be a very good idea as they are often cheaper than taking all singing and dance lessons separately. Also, you get used to regular training in all disciplines which you may need to get used to before joining a full-time three-year course if you have not had the experience or training before.

Attending a foundation course is usually no guarantee you will receive a place on the full-time course of that school once completed. Foundation courses are usually not eligible for any funding or scholarships.

> **TIP!**
>
> Consider the Year Out Drama Company (www.yearoutdrama.com) in Stratford-upon-Avon as an alternative. Telephone 01789 266 245 or email yearoutdrama@stratford.ac.uk

Drama schools offering full-time foundation courses (acting and MT)
★ Drama Centre, London: http://courses.csm.arts.ac.uk/

★ LAMDA, London: www.lamda.org.uk/

★ Mountview Academy, London: www.mountview.ac.uk/

★ Oxford School of Drama (6 months only): http://oxford.drama.ac.uk/

★ Rose Bruford, Kent (this course is designed for *international* students): www.bruford.ac.uk/

★ RADA, London (6 months only): www.rada.org/

★ East 15, London: http://east15.ac.uk/

★ Liverpool Theatre School and College (MT): www.liverpooltheatreschoolandcollege.co.uk/

Publications
Spotlight
The industry's leading casting resource comes in book form (updated annually) and via the Internet. It is divided into sections such as character actor/actress, dancers, presenters, children, leading man/female and recent graduates.

TIP!

If you miss the *Spotlight* application or renewal deadline, you may have to wait up to 18 months your entry appears in the Spotlight books! Deadlines for your photo to appear in the *Spotlight* books themselves, not on the website, are as follows:

Actors: 15 October
Actresses: 15 April
Children: 15 November
Drama school graduates (2–3 year courses): 15 October
Postgrads: 24 November
Presenters: 10 July

To register, contact *Spotlight* for details (see below). You must provide certain professional credits or a drama school course degree/diploma to be permitted to join. Your entry will appear in the book itself in alphabetical order with your photo (always submit a reproduction and never an original). Your name, eye and hair colour and agent's name will also be listed. If you don't have an agent, '*The Spotlight* 'will be listed as your contact details. You will also appear on their website with your own personal page including photos, skills, credits, personal statistics, voice clips and other details you may wish to publish. The internet website can only be accessed by professionals who have requested a login from *Spotlight*, not the general public.

For more information visit www.spotlightcd.com or contact *Spotlight* via:

The Spotlight
7 Leicester Place
London WC2H 7RJ
Telephone 020 7437 7631
E-mail: info@spotlight.com

TIP!

> Nearly all agents now submit their casting via *Spotlight* and it's therefore mandatory for most that you join.

Spotlight graduation party

This is an annual event that usually takes place in May at the Café de Paris in London. It's exclusively for CDS (Council of Drama Schools) and CDET (Conference of Drama Schools) students and brings together hundreds of performers from leading schools and colleges across the UK. The evening starts with a chance for final-year students to meet casting directors and other industry professionals. This is followed by live music, entertainment, special guests and DJs until the early hours. Tickets can be bought through your drama school or *Spotlight*'s website (details above). Final-year students get priority booking as it's essentially their graduation ball.

Castweb, Castnet and Castingcallpro

These are all services similar to *Spotlight*, where you can register your information as a performer or model in exchange for a joining fee to be spotted for auditions. I have tried several and found that it is luck which service works best for you and which registration will pay off. There are also several other services I have not listed but described below are the major ones.

Depending on the service, your information can be viewed publicly or by registered professionals within the industry who have requested permission only. Unlike *Spotlight*, these services are online only. You also receive daily information on audition news and sometimes get sent a text if you have been requested for an audition.

★ Castweb (www.castweb.co.uk): You must be a *Spotlight* or Equity member to join.
Email: info@castweb.co.uk
Telephone: 020 7720 9002

★ Castnet (www.castingnetwork.co.uk): Only for actors who have graduated from an accredited drama school (free for casting directors to search).
Email: admin@castingnetwork.co.uk
Telephone: 020 8420 4209

★ Castingcallpro (www.castingcallpro.com): This service offers various sections for UK, US and Canadian citizens. They also have a section for extras. You must be a graduate from an accredited drama school, an Equity member or have performed in at least three professional shows (extra work and non-speaking parts are not applicable). It's free to register and make your details accessible but to search for work you have to pay a fee.

The Actors Yearbook
This is an essential publication for you to have access to. It's a comprehensive reference guide to television, film and theatre and includes contact details for agents, production companies, radio, film, TV, voice-over work and much more. Available online at www.acblack.com

Contacts
Another important publication listing over 5,000 companies, services and individuals across television, stage, film and radio. This includes agents, casting directors, rehearsal rooms, digs, part-time courses, photographers, voice coaches, wigs, props, etc. Buy online at www.spotlightcd.com/shop/contacts

PCR (Production and Casting Report)
In addition to listing auditions, *PCR* (www.pcrnewsletter.com) provides weekly production news for film, television and theatre with cast and crew breakdowns and other contacts every Monday. You can subscribe annually or monthly.

The Stage
A weekly newspaper (every Thursday) providing recruitment information related to the industry, reviews, performance listings, a forum, entertainment news, an advice column, and much more. To subscribe, visit www.thestage.co.uk

Whose Where?
This is an A to Z listing of all contacts updated weekly in *PCR* and available for purchase through the *PCR* website. For more listings of publications and online casting companies, visit www.ncdt.co.uk/useful.asp and www.ncdt.co.uk/links.asp

Equity
The trade union representing those who work in the entertainment and arts industries. Members are not just actors but also dancers, singers, choreographers, backstage artists, such as stage managers, designers and directors, as well as walk-on and supporting artists and stunt performers. Equity's main function is to watch over terms and conditions of employment throughout the industry and to give advice to its members regarding all aspects of the industry.

You can join as a child student member (if attending an accredited drama school) or a youth member (professional performers aged 14–16) and as a full member if you have completed professional work and/or attended an accredited drama school. Membership is also available to opera singers, dancers, technical theatre staff, variety and circus acts, walk-on artists and overseas performers granted permission to work in the UK. You do not have to be an Equity member to be eligible for professional auditions; but some employers prefer that you are a member.

Membership benefits include help with negotiating contracts (for a small charge), free legal advice, welfare and insurance advice (tax, National Insurance, benefits, Jobseeker's Allowance guide, etc), a monthly magazine, medical support through the British Performing Arts Medicine Trust helpline, registers for casting directors that you can join, a job board on their Internet page, protection of your professional name, a list of accountants and a recommended digs list, discounts for certain services and shops, distribution of royalties and various insurance schemes, including a 24-hour accident cover. For more information visit: www.equity.org.uk

If you are a member you will find lots of helpful information under the 'members only' link. Email: info@equity.org.uk. Various branches of Equity are set up across the UK and here are their details:

Equity (South East)
Guild House
Upper St. Martins Lane
London WC2H 9EG
Telephone: 0207 379 6000
Fax: 0207 379 7001
Contact: John Ainslie

Equity (Midlands)
PO Box 1221
Warwick CV34 5EF
Telephone/fax: 01926 408 638
Contact: Tim Johnson

Equity (North East)
The Workstation
15 Paternoster Row
Sheffield S1 2BX
Telephone/fax: 01142 759 746
Contact: Nigel Jones

Equity (North West)
Conavon Court
12 Blackfriars Street
Salford M3 5BQ
Telephone: 0161 832 3183
Fax: 0161 839 3133
Contacts: Mike Cain, Mary Hooley

Equity (Scotland, Northern Ireland and Isle of Man)
114 Union Street
Glasgow G1 3QQ
Telephone: 0141 248 2472
Fax: 0141 248 2473
Contacts: Lorne Boswell/Drew McFarlane, Irene Gilchrist

Equity (Wales and South West)
Transport House
1 Cathedral Road
Cardiff CF1 9SD
Telephone: 029 20 397 971
Fax: 029 20 230 754
Contacts: Christopher Ryde, Mair James Buckley

Monologues and Acting

★

'The most precious things in speech are pauses.'
– Ralph Richardson

The lowdown on audition monologues

I know what you're all thinking – here's a list of material I can safely choose and then relax, knowing I won't make any mistakes by choosing the wrong pieces! Unfortunately, it doesn't quite work that way with monologues. There are simply too many available to compile a list and while some schools may name material they don't want to hear, in the audition information from another school there may actually be a list of the same pieces, stating you must choose from them for your audition! This is such a diverse field and trends change all the time as new plays are written and others become less favourable, having been heard too many times. The key to finding what suits you best and what you feel connected to is to do your research. See as many shows/films as possible and read plays.

Keep your eyes and ears open for a character that jumps out at you. Sometimes the best monologues can be those you have recently performed, even if it was an amateur or school production, as you are comfortable and confident about them.

TIP!

Ask professionals you know, who have seen you work/worked with you, for advice or playwrights that may suit you.

Choosing a monologue: some general advice

o Pick a character close to your playing age. If you look 18, don't choose a character that is 27, for example. Select someone you could be cast as now, rather than in 10 years time.

★ If auditioning for drama school, stick to your native accent. It's a good idea to look at plays and characters set in the area you are from, as you will be able to relate well to the general feeling of the play/monologue/character and it may therefore show you off to your best advantage.

★ Shakespeare: It's OK to audition in your native accent. Do not put on a fake 'Queen's English' accent just because you think it's required. It's not and it may just distract from the character journey you are delivering, possibly making you feel or seem unsure.

★ Make sure you read the whole play and know where your speech belongs in the context of the plot.

★ The normal length for an audition speech is about two minutes but this can vary depending on what you are auditioning for.

★ This may sound very basic, but it's something that's often forgotten: The monologue should have a beginning, a middle and an end! Don't leave your audience hanging.

★ Many people forget that one of the most important things regarding speeches is how you *start* your performance. Think about this and make a definite choice. If you're on the panel, there's nothing worse than sitting there, wondering have they started yet?

★ Make sure you know your pieces backwards. Practise reading aloud a lot and with someone you trust, such as your audition tutor (*see also* pages 217–219).

★ If you find it hard to imagine the person you're speaking to, then for practice, place an object where you have placed them. Make sure you don't rely on it too much, though!

★ If you are having trouble remembering the lines, record yourself speaking the monologue and then play it back to yourself. Also, try and associate certain phrases and words with an emotion the character is feeling at that point in time.

★ Make sure your monologue works outside the context of the play, meaning it has a life and story of its own, even if the person/people watching do not know the work itself.

★ Prepare at least five or six speeches for drama school. If they are interested in you, some panels may want to see you do several pieces and if you have not prepared for this, then you may let yourself down. If you are re-applying, learn new speeches as well as the one(s) you auditioned with last time so you show a willingness to challenge yourself (vital for training) and work on your progression as an actor.

★ Choose a piece that shows a character journey rather than just tells a story as these tend to contain more emotion. You want an active character alive with emotions: someone reminiscing about a fishing trip that they took part in won't show the panel enough! I have found that the best monologues are usually when the character speaks to someone (or a group of people) in the present tense. Of course there are always exceptions, where a character relating an incident from the past can show tremendous insight and emotional scope. An example of this would be Paul San Marco's monologue in the musical *A Chorus Line*.

★ Choose pieces that display your strengths and range as an actor. Make sure you show contrasts such as regal/earthy, drama/comedy and different energies.

★ *Enjoy* the pieces you are performing! Don't choose something you can't relate to – be *excited* about your pieces.

★ Make sure you understand all the words and/or general meaning – for Shakespeare, this is particularly important. How can you portray a character convincingly if you don't know what they're saying?

★ Generally, stay away from poems. They're generally unsuitable because they are usually more about language than a particular character. You need a piece that shows the emotional journey of a character.

★ *Never* use speeches you have written yourself – a good actor doth not a good playwright make! This seldom works and I would stay away from this option, especially when starting out.

★ Be wary of novels. This writing is not intended for performance. Some novels can work as audition material, others not. Get some advice on particular pieces from other individuals in the profession, such as your audition tutor.

★ Some people believe they have to show extremes such as crying, violence, vulgar language, nudity, and so on to prove their intensity and determination to a panel. But it's not the case. Remember that some of the most memorable performances have been those of the 'less is more' variety. You are not there to shock (most panels would not be shocked anyway, they have seen it all!) but merely to provide an insight into your talent and style as an actor. On the other hand, a choice of the above will not go against you if you feel this is the way you would like to present yourself and it suits the audition.

> ### TIP!
> If your speech includes swearing (or any other type of profanity), perform it as written. A panel will not be put off by this if it's in the original text and part of the character you are performing.

★ Cutting/pasting together a monologue – yes, this is possible and acceptable as long as you stick to simply cutting words or phrases rather than replacing or adding any words. Find some professional help if you are auditioning for drama school, as this can be an art in itself.

★ If you feel completely lost in terms of staging, etc. it's OK to ask for help (*see also* pages 217–219).

★ Make sure your monologues don't become too safe. Sometimes, if you do the same piece for many auditions (or years), your delivery can become a bit automatic. It helps to work on something new and then return to your original monologue after some time has passed. It's also a good idea, therefore, to have a repertoire of monologues.

★ Again, this may sound very basic, but do choose a monologue that's suitable for the production you are auditioning for!

★ Do not perform directly to panel members while performing your speeches (unless so directed). Pick a spot at your eye level, just above their heads. The panel wants to observe you and your performance, rather than feel like they are acting with you. Some panel members can get uncomfortable if you involve them personally in your speech.

★ Cross-gender speeches: Some speeches can be done as either male or female, which is fine as long as you make sure there's no reference to the gender opposite to your own in your monologue! The same applies for speeches written for a certain ethnic group. As long as there's no reference in the text to what colour the character is, this should be fine. Of course, if you choose a text, for example, which has strong references to a certain culture and dialect (and your own culture is completely different), this may not be so suitable for obvious reasons. Try and get advice for particular speeches.

'If you cried a little less, the audience would cry more.'
– *Dame Edith Evans*

Preparing a monologue

Here are some examples of monologues frequently used at auditions and incorporating all of the above:

Classical

★ Helena from *A Midsummer Night's Dream* (Shakespeare), Act 3, scene 2 from 'Oh spite, oh hell, I see you are all bent...'

★ Lady Macbeth from *Macbeth* (Shakespeare), Act 1, scene 5 from 'They met in the day of success...'

★ Hamlet from *Hamlet* (Shakespeare), Act 3, scene 1 from 'To be or not to be, that is the question...'

★ Flute (Thisbe) from *A Midsummer Night's Dream* (Shakespeare), Act 5, scene 1 from 'Asleep my love?...'

Modern

★ Carol from *Oleanna* (David Mamet), from 'For Christ's sake...'

★ Sophie from *The Star Spangled Girl* (Neil Simon), from 'Mr Cornell, ah have tried to be neighbourly...'

★ Tom from *The Glass Menagerie* (Tennessee Williams), from 'Listen, you think I'm crazy about the warehouse?...'

★ Matt from *Guess Who's Coming to Dinner* (William Rose), from 'Now it became clear that we had one single day...'

Monologue books

Such collections have become very popular and many of the monologues recommended are very good indeed. However, there's the danger of choosing something which is also a favourite of many other auditioning actors and you may well be the twentieth person that day to perform it, which is often the case at drama school auditions. Hence, I would advise sifting through these books, choosing a character in a monologue that appeals to you and then going away and reading the play itself. Try to find a *different* monologue by the same character not listed in the compilation books.

By all means prepare some well-known monologues but also have something different up your sleeve. In the end it's your choice but delivering something fresh and new to a panel can often work in your favour and shows you have done your research.

TIP!

Be wary of plays that are part of the A level or GCSE curriculum as these tend to be overused.

Some drama schools also have lists or comments on certain monologues they do not want prospective students to use as they have been performed too often. These can be a useful reference as they usually contain material currently in trend and possibly a good idea to avoid. The monologue regulations vary from school to school.

Overdone material

As mentioned above, it's up to you whether you choose to tackle a commonly known speech and give it your own slant or prefer to try something different. Keep in mind that if you choose well-known material you will be compared and panels may feel you have not done enough research and reading. I recommend learning a mixture of well-known and lesser-known material.

Here are some examples of overdone monologues as found in an American survey of 116 industry professionals in September 2006:

www.monologueaudition.com/Overdonewomen.pdf
www.monologueaudition.com/overdone_men.htm,
www.monologueaudition.com/overdone_shakespeare.htm

Simon Dunmore lists overdone Shakespeare:
www.btinternet.com/~simon.dunmore/

Modern and classical: what do they mean?

The break between modern and classical tends to be around 1850. Shakespeare, Oscar Wilde and their contemporaries are examples of classical playwrights. Carryl Churchill, David Hare and Jim Cartwright are modern ones. The definition of modern and classical can vary greatly from school to school, though, so it's best to read the audition guidelines carefully and to ask if in doubt whether your piece qualifies as modern or not. When auditioning for a professional production, make sure your speech suits the time the play/show you are auditioning for was written.

I have found some good pieces, so how do I prepare them?

Here are some tips to get you started:

★ Read the entire play. Make sure you know the context of your speech compared to the rest of the plot and characters.

★ Who is your character? What are they like physically? What is their history, their relationship with others in the play and in the speech itself? (If directed at someone else or a group of people.) What journey do they go through emotionally and/or physically in the speech and in the play? (These are two different types of journey.) You should be able to find most answers in the text.

★ Even though you will be performing you speech without props, scenery and a costume, create a mental image of where you are at that point and what your character would be wearing. You don't have to make a list of favourite colour, uncle's names, and so on, but use your imagination to 'set the stage' for yourself.

★ Stage your piece. Don't think you have to move to be interesting! Stillness can be very powerful and is sometimes much harder to perform convincingly than rehearsed moves. Believe in the strength of the words you are saying. Think about focus and pick a point above the panel's head as your focus. If the focus changes, make sure you find a *reason* for it to change. If you want to move or do anything, make sure it comes from instinct. Never do anything because you think you should. Try not to rely on props like chairs, you may very well find that you enter the audition space and there isn't one available.

★ Allow time to learn and, more importantly, digest a speech. It needs time to settle into your emotional and physical memory. Learning the speech the week before an audition is usually a bad idea, especially if you are auditioning for drama school and new to the whole process.

★ Accents: Be sure you are very competent at using them and practise doing the speech with an accent. Suddenly putting an accent to a speech learned in RP or your natural accent can totally throw you.

★ Don't rush, take your time! Don't feel you have to get to the end, it's not a marathon.

★ If it helps, write out your speech and highlight certain moods, mark changes of emotion, staging, etc.

★ Think about why you have chosen your pieces and how they show your strengths and uniqueness as an actor. Don't just say this is my casting type – there should be more to it than that!

> **TIP!**
>
> Don't copy speeches in the way you have seen other people or famous actors do them! This will come across as being a bad copy of someone else's performance. What you are really looking for is to bring yourself to the speech and be original, unique and you (*see also* page 47).

Speeches from musicals and film/television

Some schools happily accept these as audition pieces, others don't. It's best to check with individual schools. Speeches from movies can be dangerous as you may be too closely compared to the actor who immortalised the original role (*Lock, Stock and Two Smoking Barrels*, *Billy Elliott*, etc.) However, if you think you can offer a whole new take, then feel free. Speeches from musicals are rare to find as most musicals have songs as song monologues. However, there are some exceptions and they can sometimes make excellent audition material.

> **TIP!**
>
> Sometimes the best way to find undiscovered audition material is by going to the source itself, namely to contact theatres and theatre companies putting on new writing. Some of these list new works and their synopsis on their websites, which you can then research to see if there are any suitable characters for your audition needs. You can also ask for a list of new plays/playwrights that have been recently produced and research from there. I believe this is a very good way to find underused material, especially new contemporary monologues, which seem to become overdone very quickly.

Some UK theatres that put on new writing
★ The Traverse Theatre (Scotland's new writing theatre) has many new works put on by Scottish writers (www.traverse.co.uk/show_result.php).

★ Liverpool's New Writing Theatre (some new plays are available to buy on the website; also see the 'been and gone' section) (www.thenewworks.com/whats.htm).

★ The Warehouse Theatre in Croydon performs new writing and also holds the International Playwriting Festival (www.warehousetheatre.co.uk).

★ The New Venture Theatre in Brighton (www.newventure.org.uk/home.asp).

★ Theatre Royal Stratford East (www.stratfordeast.com/newwriting.php).

★ Hampstead Theatre, London (www.hampsteadtheatre.com/content.asp?CategoryID=960).

★ Soho Theatre, London (www.sohotheatre.com/).

★ Tricycle Theatre, London (www.tricycle.co.uk/htmlnew/index.php).

★ Finborough Theatre, London (http://finboroughtheatre.itgo.com/).

★ The Royal Court Theatre, London (www.royalcourttheatre.com).

★ The Bush Theatre, London (www.bushtheatre.co.uk).

Theatre companies performing new works
★ Northumberland Theatre Company (www.northumberlandtheatre.co.uk/index.cfm).

★ Nuffield Theatre, Southampton (www.nuffieldtheatre.co.uk/cn/nuffield/nuffield.php?section=nuffield).

★ Out of Joint is a theatre company dedicated to new writing (www.outofjoint.co.uk/).

★ Show of Strength Theatre Company, Brunel (http://showofstrength.org.uk/).

★ Theatre Absolute, Coventry (www.theatreabsolute.co.uk/home.asp).

★ White Bear Theatre Club, London (www.whitebeartheatre.co.uk/).

Also, 7:84 TC Scotland, 333 Woodlands Road, Glasgow G3 6NG. Telephone 0141 334 6686. And for Welsh new writing, Sherman TC, Senghennydd Road, Cardiff CF2 4YE. Telephone 01222 396844.

Plays and Playwrights 2007
www.amazon.com/Plays-Playwrights-Martin-Denton-editor/dp/0967023491
This is the eighth volume of an annual anthology of plays recently produced in New York by emerging playwrights. It may be worth having a look at this (as well as the former seven volumes), although characters and setting may be American, which is not ideal for drama school auditions when you are preferred to audition with your native accent. However, some monologues and characters may also be suitable for British accents, depending on the play. It's definitely worth a look when hunting for contemporary material.

In Yer Face Theatre (www.inyerface-theatre.com/az.html) offers a comprehensive 'A–Z of new writing'. Although some material may again be very popular (Sarah Kane), it's worth looking up the lesser-known playwrights mentioned and their works.

Direct links to monologues
Please note that I cannot guarantee *all* the material will be useful for auditions, although many of the monologues will be of interest. Some may be very overdone, others written by non-professional playwrights, which may not be an ideal choice. If in doubt, ask an industry professional for help.

www.whysanity.net/monos/
www.playdatabase.com
www.shakespeare-monologues.org/
www.monologuearchive.com/
www.monologues.co.uk/
www.theatrehistory.com/plays/monologues.html
http://members.aol.com/lockslett3/monol/monolg.html
www.members.tripod.com/denmark01/naranja/
http://epicwords.tripod.com/monologues.html
www.actorpoint.com/monologue.html
www.matthewaeverett.com/search/index.php

www.geocities.com/akatsavou/monologue_en.html
www.geocities.com/foxfire321/monologues-from-plays.html
www.trainedactor.com/classroom/choose.html
www.geocities.com/foxfire321/Girls-World-of-Theater.html
www.twiztv.com/scripts/
www.monologueaudition.com/
www.notmyshoes.net/monologues/
www.btinternet.com/~simon.dunmore/
www.theatrefolk.com/spotlight/download/3
www.stageagent.com/monologues.shtml
www.jimmybrunelle.com/ (also for kids and teens)
www.angelfire.com/realm/theatre/femalemono.html
www.artsonthemove.co.uk/resources/scripts/scriptsyoung.html
www.artsonthemove.co.uk/resources/scripts/scriptswomen.html
www.sunnyhillsdrama.com/women%20monologues.htm
www.sunnyhillsdrama.com/men's%20monologues.htm
www.theatrehistory.com/plays/wedekindmono.html
www.broadwayworld.com/board/readmessage.cfm?thread=871066&boardna
me=student&dt=27

And for monologues from musicals, visit
www.musicaltheatreaudition.com/shows/1materials/index.html.

What belongs in a monologue audition repertoire?

> 'I didn't like the play. But I saw it under unfavourable cir-
> cumstances – the curtains were up.' – *Groucho Marx*

I advise you to have at least five or six speeches in your repertoire; also when
auditioning for drama school. Have an example from each of the following
categories:

★ A modern comedy speech.

★ A modern dramatic speech.

★ A comedy speech from Shakespeare.

★ A dramatic speech from Shakespeare.

★ A further classic speech, such as Oscar Wilde or a Pinero in case they ask for classical but non-Shakespeare.

★ Any additional speech that shows off a special skill like an accent, juggling, acrobatics, etc.

The more speeches you have, the more material you have to choose from for auditions. Also the more practice you will have delivering different kinds of material.

Audition coaches

'When you're a young man, Macbeth is a character part. When you're older, it's a straight part.' – *Laurence Olivier*

Whether for professional work or drama school auditions, some of you may feel you need feedback from that 'outside eye and ear' regarding your audition material. Have you picked the right piece? Do you feel uncomfortable with or uncertain about your staging? Perhaps you want to know if you are coming across well to those watching and listening? Maybe you find it impossible to track down a piece to connect with in the first place?

The audition tutor (or audition coach) can prepare you for auditions. They will not teach you how to act, nor will they tell you what to do, where to walk or when to move your arm, and so on. Some people prefer to have an audition tutor, while others don't, and you do not have to use one to be prepared for auditions. Here, there's a fine line as there's always a risk that the information and 'help' you receive can be inhibiting and/or negative.

TIP!

Working with an audition tutor is like rehearsing your pieces with a director and working with the feedback you get and improving your performance in this manner.

Some drama schools state they prefer you not to have any coaching for your pieces. Who you choose to trust is entirely personal, so go with your gut feeling on this. For some people, help from an audition tutor can be a vital factor in improving their confidence and they learn ways to unfold their natural talent so audition panels can see exactly what they have to offer. Drama schools look for talent rather than the perfect performance and although some schools advise against using a tutor, as the number of applicants for schools continues to rise, it may be that the more prepared you can come across, the better.

After having real trouble trying to locate suitable monologues for my drama school auditions, I decided to contact the local adult college head of acting for help. For me, this was a very good decision. Not only was I reassured that my pieces were absolutely fine, but I was also given creative encouragement in the ways to approach them and how to pace myself. Basics such as when to start my pieces, where to stand in the room and whether I was audible enough were covered. I was given the confidence I lacked due to inexperience to perform to the best of my ability. But this is my own experience and others I know were offered training places on their own instinctive accounts of performing monologues without any assistance. Again, there are no rules, but don't be afraid to ask for help if you feel you need it.

What makes a good audition coach?
★ An audition tutor should be someone who is (or was) either a professional actor themselves or involved in the business in other ways. They might be a casting person, possibly an agent, a director, a drama school tutor/director or someone who used to teach at drama school, or a person who has been on drama school and/or professional audition panels. They should not be a close friend or family member as they are too close to you.

★ They will give you notes without being negative or putting you down and will offer constructive criticism.

★ They will encourage you to be truthful to the text, in the moment and be honest about everything you do.

★ They will give you helpful exercises, encourage you to try things in different ways, make definite choices and never make you feel inhibited. In addition, they will be polite, not shout or swear at you.

★ They won't tell you what to do, or get up and show you what to do or want you to simply copy their actions. They know this is your interpretation and that there's no single right way to perform a monologue as long as you are in the moment and true to the text. They will help bring out your particular style and strengths.

★ They may give you tips on line memorising, projection and other technical aspects of a monologue performance and will help you stage the pieces.

★ They will make you feel confident and more relaxed. Also, they'll encourage you to find your own monologues, but will recommend plays and playwrights for you to consider as they have a very good knowledge of what material is out there.

★ A good tutor will tell you when they believe you are ready to perform the piece, although they'll also make sure that you too feel ready. Audition teachers can also be helpful with staging and other issues, so take your songs to them.

Note that teachers (university tutors and GCSE/A-level drama) are often not a good choice for audition tutors. Although their academic knowledge may be outstanding, they may lack the professional industry knowledge and experience. Also, they tend to approach monologues from an academic rather than performance point of view. To sum it up, a good audition tutor will open acting doors, help break down any barriers you may have, clarify things and give you the confidence to show off your talent, potential and uniqueness as a performer to your best possible standard.

Where can I find someone to help me?

There are various places you can look although a personal recommendation is usually the best way. Ask around in your amateur group, your local youth theatre or Stagecoach. Also try The Actors Centre, *Contacts*, Actors Temple (www.actorstemple.com/one2ones/), the NCDT notice board (www.ncdt.co.uk/noticeboard.asp), dance, music and acting colleges of any kind that have notice boards or online notice boards. You can also ask at your local theatre and check *The Stage* classified section. *See also* pages 275–296 for further contact details.

> **TIP!**
>
> Check out drama school websites as they sometimes do audition technique weekends or weeks (*see also* pages 339–345 for details of summer courses).

How much will I have to pay?

At the Actors Temple in London you can attend a 45-minute session for about £20 at the time of writing. Audition tutors that are well known and have an excellent track record for helping people usually charge more, about £35–40 per hour. Again, outside London prices are usually lower.

Singing

★

'Look. I'm 40. I'm single and I work in a musical theatre – you do the math!'
– *Nathan Lane*

Types of musical theatre audition songs

What songs are available and when are they suitable?
Choosing a suitable song to sing for an audition can be almost as important as the singing and performance itself and it's vital that you pick material that shows you and your talents off to best advantage. I remember a girl singing 'Music Of The Night', who was auditioning for *Mamma Mia*. Not only did she try to sing it in the original male key (which was extremely unsuitable for her voice), it was also a highly inappropriate song for that type of show.

Singing for drama school auditions
For musical theatre courses, panels want to see the particular strengths, style, talent and casting type you have to offer, whether you have started to discover who you are as a performer and what type of material suits you. Here are some of the things they'll be looking for:

★ A character and journey throughout your pieces. The acting should be the first and foremost thing in your mind, you should make definite choices and let them lead your performance. *See also* the advice on how to act a song, pages 226–227.

★ Pieces that show off your singing range but still lie comfortably within it. Make sure you can hit all the notes comfortably without straining.

★ A contrast of pieces. Don't prepare all your songs by the same composer or same era, choose contrasting pieces. Show off different sides and styles.

★ If you do decide to present well-known material, have some unusual choices prepared too. This will show you have not just chosen the first popular MT tune you could think of that's currently on in the West End.

★ Choose pieces that you are good at and that suit your type. Don't sing 'The World's Fattest Dancer' if you are a slim and petite! Equally, if you find songs with a falsetto difficult, stay away from this kind of material and choose something that is more you.

For audition tips regarding acting courses, where singing is not such a deciding factor, *see also* pages 239–241.

Singing for professional auditions

In addition to the above-mentioned, panels looking to cast a professional production don't just want to see if you can sing. They want to know how you, your skills, your talents and look can suit and benefit the particular production they are casting. Therefore, it's important to do your research about characters, time/setting and the musical style of the show you are up for. Choose songs accordingly. It's usually a good idea to select audition material (or at least one of the pieces) from the composer of the particular musical for which you are auditioning. This is especially relevant when you are asked to 'prepare a song in the style of the show' or similar instructions.

This means that if you are auditioning for Rodgers & Hammerstein's *Oklahoma!*, they will expect to hear musical pieces from the same era and in the same sort of musical style. It would therefore make sense to choose your audition material from the Rodgers & Hammerstein repertoire. For example, if you pick a pop song or a Jason Robert Brown piece, it will have little relevance for the panel as to whether you are suitable for the style of music and singing required for *Oklahoma!* It's quite possible they may not see your potential for any roles in the show they are casting. Try and find songs similar in feeling and style to the character/show you are hoping to be cast as. Here are some examples:

Freddy (young leading man in *My Fair Lady*) – 'She Is Not Thinking Of Me' (*Gigi*).

Mr Lundy (mature leading man in *Brigadoon*) – 'The Impossible Dream' (*Man of La Mancha*).

Johnny (feisty leading man in *Dirty Dancing*) – 'I Can't Stand Still' (*Footloose*).

Auditioning for a male dance part – 'Stepping Out With My Baby' (*Easter Parade*).

Scar (villain in *The Lion King*) – 'Another Pyramid' (*Aida*).

Male ensemble for *Parade* (Jason Robert Brown) – 'She Cries' (*Songs For a New World*).

Public Enemy (comedy/character in *Anything Goes*) – 'Brush Up Your Shakespeare' (*Kiss Me, Kate*).

Rosabella (ingénue lead in *The Most Happy Fella*) – 'I've Never Been In Love Before' (*Guys and Dolls*).

Mrs Potts (mature leading lady in *Beauty and the Beast*) – 'If He Walked Into My Life' (*Mame*).

Auditioning for a female dance part – 'Go Into Your Dance' (*42nd Street*).

Velma (the bad girl in *Chicago*) – 'The World Goes Round' (*New York, New York*).

Ado Annie (comedy/character in *Oklahoma!*) – 'I'll Show Him' (*Plain and Fancy*).

Female chorus for *Jekyll and Hyde* – 'Gold' (*Camille Claudel*).

The following are song types that are part of the audition process for most musical theatre and play auditions. There are, of course, many more types of song, such as Torch, Point Number, etc., but below you will find explanations of the main types of songs you will be asked to prepare for an audition.

Ballad

This is a story in song, which can be romantic, sentimental or dramatic with a slow tune. In musical theatre, an example of a romantic ballad would be 'If Ever I Would Leave You' from *Camelot*, while 'How Many Tears' from *Martin Guerre* is an example of a dramatic ballad. There are also differences between the classic musical theatre ballad, such as 'If I Loved You' from *Carousel* and the modern musical theatre – 'Christmas Lullaby' from *Songs For a New World*, for example. The final type of ballad in musical theatre is the pop ballad, such as material from the musicals *Aida* or *Rent*. For females, ballads can be either sung in lyrical voice ('Think Of Me' from *Phantom of the Opera*) or with a belt quality ('Someone Like You' from *Jekyll and Hyde*). You can choose any variation of ballad for your audition for drama school. As mentioned previously, for professional auditions it is beneficial to pick material in the style of the show for which you are being seen (*see also* below).

Character
This is also sometimes known as comedy song. These are pieces where the performer portrays a certain type of character (the villain or the funny side-kick, for example) and usually include either comedy or a direct correspondence with the audience. Examples are: 'Be Prepared' from *The Lion King*, 'Popular' from *Wicked*, 'I'm Calm' from *A Funny Thing Happened On the Way to the Forum* or 'Little Girls' from *Annie*.

Up-tempo
Basically, this is a very fast song. There are many different examples, which can be romantic ('Almost Like Being in Love' from *Brigadoon*), dramatic ('Mein Herr' from *Cabaret*), modern ('I Can't Stand Still' from *Footloose*), classic musical theatre ('I'm A Bad, Bad Man' from *Annie, Get Your Gun*) or character/comedy ('The World's Fattest Dancer' from *Fame*). Most character and comedy songs tend to have an up-tempo element.

Patter song
This is very fast and very wordy. Examples include 'Modern Major General' from *Pirates of Penzance* and 'Words, Words, Words' from *The Witches of Eastwick*. These songs may be required and are useful for the actor who sings, as they do not always require a lot of range (the character of Professor Higgins in *My Fair Lady*, for example), although they still can.

Classical
Pieces from opera and operetta are not required as often as the other types of songs. Classical material is usually only suitable for auditions for shows such as *Phantom of the Opera* and work by Gilbert & Sullivan. I suggest you stick to musical theatre pieces unless those auditioning specifically say they are open to classical material. Most musical theatre courses state in their audition guidelines that classical material should not be used for course auditions.

Rock/pop/modern
Some drama schools are happy to allow pop and rock material (Mariah Carey,

Dido, Stevie Wonder, etc.), while some are not. It's best to read the audition guidelines carefully. For professional production, rock and pop songs can be used if suitable for the show, such as *Mamma Mia*, *We Will Rock You*, etc. as often these are specifically requested.

The 'all-in-one audition' song

In my opinion, this is the ideal audition song. An 'all-in-one number' is a song of about two to two and a half minutes (or sometimes three minutes), sometimes 3 minutes, which shows a definite character journey with a beginning, middle and an end. It tells a story with excellent lyrics (the composer has got to be good, for example Sondheim, Harold Arlen, and so on) and strong character definition. These are the best audition pieces because they are like sung monologues. You can immediately show a strong acting journey through song and I would say that some of these songs are almost foolproof because they are structured so well.

These songs are usually very well known, popular and overdone, hence I have listed samples of not so well known ones in my recommended song list. Well-known examples include: 'On My Own' from *Les Misérables*, 'Adelaide's Lament' (*Guys and Dolls*), 'Some Enchanted Evening' (*South Pacific*), 'Send in the Clowns' (*A Little Night Music*), 'Reviewing the Situation' (*Oliver!*), 'Mister Snow' (*Carousel*). Songs with more of a pop nature are more 'sung as thought' numbers, meaning they are sung by the character, while he/she is in a certain mood/dilemma. Often pop songs have no full character design as such (characters and acting are not so strongly represented in pop material, being a different musical field). However, what audition panels want to see you do is perform and act a character journey and song, not just hit top notes in an interesting way with trills, and so on. It's different if you are auditioning for a pop musical, of course, but if you choose to do a pop song for your drama school audition, make sure the contrasting song is an excellent all-in-one number.

The beauty of a great all-in-one number is that if you nail the character, just sing the lyrics as you are in the moment, think about the character journey and pick a song in your range then it should really show off your strengths. I don't want to use the phrase 'automatically' as that suggests a lazy performer, but good lyrics count for a lot. If you pick a song that is not so well written or unsuited for audition purposes, it's much harder to present it and consequently your talents and strengths may not come across as well.

Unsuitable songs

★ Chorus numbers – For example, 'Thank You Very Much' from *Scrooge* or

'Be Our Guest' from *Beauty and the Beast* – they are not meant to be sung by one character only.

★ Progression songs/songs explaining the setting – Examples of these: 'You Did It' from *My Fair Lady* or 'Henry Street' from *Funny Girl*, as they are not usually suited for one character journey; also often they do not have enough character range as this is not what they were constructed for.

★ Duets – These *can* be used if you edit appropriately ('I Have Dreamed' from *The King and I*). Some duets such as 'Sue Me' from *Guys and Dolls*, or 'Anything You Can Do, I Can Do Better' from *Annie, Get Your Gun* are not impossible for a solo version as the whole song depends on the characters interrupting and topping each other. If in doubt, ask a professional and/or your singing teacher for help. As an example of how *not* to make use of a duet, I remember once witnessing a lad singing both parts (at once, as they were cutting into each other) for an audition!

★ Opening and closing numbers – 'Another Opening, Another Show' from *Kiss Me, Kate*, for example, can cause similar problems to progression songs and again, does not have enough of a character journey.

★ Songs you wrote yourself/were written by a friend or relative – Unless your relative happens to be Oscar Hammerstein, of course, these are best avoided! Stick to tried-and-tested material that is critically well acclaimed.

Choosing a song for a pantomime audition

There are two types of pantomimes: classic and modern. In the classic version, the lead male is played by a girl ('principal boy'), while in modern pantomime cross-gender casting does not usually take place, apart from the dame. Also, classic pantos tend to prefer Disney and classic MT musical material, while modern ones often consist of pop songs. To read more about the history of pantomime and the differences between various forms, visit www.its-behind-you.com/

Your audition material needs to vary depending on what kind of pantomime you are up for. Usually, as with most auditions, you will be asked to prepare two contrasting songs, so it's good to have ideas for both in your repertoire. As the princess for example (Snow White, Cinderella) you may do well singing a song such as 'Some Day My Prince Will Come' from the Disney movie if classic. 'I'm Not That Innocent' is good if modern and poppy. As principal boy (auditioning as a girl) you may sing 'Stop In The Name Of Love'

(Diana Ross) if modern, or 'The Lady Is A Tramp' if classic. As principal boy (auditioning as a man), songs like 'If I Can't Love Her' (*Beauty and the Beast*) for a classic panto or 'She's Like The Wind' (*Dirty Dancing*), if modern is required. For Buttons and other similar comedy side-kicks, try material such as 'Tonight At Eight' from *She Loves Me* (classic) and a chart pop song for modern. The dame is a tough one and it really depends on your type of dame, though. Here song recommendations are difficult to make. For evil queens, fairies and similar characters, 'If You Believe' from *The Wiz* can work for both classic and modern. Chorus in pantos tend to be dance-orientated, so it's probably best to sing a happy, fun, positive type of song.

Practical tips for your audition
What does it mean to 'act a song'?
For MT songs, acting a song makes sense literally, as you are singing in character and therefore have the accent of that character, and so on. If the song is not from a show, it may still be from a movie, like *Moon River*, in which case again you have a character to base it on. Of course you do not need to stick to that particular character. You can create and choose any character you like so long as you are truthful and in the moment and make definite choices. By 'acting a song' what is initially meant is *giving value to the lyrics*. That means you pay attention to what you are saying and are being in the moment, as if you are saying those words for the first time as they pop into your head. It's like a monologue except you have a tune to go with it. Many singers do their songs as monologues for practice so they can really concentrate on the lyrics. The tune is just the 'underscore' for what you are saying.

A typical mistake singers make is to concentrate on the notes (particularly if they are high or difficult) and forget what they are saying and why. Or they sing a top note extremely loudly because it is a top note when the lyric may ask them to sing that note softer or give it less emphasis. A song is meaningless and empty if you don't give the lyrics meaning. Otherwise the audience just hears a nice voice and a good tune, but not much more than that. What makes an extraordinary singer is not just tonal quality, phrasing, style and to a degree range but also the ability to interpret the song. Done well, it sounds as if they invented the words on the spot and say them for the first time; every single person in the audience feels drawn in, as if the song is being sung to them individually. Every song tells a story. Think why someone is singing that song at that particular moment in time and what each word means.

Another important consideration is that when speaking a song as a monologue you need to go over the usual breaks and phrases of the way the music dictates it and re-phrase according to a speech.

Don't necessarily allow the tune or placement of the notes determine the phrasing and emphasis of the word. Just because a word is placed on a top G does not necessarily mean it needs the most emphasis and volume. The way you sing a song should always be connected to the journey of your particular character.

Picking a song for your age range

For musical theatre auditions (especially drama school), choose a song sung by a character in your age range. Don't sing a song where the lyrics imply the character is much younger or older than you. You want to be able to relate to your chosen piece. It's important to present a panel with material and characters they can see you playing now, rather than in 10 or 20 years' time! Unless, you are of course professionally auditioning for an older part. Some songs may be 'ageless', meaning the lyrics don't suggest a certain age, in which case it's fine to present them at all ages.

Preparing your sheet music

When taking songs to the audition, make sure they are easy for the accompanist to work with. Many people photocopy the music, then tape the pages together with clear tape from the back (one piece top, one middle, one bottom) and highlight key changes, etc. Or they file the photocopies in pocket holes (see-through files with holes on the left side) which can be placed in a folder. The most important thing is that the pages can be easily turned, which is often not possible with a book, especially if it is new or rarely used.

> **TIP!**
>
> Bringing a backing track instead of sheet music is not the norm for either drama school/similar course or professional auditions. If you have a backing track, feel free to take it along but make sure you also have sheet music as 99 per cent of the time the panel will expect you to have prepared sheet music. Backing tracks are more commonly used for cruise ship and band/music group auditions.

Transposing songs

Generally, I recommend singing the song in its original key. There are two reasons for this. The first is that if you transpose a song down, the panel will have a subconscious negative memory because they will have heard what you *can't* do, namely they will remember you *can't* hit that original top note, which is why you had to transpose the song down. They'll also wonder why you didn't just choose a different song that sits better in your range in its original key. If you transpose a song up, again they'll wonder why you didn't choose a song that is higher placed to show off top notes. The second reason is that transposing a song can change the entire feeling of the song and how it comes across, even though you may only have gone up or down by two or three keys. Singing a soprano song as an alto (and vice versa) can sometimes make a big difference, depending on the song. This does not apply to all material but generally songs change in feel if you alter their key. Also, some songs (many jazz standards, for example) were written in male and female keys as they can be sung by both sexes, in which case again, it's fine to use a different key. Finally, if you wish to sing a song usually sung by a male character (or vice versa), transposing up or down to the required gender key is also acceptable. Make sure that you get professional help with this, though!

If you do choose to transpose a song then be prepared to answer questions and give a reason why. In the end, it's your choice and some people have been successful in presenting transposed material but generally panels prefer songs in their original key.

> **TIP!**
>
> If you find your particular song is part of a musical theatre anthology or similar songbook and it has been transposed up or down on one of these compendiums, I would say that it's safe to use this version as it has been generally approved by the industry.

Singing songs written for opposite sex

This is fine as long so the key works (see above) and the lyrics do not conflict with your gender. Sometimes a cross-gender song can be a refreshing change for a panel and artists such as Linda Eder (*Man of La Mancha*) have made it their signature. Some panels, though, are not greatly in favour of cross-gender auditions, so again, be prepared to answer questions if they ask why you made that choice.

Changing lyrics and notes in songs

Never change the tune of a song! There's a reason why the composer wrote it a certain way and they would almost certainly not wish to hear it performed any differently. If you wish to finish the song's final note higher or lower than written, this is sometimes possible, but check with a professional. Note that the above applies to MT and you *can* improvise and bend the notes, etc. when it comes to jazz tunes and standards. If you are changing lyrics, only do this to solve gender problems when singing material usually sung by the gender opposite to yours, and again, try and find a professional to help you.

TIP!

Always choose a song within your range! It's better to sing something less rangy, but well and in tune, rather to scream or squeak out a top note you really can't hit that well. Present what you are good at, pieces that show your singing and acting range and most importantly, *enjoy* singing the material you present. If you don't like it, how can you possibly convince those observing?

Staging your songs

The most important thing to remember is that an audition is like a mini production. It has a beginning and a middle and an end. You are taking the panel on a journey. You are not singing simply to show a top C or to display an emotion. This is certainly part of your performance, but to make your character (and what you are singing/your acting journey believable and exciting to watch), consider the following:

★ Where is your character in relation to location and time period? Are they a nineties drug addict living on the streets (*Rent*) or an upper-class aristocrat in a corset at the turn of the century (*The Woman in White*)? This can make a vast difference as to how you present your song, how your character would stand, posture, and so on.

★ Are they singing to anyone in particular? What is their relationship? What has happened in the past that has influenced their relationship? You do not have to follow the actual storyline of the musical; you can make up your own as long as it is clearly thought through.

★ What is the reason for your character starting to sing this song, what is the trigger in the story? As above, you can again make up your own reason, if you wish.

★ What journey does the character go on? Is there a resolution at the end?

★ Staging does not automatically mean you have to move. There's nothing worse than watching a performer waving their arms and hands about for no apparent reason. If you make a gesture, make it definite and commit to it. Have a reason why you choose to move. Don't gesture just because you think you should, always follow your instinct.

★ Once you have started to perform your song, never move backwards, only diagonally, to the side or forwards. Moving backwards creates distance between you and the panel and therefore your performance. It can also come across as apologetic and/or negative.

★ Practise your song as a monologue (*see also* page 226).

★ *Never* copy anyone else! Be yourself and give your own interpretation. Otherwise you will just come across as a Liza Minelli or Philip Quast tribute, which is only of interest if you are auditioning for that type of show (*Rat Pack The Musical*, for example).

★ If you are staging dance moves, make sure they look like part of the whole performance rather than someone singing who suddenly goes into a few random dance steps! Be aware that they have to connect smoothly to create a full picture.

For advice on how to interpret lyrics and how to act a song, *see also* page 226. Also, have a look at the staging advice for monologues (page 212) as much of this applies to staging a song.

> **TIP!**
>
> If you are reapplying to the same school/course, learn new songs as well as the ones you prepared/performed the year before. Schools may remember you and even your piece (they do keep records). They will want to see some development since the last time they saw you perform as their reason for rejection may have been that they thought you were too young or not mature enough vocally or something similar. If you sing the same song then you may come across as unwilling to learn new material or not wanting to push your own boundaries and explore/create. In a worst case scenario, they might see you as being lazy! By all means take along the song from last year, but have something new up your sleeve too.

Vocal ranges and voice types

To discover your vocal range, find a piano and simply sing through the scale from the lowest possible note you can sing to the top note. The same procedure applies for your belt range. You may find it helpful to involve a professional/singing teacher for further clarification and if you cannot read music.

The vocal ranges listed below (from lowest to highest) should be taken as a general guide. Numbers indicate which note is meant. For example, C4 means the 4th C (counting from left to right) on a piano keyboard. B2 indicates the 2nd C, A5 the 5th C, etc.

Soprano: A3–C6
Mezzo-soprano: A3–F5
Alto: G3–D5
Tenor: B2–G4
Baritone: G2–E4
Bass: E2–C4

For more information on vocal ranges, types of voices and singing, visit www.vocalist.org.uk

TIP!

When including your singing range on your CV, make sure you put notes where you sound in tune, are strong and comfortable (no screeching or screaming!) and you can hit every time, even with nerves in an audition situation.

Accompanists

'Has anybody ever seen a dramatic critic in the daytime? Of course not! They come out after dark, up to no good.'
– P.G. Wodehouse

An accompanist is a person who musically supports an individual or choir, and for our purposes, on the piano. He/she is *not* a pianist as he/she fulfils a totally different role. While a pianist's prime aim is to interpret a piece of music to technical perfection, personal style and perform this to an audience, an accompanist is there to serve the singer(s) and their performance. Professionals sometimes use accompanists to practise their pieces before auditions.

Most professionals will be able to tell you all sorts of stories about accompanists. I have worked with some wonderful ones in the past, as well as some that turned out to be a complete nightmare. I remember doing a gig at a cabaret venue, where the pianist hired for the evening proceeded to get completely drunk as the performance went on. I was on last, at about midnight. I got through about half of the first song when I was interrupted. Out of nowhere my accompanist dropped the sheet music and started to play from the middle of my second number! After several attempts to clarify to him what I was doing and him responding with merry renditions of Bach and Chopin tunes (not in my planned repertoire, it was a jazz venue), I just shouted 'Cut!' and legged it off stage as fast as I could!

A good accompanist…

★ Will have a large repertoire of songs, with or without sheet music, although very good accompanists know most popular songs by heart.

★ Will have excellent sight-reading skills and be able to play music on the spot.

★ Can arrange/rearrange songs if need be and transpose (via computer or hand writing) into a different key (they may charge extra for this).

★ Will make it his/her prime aim to follow the singer and his/her interpretation.

★ Is able to adapt to different singers and their styles quickly and smoothly.

★ May have experience of playing 'in the pit' (in the orchestra) for professional musicals and may have experience accompanying cabaret acts or concert singers.

★ Will have excellent musicianship skills and an great ear for chords.

★ Has experience accompanying singers. If you need an accompanist for musical theatre or jazz standards, make sure you find someone with this kind of experience as it can vary greatly from the classical type of accompaniment that is not as 'loose' generally.

★ May be able to transpose keys on the spot without music, although only the very best accompanists accomplish this skill to perfection.

Really, accompanying is a unique job and often excellent accompanists are also professional musical directors and can be highly sought after. Some professionals take their own accompanist along to auditions as it makes them feel less nervous and they know their accompanist understands their songs and their voice and style perfectly.

So where can I find an accompanist?

Again, recommendations are usually the best way to go. Ask singing teachers and other people in the business. Check notice boards at music colleges and universities; also theatres, cabaret venues, The Actors Centre, music library notice boards, any place to do with the performing arts. Try www.yell.co.uk or a music directory. Check out Music Angels www.website.lineone.net/~galbraith-woods/Music%20Angels/ and visit this useful site listing accompanists all over the UK: www.uk-piano.org/piano-accompanists/.

How much will I have to pay?

Usually, anything between £20 and £40 per hour in London. Rates outside London can be cheaper. Some accompanists give you deals if you go and see them regularly.

> **TIP!**
>
> Drama schools and professional auditions usually provide accompanists.

Sheet music, backing tracks and transposition services

'Music is the shorthand of emotion.' – Leo Tolstoy

It is the worst feeling in the world when you have found a song you really like and are then unable to locate the sheet music. This has happened to me so many times, not just when starting out. I remember trying to copy out a song myself with my (very) basic music theory skills from a song on a CD – failing miserably.

The main stores for sheet music are Chappells, Foyles and Dresscircle, all located in London, but they also have mail order and you can order online at some. Chappells sells a large variety of backing tracks (including a inexpensive book that lists all backing tracks on offer) and sheet music, as does Foyles and Dresscircle.

Chappells

In my view, the best and first place to look for any sheet music. If it is out of print they may also recommend where to look instead.

152–160 Wardour Street (they used to be based near Bond Street but have moved)
enquiries_bs@chappell-bond-st.co.uk
www.chappellofbondstreet.co.uk/
Telephone: 020 7491 2777

TIP!

Chappells now offer a fantastic online search facility for sheet music.

Foyles

Two stores, one in Charing Cross Road, the other in the Royal Festival Hall near Waterloo in London. Visit www.foyles.co.uk/foyles/index.asp for further details.

Dresscircle

57–59 Monmouth Street
Upper St Martin's Lane
London WC2H 9DG
info@dresscircle.co.uk
www.dresscircle.co.uk
Telephone: 020 7240 2227

Below, I have listed some sites providing catalogues of available backing tracks (often difficult to find and unusual). These sites also offer a music transposition service if you need songs in a different key or transcribed from a CD as the sheet music is not available and/or out of print:

www.musicalmidi.net/ – Fully orchestrated backing tracks, also for full musical scores. They also offer transpositions of keys and transcriptions and they can turn a piece of music into a backing track/midi file (a song file you can save on a midi disk and also save on your computer) as well as into a sheet music piano copy or 17-piece arrangement.

London arrangements have a huge online catalogue of available backing tracks and also make them to order. Apart from backing tracks they also transpose sheet music and transcribe from CDs. Pay and order online.

30 Maryland Square
London E15 1HE
Telephone: 020 8221 2381
Fax: 020 8926 2724
www.londonarrangements.co.uk
E-mail: enquiries@londonarrangements.co.uk

www.standardstrax.com/ – a further website offering backing tracks
Also try:

www.ameritz.co.uk
www.musicalcreations.com (based in the US)

For online sheet music (which you may be able to pay for and download
instantly, depending on the site), visit:
www.pianofiles.com – great site where you can register and trade sheet
music with other users for free
www.sheetmusicuk.com
www.musicroom.co.uk
www.sheetmusicplus.com
www.sheetmusicdirect.com
www.8notes.com
www.musicnotes.com
www.sheetmusicnow.com

These are just a few examples and there are many sheet music services online
to choose from. Also check out EBay, Amazon and www.halleonard.com, who
are the publishers for a lot of musical theatre related sheet music. Riseman on
www.riseman.com/auction.php?min=401 also has regular auctions for sheet
music and you may be able to obtain a rare, out-of-print piece that way.

TIP!

If you are using sheet music for personal study and having a hard time
finding your desired piece, contact Weinberger's, who will probably
offer you at least perusal of the material and may possibly send/fax
you a copy - www.josef-weinberger.co.uk/weinberger/index.html

Finding sheet music outside London

I suggest ordering and buying online. Some services will let you download the music and print it off straight away once you have bought it. For music shops in your area, check out www.yell.co.uk

Libraries and sheet music

Apart from trying your local library (you would be surprised just how many of them actually do have sheet music), there are three main places in and around London. These are the Victoria Music Library in London, The Performing Arts Library in Dorking, Surrey and the Barbican Music Library, where you can borrow sheet music for free. For full details, see page 78.

Photocopying sheet music

This is problematic because basically it is illegal and libraries have warning signs above their photocopiers stating that it is against the law. However, many people do photocopy sheet music for audition and studying purposes. *See also* page 228 for more details on how to present your sheet music.

> **TIP!**
>
> Make sure that the key of the song you have been practising listening to a CD in your bedroom is in the *same* key as your sheet music!

Sight singing, reading music and music theory

'Wisely, and slow. They stumble that run fast.'
– William Shakespeare

Some people panic at the mention of this, but don't despair: it *is* something you can learn. I remember first learning to sight sing when I did my Guildhall singing exams at the age of 17. I was lucky as I had good piano skills and could read music from an early age, but even so it takes some time to connect the dots on the page to your voice.

Sight singing is reading and performing a piece of music without having seen it before. To sight sing you have to be able to read music and follow a score (the music). Music theory incorporates all elements of how music is written out so that the musicians and performers can read it like a 'script'.

Being able to read music and sight sing is an extremely useful skill to have as it saves time and money. It can also make you popular for jobs such as last minute understudying, and is a good skill to have, should you need to learn a score quickly, if you are hired short notice and don't get much rehearsal or you are a session singer (sing for commercial jingles). Not all professional performers sight sing and read music but it is extremely beneficial when rehearsing for a professional musical. Some people have more natural talent for this than others as they may have perfect pitch (be able to identify a note when it is sung/played) or a very good ear or sense of rhythm. It's a skill that can be learned, though – anyone with a feeling for music can improve and conquer this.

There are various pieces of software available (some for free) that can help you to learn how to sight sing. Some of these are:

Happy Notes Games - www.happynote.com/music/learn.html
Learn piano chords online -
www.electricbluesclub.co.uk/learn_piano_chords.html
Sight singing trainer - www.earpower.com/ssing.php

Some basic sight singing tips
★ Look at the time signature of the first bar to establish what you are counting in.

★ Recognise the beat of the bar in which you start.

★ Read the words in the rhythm of the music.

★ Clap the rhythm.

★ Find out where in the accompaniment you get your first (or starting note) from.

For more information, visit:

www.musictheory.halifax.ns.ca/ – free online lessons and help sheets
www.abrsmpublishing.com/publications/1267 – examples of sight singing tests

Sight singing/music theory is taught at all renowned MT courses and is also usually part of the curriculum of singing exams offered by institutions such as the Royal Academy of Music and Guildhall School of Music and Drama.

TIP!

It's *not* mandatory to have these skills when auditioning for an MT course! These are skills you will learn during your time on the course and then be tested on before you move on to the next term/year. When auditioning for a classical singing or opera course, some knowledge of sight singing and being able to read music will be required.

Singing auditions for acting courses and actors

'Gardens are not made by singing "Oh, how beautiful," and sitting in the shade.' – *Rudyard Kipling*

Many actors seem happy to present a number of speeches at their auditions but crumble into a big heap when they discover they may have to sing. 'I can't sing!' is a phrase often used and many are defeated before they even start. So how can you conquer a singing audition if you are not a singer?

Singing auditions for acting courses

Drama school panels auditioning prospective students for acting courses usually look for the following:

★ Interpretation of text through song (basically acting a song and making strong character choices).

★ Whether you can carry a tune.

★ If you have the guts to sing in performance as some plays may require it.

The singing will not be a deciding factor for these courses, I knew plenty of people at drama school who were not good singers by any means but still got a place. It has more to do with the acting than the actual singing part of the song. You can sing any type of songs really, but I recommend you stick to something where you can tell some sort of story/develop a character, which is why MT songs are usually a good idea. Have a look at my recommended song section on pages 303–335. I have marked songs which are good performance material for 'actors who sing', rather than singers. Folk songs and music-hall material is fine and a great idea if it has to be unaccompanied.

Also, it doesn't really matter if you go off a semitone or so as long as the piece sounds generally tuneful. They are not looking for a singer, rather an actor not afraid to use his/her voice in a song if the part requires it. I recommend a singing lesson or two, though, just to get a few tips and to run through your piece on the piano; also practise it unaccompanied in front of someone. Check the audition regulations as to whether they want accompanied or unaccompanied.

The schools usually expect a chorus and a verse – 'or 16 bars' is the famous expression. That should be sufficient. So how do you pick the right starting note? Well, if a piano is conveniently placed in the room, then ask if you can use it! The chances of that happening are not high, however, so practise without a starting note and don't worry too much about getting it perfect. Again, it's more about being positive with your acting choices. You can always bring a tuning fork along, too.

> ### TIP!
>
> Check in advance whether the schools/casting people wish to hear you sing unaccompanied or if you will need sheet music.

Actors auditioning for MT or similar productions that require singing
In addition to all the above, I think the most important thing for actors to realise is that they are not 'competing' with the trained singers attending the same audition. Although you will work on a song in the same manner as an MT professional (*see also* pages 226–232), you are being seen as an actor who sings, rather than as a trained singer. The panel has viewed your CV and is fully aware that singing is not your main strength. Therefore they're not expecting you to perform the most difficult song ever written with the most challenging top notes. Rather, they probably have a particular part in mind for you that does not require a large vocal range/a trained singer/solo singing, or a combination of any of those (Henry Higgins in *My Fair Lady*, for example).

First and foremost, professional panels auditioning actors for a musical or similar will be looking to see that you feel comfortable with your voice and using it in song. Also that you are able to create a fluent transition between the acting scenes and the singing. I mentioned earlier that singers often break down songs and practise them as monologues, changing emphasis on certain words, and so on to give appropriate value to the lyrics. The gap between speech and song is not as wide as some actors think. As with a monologue, the most important part of performing an MT song is making character choices and conveying a journey of some kind.

Your choice of song is vital in making you feel more at ease in a field that's a bit out of your comfort zone. Yes, the song has to be appropriate for the character and/or show you are being seen for but it also has to be something you enjoy performing and are not terrified of! When choosing your song, focus on the acting journey and the character. Don't worry about finding something suitably difficult vocally. Stick to songs you can connect to and feel secure singing.

> **TIP!**
>
> *See also* pages 226–232 for my comments on some material in my recommended song list, which I feel could be appropriate for actors or those with little singing experience/training.

As already mentioned, have a look at folk songs and music hall material. Gilbert and Sullivan have written some wonderful patter songs (*see also* page 223) that can be perfect for showcasing actors. If you have a good ear for music and just lack the training, Sondheim material can be useful (*see also* recommended songlist, pages 303–335).

For a basic idea of how your voice functions, how best to use it without causing damage, assistance with song choices for your vocal range and preparing the actual performance aspects of your song, I recommend you see a singing teacher. It's important that your teacher not only works with you on your voice technically but also prepares you for the practicalities of an MT audition. See also pagess 87–90 for information on the process of MT auditions.

Choosing a singing teacher

'Good teachers are costly, but bad teachers cost more.'
– *Bob Talbert*

There are no set rules on how to find a good singing teacher. It's usually trial and error. At first, singing lessons will seem strange to a new starter as you are confronted with unusual vocal and physical exercises, which appear to have nothing to do with singing a song. I remember at the age of 14 being made to lie with my back on the floor and sing a sequence of 'hahas' while rolling on my back. Different teachers use different methods and there's no one way that's best for all. You just have to see what style of teaching suits you and your voice. As long as you feel a positive difference in your voice and that you are making progress and developing, the teacher is good for you. It's important to find a teacher you feel comfortable with, who gives you constant constructive criticism.

Don't be afraid to try out different teachers and switch if you need to. It can take time to find the right teacher. If you are starting out in singing, don't worry too much about sounding bad in your lesson, doing exercises perfectly or what they mean for your future singing. Think of them as your building blocks to improve the natural vocal talent you already have. Some may work for you and others may not. After a while you may not need to refer to them anymore, it depends on the individual.

Where can I find a good teacher?
The best way to get a teacher is usually through personal recommendation. Ask friends, people at your school, in your amateur/youth theatre group or at local adult colleges and music colleges. Contact Stagecoach (www.stagecoach.co.uk/) as they often have a list of teachers who also teach adults and *Contacts* too has many listings. Local music shops and libraries are good places to check, as are dance schools, your local choral society or church, any place related to singing with a notice board. The Incorporated Society of Musicians (www.ism.org/home.php) has a register of teachers with a recognised professional qualification, a reference and teaching experience. The Actors Centre (*see also* page 281) offers singing tuition for professionals but you have to be a member.

> **TIP!**
>
> Contact drama schools in your area. Most of their full-time singing teachers will also tutor additional private students at home and they may well be interested in taking you on for extra income on top of their drama school teaching pay.

Other ways to find a teacher
Various websites exist with a list of teachers so you can search for a tutor in your area. There's no guarantee, though, on the standard of the tuition. If you wish to pursue this route, it's very much a game of trial and error:

www.vocalist.org.uk/singing_tutors.html
www.singing-teachers.co.uk/
www.vocaltutor.co.uk/
www.gumtree.com/london/music-tuition_145_1.html
www.realukmusic.co.uk/east_midlands_music_teachers.htm

For a guide to singing, the voice and terminology, visit www.vocalist.org.uk.

Questions to ask any prospective teacher
★ How long have they been teaching? Who have they taught? If you wish to enter the professional world of MT or are an actor who sings, it's best to go to a teacher with experience of teaching professionals and/or drama school students in this genre.

★ How long will the lesson last? Most lessons tend to be 45 minutes or an hour although some can also last just 30 minutes. It depends on the teacher and the strength of the voice of the student.

★ Do they have any performing experience? Again, this can be useful if you are auditioning for MT. Good performers do not necessarily make good teachers (and vice versa) so this is not a vital criterion but it can be beneficial. You need someone who knows musical theatre, can recommend audition material, who understands what suits your voice, someone with insider knowledge of which pieces are currently overdone or likely to be most suitable for you and your voice.

★ What is their musical background? You do not necessarily need a music degree to be a good teacher but you should still have experience of sight-reading, music theory and be very clued up on the technical aspects of the voice.

★ Can they play the piano well? If not, do they have an accompanist who plays for their lessons? This is fine if they are not good pianists but the last thing you want is a teacher who stumbles through your pieces, puts you off and wastes time in the lesson.

> **TIP!**
>
> Ask if you can have a trial lessons before you commit to a regular arrangement.

Can a teacher with a classical background tutor me if I want to be a musical theatre performer/actor who sings?
From personal experience I can say that the basis of all singing is a classical foundation, so teachers with this sort of background are usually great when you are starting out and want to learn the basics for a secure

foundation. Most importantly, it is a singing teacher's job to build voices. In terms of musical theatre auditions, however, I have found that teachers who have a solely classical background know very little about the *acting* journey of a song. I'm not saying that opera and classical singers do not show emotion while singing and do not have a character journey, but they are different fields and types of singing. Classical singing places the emphasis on the *sound* while MT is all about the character journey, the *acting* and giving meaning to the lyrics. In classical singing everything must be sacrificed to achieve the perfect sound, whereas in MT it must all be sacrificed to achieve the 'perfect' acting journey and characterisation. Of course your sound remains important and it must be securely rooted and produced properly, but in MT you are using song as a tool to tell a story.

Also, classical singing (and therefore training) uses the same sort of sounds regardless of the piece of music you are singing, meaning the tonal quality of the sound you produce is the same whatever character you perform. In MT this is not the case as different vocal techniques are used, which are not found in classical singing. These include the famous so-called 'belt', speech quality, falsetto, and so on to portray different characters, emotions and states of mind. Your teacher needs to be aware of all this and to have an idea how your specific vocal talent can incorporate this and produce different sounds safely without damaging your voice. Therefore, I would say by all means go and see a classical teacher but when preparing for drama school and professional MT auditions, find a teacher with the appropriate knowledge and experience of this field. It's possible to have both: a classical teacher for technique training and a second teacher to concentrate on MT sound and repertoire.

How should my teacher help me prepare for MT drama school/professional auditions?

Apart from working on your voice, of course, your teacher should assist you with the following:

★ Choosing material suitable for your voice, casting type and MT auditions generally.

★ Assisting you with cutting songs and also creating 16-bar versions.

★ They may have suitable sheet music available for you to borrow.

★ Also, they may recommend shows and composers.

★ They will have a general knowledge of music – they will be able to write down the occasional chord, possibly change the ending of a song to a higher/lower note and mark the sheets accordingly and know what key you are singing in.

★ They will explain the music to you so that you can then in turn describe it to the pianist at your relevant audition. If your teacher does not play the piano then they should have an accompanist present who is able to help you with all the above points.

Male or female teacher: which is better?
This depends on the individual and what you prefer. Some people prefer teachers of the same sex as they feel they can relate better. It's a personal choice really.

What your teacher should *not* be doing
Your teacher should *not* be forcing your voice. He/she should be honest and truthful about you (which can sometimes be hard to hear) but never rude. They should never swear/shout at you or be unpleasant. Your voice should not hurt after the lesson and you should not be hoarse. Your teacher may tell you to leave certain pieces of music for the meantime if your voice is not ready. That's fine, however the teacher should never put limitations on the type of material you sing. All singers who have a certain vocal talent are able to work on all kinds of songs, although they may specialise in or have a stronger talent for certain types of singing.

Just for the record…
Singing can only be taught to a degree. You are either born as a singer or you are not. You are born a soprano, mezzo, tenor, etc. and cannot change this through training although you may add a few notes to the general range of your voice or strengthen existing ones. You are born a belter (see http://vocalist.org.uk/powerful_vocals.html for details) and you can only be taught this technique to a certain degree. You won't suddenly be able to sing like Idina Menzel in *Wicked* simply by going to see her singing teacher. Never force your voice to do anything that it's not naturally built to do.

> **TIP!**
>
> If you feel in any way uncomfortable or inhibited with the training you are given, then leave. You do not have to stay so as not to make your teacher feel bad. You are paying for a service and if you are not satisfied with it then you have the right to choose another teacher.

Cost of lessons

This varies and London is of course more expensive. I would say that a professional lesson consisting of one hour by an experienced teacher in London with a record of successful professional students is usually £40 per session upwards. Most professional performers I know pay between £35 and £60 for their singing lessons depending on their teacher. Costs can rise astronomically if the teacher is well known but I personally do not think this is always necessary unless you have serious vocal issues that need to be dealt with. Outside London prices vary and at The Actors Centre you can get a 45-minute lesson for £24 an hour. Book early as teachers are very popular and you also have to pay the £55 annual membership charge.

What age is best to start singing lessons?

This depends on the individual but I would say anything regular before 13 or 14 is too early really and some teachers recommend 16. If you are attending a stage school you will have private singing tuition at a younger age but from personal experience I can say that I recommend waiting. Usually the breaking of the voice for the male tends to be a strong factor in this. Girls also go through a voice break (but it is far less pronounced than the male one), which usually coincides with them starting to menstruate (a sign of maturity as the voice has reached an adult stage of development). Most people don't start private lessons until 16 or 18, which is also fine. Those whose voices mature earlier can benefit from teaching at an earlier age and some voices mature later.

> **TIP!**
>
> A good singing teacher should be able to tell you if your voice is ready for lessons or not.

Looking after your voice

'Sickness comes on horseback but departs on foot.'
– Dutch proverb, sometimes attributed to William C. Hazlitt

One of the worst things that can happen to a performer is when they feel a cold coming on, or they sense they are losing their voice and they know they have an audition or performance coming up. This is especially bad if you are in a run of a show where it's your job to perform to your full capacity eight shows a week. I learned this the hard way when I was in an amateur production of the musical *Hair* at the age of 14. The opening night had gone extremely well and most of the cast proceeded to party afterwards for a couple of hours, surrounded by smoke and having to shout above the music. The next morning I woke up and my voice had gone. For the rest of the run I had to remain completely silent and mime in the chorus while another girl took over my solo parts. I was devastated! So, how do you get through a show or presenting your songs to a panel when your voice is far from its usual strength?

Each voice is different so ask a professional singing teacher and your GP for advice regarding your own voice and the illness you are suffering from. In certain cases there's nothing you can do as sometimes the voice simply goes and the vocal chords are so infected you cannot sing (laryngitis).

There are no miracle cures here. If you are sick, you are sick and there's nothing much you can do about it but rest. There are ways to try and prevent or stall a cold from coming out/getting worse before an important day, however. Here are some tips:

★ If you feel that tickle in the back of your throat, painful sinuses or anything out of the ordinary regarding the health of your voice, keep quiet! Don't sing. Restrict speaking to a minimum. This really does pay off. Only sing on the day of your performance/audition by doing a good, full warm-up to the ability of your current vocal state. (Rumour has it that Celine Dion spends several days without speaking before an important concert tour, just to make sure her voice is in the best shape it can be.)

★ Stay away from medicated pastils as they can numb your voice. Instead take a Vocalzone (see www.vocalzones.com/ for a description).

★ Drink lots and lots of water, herbal teas and fruit juice. Stay away from fizzy drinks, coffee and alcohol – they can dry out the voice.

★ Gargle with honey and lemon or salty water (if you can bear it!). Don't gargle with medical solutions – these dry out your throat.

★ Rest as much as you can. Stay in bed if you can. This may seem a bit over the top for a common cold but you need to do all you can to help your voice recover and get better.

★ Milk and dairy products can clog up the vocal folds, so avoid them as you probably have enough mucus to deal with already if suffering from a cold or flu.

★ Avoid smoky atmospheres and, if you smoke yourself, try to stop.

★ Continue eating healthily and get plenty of sleep.

For more information, visit www.vocalist.org.uk/vocal_health_links.html and also The British Association for Performing Arts Medicine (www.bapam.org.uk/.). If you are suffering from constant vocal problems (hoarseness, pain, strain, etc.), consult a voice expert immediately to prevent nodules and other vocal damage.

What belongs in a professional musical theatre song repertoire?

'There is a traditional trick that theatre people have played as long as I can remember. A veteran member of a company will order a gullible newcomer to find the key to the curtain. Naturally, the joke is there is no such thing. I have been in the theatre over fifty years, and I don't think anyone would consider me naïve, but all my life I've been searching for that key. And I'm still looking…' – *Richard Rodgers*

Professional musical theatre performers usually have a repertoire of songs at their disposal for audition purposes. If you are/will be attending an MT course, finding suitable audition songs and learning how to present them will almost certainly be part of the curriculum. Sometimes auditions can come at very short notice, in which case it's good to be prepared. I have received a call at 9.00pm to audition for a musical the next morning, leaving no time to learn a new song suitable for that particular show. Some audition panels request that you 'bring along a selection' and may want to hear you perform anything from Cole Porter to a folk song. This is particularly so with new musicals. I remember once getting a call for an audition for a series of new musicals to be presented at a festival. I asked my agent what the casting director had requested in terms of songs. 'Oh, just bring your entire folder, they will pick something' I was told. I would have stood there looking quite embarrassed had my song folder consisted of only two or three numbers! The following types of song should be included in your audition song repertoire:

★ A modern ballad ('modern' meaning the song/musical was written in the 1980s or later) from a musical such as *I Love You, You're Perfect, Now Change!*, *Nine* or *The Secret Garden*.

★ A modern, up-tempo song from the same era as above.

★ A classic musical theatre ballad ('classic' meaning written before 1980) from a musical such as *Funny Girl*, *Cabaret* or *Gigi*.

★ A classical musical theatre up-tempo song from the same era as above.

★ An Andrew Lloyd Webber piece – although these are overdone generally they are sometimes requested by panels and are, of course, suitable when auditioning for shows actually written by Lloyd Webber, such as *Phantom of the Opera*, *Cats*, etc.

★ A character or comedy number, something like 'Dance Ten, Look Three' from *A Chorus Line* or 'Where Is The Life That Late I Led?' from *Kiss Me Kate*.

★ A Sondheim piece. Better yet, have two: one ballad, one other.

★ Anything by Noel Coward.

★ A pre-1930s piece such as anything by Ivor Novello.

★ Something classical or from an operetta; also a Gilbert and Sullivan work such as 'Poor Wandering One' from *The Pirates of Penzance*.

★ A folk song can also be useful (for a selection, visit www.melodylane.net/folk.html).

★ A pop or rock song: this can be from a pop musical such as *Footloose*, or it might be a pop or rock number by a recording artist like Whitney Houston, Celine Dion, etc.

★ A standard – 'Fly Me To The Moon', 'I Got Rhythm', 'The Lady Is A Tramp', for example.

★ A song suitable for a panto audition (Disney material can be useful for this).

★ A patter song (this can be the same song as your comedy/character number).

These are the basics. Generally, it pays off to have at least one piece by the following:
Kander & Ebb, Kurt Weill, Cole Porter, Jason Robert Brown or someone equally modern (Ahrens & Flaherty, William Finn, for example), Rodgers and Hammerstein, Bernstein, Gershwin, Jerome Kern, Dorothy Field, Harold Arlen, Jerry Herman, Lerner & Loewe, and possibly Rodgers & Hart, Bock & Harnick, Jule Styne, Frank Loesser, Maltby & Shire, Stephen Schwartz, Maury Yeston and Irving Berlin.

> **TIP!**
>
> Music-hall songs are also great for lesser-known character/comedy pieces. If in West London, definitely have a look around Portobello Market (Ladbroke Grove or Notting Hill tube) for some old sheet music and have a listen to artists such as Marie Lloyd.

For many auditions it's a good idea to sing a song from the same composer as the show for which you are auditioning. Covering most of your composers in the first place can save a lot of panicking!

Well-known or overdone songs
Most professionals have these in their repertoire as 'extras' meaning they are not a part of their usual repertoire. However they do have a good knowledge of them in case audition panels suddenly ask for 'something that's really well-known' – which can happen on the spot or in advance.

Requests for well-known songs are particularly popular for cruise ship and panto auditions, or for productions such as *Night Of The Musical*, which are compilation shows of well-known musical theatre material. Examples of these include: 'Maybe This Time' from *Cabaret*, 'I Could Have Danced All Night (*My Fair Lady*), 'Bring Him Home' (*Les Miserables*) and 'Music of the Night' (*Phantom of the Opera*).

A word on Sondheim

It is often stated that Sondheim is not a good composer to use as audition material due to the level of difficulty and sophistication of his arrangements. For drama school purposes I am inclined to say that a Sondheim piece is fine as the accompanists are very used to playing his work and know the material well. For professional auditions it really depends on your accompanist. I suggest you stick to the less complicated Sondheim material (in terms of the piano arrangement) or bring along other, alternative songs just in case you hear the accompanist bashing along badly for the person/people before you! Here are some examples of Sondheim that can be difficult to reproduce well:

★ 'Everybody Says Don't' from *Anyone Can Whistle*, 'Not Getting Married Today' (*Company*), 'Putting It Together' (*Sunday In The Park With George*).

Sondheim not quite so challenging to play (although *nothing* is ever unchallenging by Sondheim):

★ 'Not While I'm Around' from *Sweeney Todd*, 'I Remember' (*Evening Primrose*), 'Sooner Or Later' from the movie *Dick Tracey*.

Make it easy on yourself! Keep all your audition songs in one place (preferably a folder), photocopy those songs in a book, put them in a clear file and transfer to a large folder. Divide into sections such as Sondheim, comedy, rock/pop, etc. I keep two folders now, one with 'main audition material' and the other called 'second choices and other stuff'. If you get a sudden call, you can just grab your folder and rush to the audition. I actually keep a folder at my relevant temp job, so I don't have to rush home and get my music if time is running short!

Dance and Movement

**'Remember, I did everything Fred Astaire did,
but backwards and in high heels'**
– Ginger Rogers

Mamma mia, here we go again…

Mamma Mia, one of the West End's biggest hits, was having its annual recast during my first few months out of drama school. Dance was still a big concern for me back in those days so I thanked the stars when I was informed that it would be 'singing only' for round one. I arrived at the 'Soho laundry' with time to spare, which was just as well as the ancient lift took up most of my remaining extra minutes as it creaked noisily towards the top of the building. I glanced around the room but did not recognise anyone, so decided to have another listen to my song on my Discman (*yes*, it really was that long ago!). The singing went well and the panel were tapping along to the beat of my number and generally seemed to enjoy themselves. I allowed myself a tiny sigh of relief. 'That was great, now could you please get changed so we can see you for the dancing in half an hour?' I froze. No-one had mentioned dancing and I had none of my gear with me. 'Erm, isn't that happening another day?' I weakly asked. 'No, it's today' was the bright, smiley response. 'Unfortunately I was not told to bring any dancewear' – maybe this would give me the few extra days I needed to mentally prepare for a dance call. 'Oh, that's OK. Just wear what you're wearing now, that's fine'. I was wearing a short skirt with fishnet hold-ups and a tight blouse!

Stay calm, stay calm… I decided to ask around the room if someone would lend me more suitable attire. The girls were friendly and helpful if nowhere near my height. I ended up in jazz pants that were far too short, someone's spare pair of pink socks, a purple T-shirt with 'I'm the star and you know it' printed on the front in silver glitter and a pair of shoe laces taken from my trainers to hold my hair back. I was assured I looked 'groovy' but I could not have felt more uncomfortable than if I'd been asked to wear a leather thong bikini to dance in. Nevertheless, the show had to go on. I tried my best to look professional in my stylish ensemble. Sadly, the socks were comfortable, rather than practical. I lost my balance on more than one occasion and was finally asked to remove them, resulting in me squeaking across the floor noisily in bare feet. Hey, at least I was getting noticed – any publicity is good publicity, right? Apparently not true, as I was not asked to stay for the third round (acting) that day. But I learned my lesson: always bring dancewear to any musical theatre audition.

What to wear

Once you've accepted a place at drama school a list of dancewear necessary for your course will arrive on your doorstep. Never mind the cost involved in purchasing it all, what do the clothes and shoes actually *look* like and which ones are best?

An explanation of general dance and movement related terms
Here is a quick guide to your new wardrobe:

★ Character shoes: These are usually black, off-white or brown. They are used mainly by females and have a heel (the degree of heel varies from shoe to shoe) and also a leather sole so you don't make a noise when walking across the stage. They are not meant for outside wear, just inside and stage. Men's character shoes do exist but they are usually known as 'ballroom shoes'.

★ Tap shoes can have metal taps on the heel, toe or both (go for both if you are a MT student/professional). Either they resemble character shoes with taps or they are like trainers (with shoelaces) with taps.

★ Ballet shoes come in leather, plastic or canvas (the most expensive). The sole is usually leather. It comes down to personal taste which type you prefer. They usually come in black, pink or white with an elastic band that you have to sew on to the shoe to hold your foot in. Ballet shoes usually look like little slippers although there are also versions with shoelaces.

★ Jazz shoes can be made of plastic or leather and have different soles (soft leather, suede or plastic), with a split sole or not. There are many different types of jazz shoes. Most of them look like a soft version of trainers (as with shoelaces). It's best to look around specialist shops to see which type suits you best.

★ Capezios (trainers for the dancer): Sturdy, these tie up with shoelaces but with a split sole designed for dancing. They are named after the company who makes them.

★ Jazz pants are tight-fitting, elasticated long trousers usually made of Lycra. They widen out at the bottom (a bit like a boot-cut in jeans).

★ Leggings are tight-fitting trousers made out of Lycra. They're like tights but made from stronger material and have no feet.

★ Practice skirt: This is black, ankle-length and flares out from the waist. It's made out of heavy material. You can buy these at dance shops or make them yourself.

> **TIP!**
>
> Some colleges also offer the services of their wardrobe department so you can have practice skirts custom made for you in exchange for a fee. Sent in your measurements and a cheque and you will usually receive the skirt during your first week of starting the course. Not all drama schools do this, so check with your school.

★ Joggers/jogging bottoms are what the name states: jogging pants that are usually drawstring, loose, long and made of cotton.

★ Leotard: The best way to describe this would be to say that it's like a bathing suit. There are many different types – long sleeve, short sleeve, straps, high neck, backless, crossed at the back, double crossed. Again, it's up to you which kind you prefer but females with larger breasts should try and stick to types that really 'hold it all in' for extra support.

★ Dance tights are like regular tights except they're a lot more resistant and with a hole at the bottom of the foot (so you can roll them up if need be). They are usually pink, black or white.

★ Legwarmers are like large woolly socks without the foot part. They can be worn loosely around the ankle or pulled up to the knee and are usually made of cotton.

★ Blacks: A term used by drama schools to determine movement wear that is all black in colour. This usually consists of a fitted T-shirt and either jazz pants or joggers.

★ Jockstrap: A man's undergarment consisting of an elastic waistband with a support pouch for the genitals and two straps extending from the bottom of the pouch across the buttocks to the waistband. It's usually white or black in colour.

★ Ballet skirt: This is made of very loose, lightweight (sometimes see-through) material and is a knee-length skirt tied around the waist.

★ Pointe shoes enable dancers to dance on the tips of their toes. They are made of satin and shaped like a slipper with no heel. The part of the shoe covering the toes is made of layers of fabric glued together in the shape of a 'box' then hardened. Soles are made of hard leather to prevent shoes from bending and to help support the foot. To make sure the shoe stays on tightly, dancers sew satin ribbons to the sides and tie them securely around their ankles.   Normally pointe shoes are worn by females but male dancers may wear them for certain roles such as the ugly stepsisters in *Cinderella* or Bottom in *A Midsummer Night's Dream*.

Where can I find everything?

Below is a selection of shops. Many shops that sell dancewear do not have websites so it's best to have a look in www.yell.co.uk or your local phone directory to see what's available in your area. Some places do student discounts, so have your NUS (National Union Students) card ready. I recommend going into a shop if you are a dancewear 'newbie' to try on lots of different things and familiarise yourself with what's available. Finding out your size can be very different for dancewear/dance shoes to regular clothing.

> **TIP!**
>
> You can always write down the exact size and make of a garment and then order it online for less money if you can wait!

www.dancia.co.uk – Shops are located in Glasgow, Edinburgh, Nottingham, Birmingham, Norwich, London, Ewell, Slough, Whetstone, Oxford, Dorchester and Brighton.

www.beverleydancewear.co.uk/ – East Yorkshire.

www.rainbowdancewear.co.uk/ – Aberdeen.

www.thedancersshop.co.uk/ – Basingstoke.

www.dancewear-edinburgh.co.uk/ – Edinburgh.

www.dancewear.co.uk/ – London (also called Porselli).

www.twinkletoesdancewear.co.uk/ – Helensburgh.

www.dancewear.org.uk/ – South Ruislip, Middlesex.

www.blochworld.com/ – stores all over the world.

www.sansha.com/ – London.

Gamba, 3 Garrick Street, Covent Garden, London WC2E 9AR.
Telephone: 0171 430 0704. Postage: Leotard £1.50, shoes £2.50.

www.freedoflondon.com/ – stores all over the UK. Check out the store locator to find your local branch.

Pineapple Dance Store (www.pineapple.uk.com/shops.htm) has stores all over the country.

Web directory for dancewear:
www.giantexplorer.com/result/Dancewear&source=goog

For an extensive website listing dance shops all over the UK, visit:
www.danceweb.co.uk/ps/Footwear/

A selection of online stores
www.totaldance.co.uk/

www.dance.ie/

www.shoppingmary.com/

www.katz-dancewear.co.uk/

www.thestudiodanceshop.co.uk/

www.dancedirectworld.com/

www.dazzlem.co.uk/

www.totaldance.co.uk/

www.danceworld.demon.co.uk/

www.wearmoi.co.uk/

www.dancewearforyou.com/

www.backbaydancewear.com/

How can I save money?

If you are an actor and/or looking for blacks you don't have to go to an expensive dance shop to find them. Places like Primark and M&S have regular joggers and T-shirts at a fraction of the price of a dancewear shop. Try second-hand and discount online dance stores, too:

www,dancedepot.co.uk/

www.discountdance.com/

www.adadance.com/

www.all4dance.com/

www.dance4less.com/

There's also e-Bay!

Dancewear for special sizes

If you are tall and/or larger than average, the following will be able to help you:

Long Tall Sally (www.longtallsally.com) – Stores are located all over the country and you can also order online. While they don't do typical dancewear, you can find joggers and jazz pants there and items such as shrugs and sweat jackets with legs and arms that are long enough.

Another useful place is Topshop (www.topshop.com) tall section that often has good-quality black T-shirts at a reasonable price and joggers/jazz pants type clothing with 91/96cm (36/38in) inside leg.

Guys, try High and Mighty (www.highandmighty.co.uk/). Again stores are located all over the UK and this is clothing designed for the large and taller man.

What if I can't dance?

When a male dancer in Noel Coward's London revue *Sigh No More* forgot to wear the proper support, Noel said to the choreographer: 'For God's sake, go and tell that young man to take that Rockingham tea service out of his tights!'

When I first decided to pursue a career in this profession I could not dance at all. I had tried various jazz and ballet classes when I was a child but had either been asked to leave – or they had allowed me to stay out of pity! Dancing was not natural to me but this did not bother me too much. I took a few dance classes before auditioning for drama school at the age of 17, also after attending the summer course at GSA and noticed just how good some of the other aspirants were. However, I was told at the time that it was important to be good at 'two out of the three required musical theatre elements'. I therefore concluded that since my singing and acting seemed to be of the required standard, I did not need to worry too much about dance as I could learn that once I started full-time training. As it happens, I was wrong! A year later, I was rejected by the head of dance at GSA due to lack of dance training.

Since my days of auditioning for drama school, competition has become even stronger and it's now more important than ever to train in dance even if you think your other talents may carry you through. Most of the time they won't! I ended up at Mountview, which offered me a place that same year despite my lack of training. However, I was the weakest dancer in my year and had to put in many hours of extra work to be anywhere close to the required standard and also to be able to pass the annual dance exams. My meagre dance training also became a problem later at professional auditions. I decided I would not give up and would continue training regularly after I graduated. Although I will never be up to the standard of some, I was recently asked to join the final round of auditions for a musical based purely on my dance audition and am now able to put 'intermediate dance' on my CV. Persistence in the dance field will pay off! Don't give up without giving it a try.

If you wish to pursue musical theatre as a career and have not danced then start dancing yesterday! Dance is an important part of musical theatre and although of course some musicals require more dance skills than others, it's essential to know how to move and have some technique to back it up. There are too many people about now who can class themselves as 'triple threats' for you to ignore the dance field anymore, so it's recommended you start dancing as soon as possible. You may think you have two left feet, are totally inflexible and can't follow a routine to save your life but not for the first time do I have to refer to the old adage: practice makes perfect. And some of you may be better than you give yourselves credit for. You may never be good enough to star in *Chicago* or be able to do the splits but that's not the point. You are not expected to be the next hot dance star in the West End! It's fine if dance remains your weakest of the three disciplines but it's important that you know the terminology for choreography (even shows like *Phantom of The Opera* or *The Woman in White* are choreographed) and how to perform the basics. It's about moving comfortably on a stage and most importantly looking comfortable, smooth, fluid and agile.

At professional dance auditions you will need to be able to pick up a routine (often from the actual show for which you are being seen) within 10 minutes and then perform this to the panel in small groups. Most times there will not be a mirror, no-one in front of you to watch and no dance teacher dancing the routine with you. You literally have 10 minutes to (a) learn a routine and deliver it perfectly and (b) perform it well, act it, give it character and make yourself stand out from the rest of the crowd of talented performers. And that's even if you state 'basic dance' on your CV and they know it's your weakest discipline. Years of lessons and practice are required. A musical theatre performer who performs their dancing well but has weak (or no technique) is a risk. This person will (a) show up badly against the other trained dancers and (b) will probably be susceptible to injuries and have to miss shows as their body can't cope with the stress of several shows a week.

Many actors who are training or working in non-musical-theatre-related performing jobs do ballet. We frequently have actors join our ballet class who want to gain a better feel for the movement of a Shakespearean or Restoration play. For the actor dance is not vital (although it is always useful and the more skills you have, the better) but for the musical theatre aspirant and performer it's unavoidable.

> **TIP!**
>
> Keep in mind that most of the time when you are starting out you will be auditioning for chorus/understudy. This means you will need to be able to sing and act to a high degree for the role you are covering but you also need to dance to be in the chorus when you are not on as the understudy.

How should I prepare for a career in musical theatre if I'm not a natural dancer?
Starting your dance training as a teenager is fine. You don't have to begin at the age of five to have a chance! Many people start at 13/14/15. This is a good age to train regularly, although of course the earlier you begin, the more proficient you may end up. I would advise doing one hour of ballet (the basis of all dance and physically speaking the toughest of the

dance forms) and one hour of jazz/modern per week as a minimum for at least two years before you start auditioning for musical theatre courses. If you have time by all means add tap to your repertoire but it's not vital. You will be taught this at drama school and not be expected to have knowledge of this type of dance – unless auditioning for very dance-orientated musical theatre colleges. Classes like Pilates can also be useful to increase your flexibility.

It's important that you take a class where you have to learn a routine each week as this promotes your physical memory, vital for any future dance auditions. Try to go to the best possible dance class in your area. If anywhere near London, I recommend Pineapple in Covent Garden or Danceworks in central London. Some people come all the way from Bristol, Eastbourne, even Cardiff each weekend to take class there! The higher the standard of teaching, the better you will be prepared. Ask teachers for advice and do trial classes if you are not sure where you belong. Try to choose a class where you are not one of the best so you still have to push yourself. See also pages 276–278 for links to websites listing dance training in your area.

> **TIP!**
>
> The only way to improve the speed at which you learn a routine is to practice. And the more you do it, the more comfortable you will be.

Some people do not start their dance training until they attend drama school. However, these cases are becoming much less frequent as there are simply too many people about who can dance and sing *and* act! Some schools offer courses with very little focus on the dance element. Be aware though that if you go into musical theatre as a profession and disregard one of the three main elements of this art form you will very possibly be at a disadvantage when competing for work so you will be limiting yourself.

The dance audition: tips and advice

'Dance first. Think later. It's the natural order.'
– *Samuel Beckett*

If you are not a natural dancer, this type of audition can be particularly scary. Everyone seems to look as if they know exactly what they are doing while you can't wait till it's over! I used to have nightmares before my dance auditions and probably ruined my chances simply by looking like a rabbit in the headlights instead of appearing cool, calm and collected and ready to give it a go to the best of my ability. These are a few tips that I can pass on:

★ First of all *relax*. People may look like they know what they're doing but most of the time they are equally nervous and anxious. It's often an act!

★ Make sure you warm up in plenty of time and have stretched to the full extent of your individual level of flexibility.

★ Try and enjoy yourself! Although this is hard, a positive attitude comes across in your dancing so the happier you are with what you are doing, the more it will show in your dance. If you look like you don't want to be there, the panel will notice and wonder why you attended in the first place.

★ Even if you mess up the entire routine try and finish in the right position at the end to make a confident and strong stand. Many panels look at the final pose as a determining factor.

★ Make sure you stand at the front so you can see what is happening. Don't let anyone push you to the back. You have as much right to be in front as they do!

★ Try and find a character for your dance. Don't just repeat the moves. You are also an actor so bring that across in your dance, in your face and your physicality.

★ *Don't* look down! Even when your feet are totally wrong, if your face is alive and full of character and facing the audience/panel confidently and you look like you know what you are doing, the battle is half won.

★ Make all your movements definite and big. Don't be timid and limp. Dance is about energy and strength so show off! Be interesting!

★ Remember that knowing the steps is not enough. Some people may mimic the steps to perfection but are boring to watch. You are there to entertain as well as show a perfect split jump.

★ If you don't know the steps to save your life, fake it. Invent something: don't just stand there and do nothing!

Other Related Jobs

'She stopped the show – but then the show wasn't travelling very fast.'
– Noel Coward

Corporate acting and role-play

This particular type of acting involves you playing the part of someone involved in a business field like banking, law, medicine, and so on. You will usually act out a certain situation in front of a group of lawyers, bankers, doctors, etc. to teach, train and inform. This type of training is often used to encourage better communication in companies, train managers how to treat and manage their staff, prevent lawsuits (racism and equal opportunities claims) and generally improve the structure of a company. For example, you could be playing the scenario of a rude boss who takes out his anger on his secretary and treats her in a professionally unacceptable manner (shouting, swearing, and so on). After discussions with the group, you will then proceed to act out the 'corrected' scenario where the secretary is treated in a professional manner. Usually scripts will be given to you before the day to learn. You may also take part in improvisation, acting or similar workshops with a team of corporate staff.

For this type of work you will most probably need a suit, the ability to feel comfortable in a corporate environment, teaching skills and good organisation skills.

Role-play can also include Murder Mysteries and related performing work.

Where can I find this sort of work?

You need to apply to a company (listed in *Contacts*) who will send you out for role-playing work. They are like an agency but you don't pay them any commission (they are paid by the companies who use their services). Some examples are Laughlines (www.laughlines.net/) and Terri Wiltshire Associates (www.twaroleplay.co.uk/). Most companies want to train you before sending you out to work. Usually they will not pay for your training and expect you to invest time and money yourself. The Actors Centre holds workshops and classes for corporate acting and similar work as preparation for joining a corporate acting agency.

What can I earn?

Role-play can be extremely well paid (up to £400 a day for a few hours work) but rates vary according to experience and demand. Due to the high rate of pay, this type of temporary work has become extremely competitive so it pays off to have contacts who can recommend you.

> **TIP!**
>
> Warning: This type of work can involve a lot of travel all over the country and you may therefore be unavailable for auditions.

Extra or walk-on work

> 'Work isn't to make money; you work to justify life.'
> – *Marc Chagall*

To put it frankly, *anyone* can be an extra (also known as a supporting artist) if you are prepared for irregular work and willing to put up with unsociable hours. Extras are not regarded as actors, although some may have acting skills and talent. They come in all shapes, sizes and ages, depending on what is required for each television or film scenario.

Being an extra can be a good part-time job for students (16 years-plus due to regulations) or those wishing to be a part of the industry without actually working as professional actors. It's not a route into television or film fame and does not require training.

> **TIP!**
>
> If you want to be a professional actor, extra work is usually not a stepping-stone to larger roles and agent representation. Often actors' agents strongly discourage their clients from doing extra work as it undermines their status.

What does extra work involve?

First of all, flexibility! You need to be able to attend a shoot at very short notice and be willing to travel to the shooting location. Work may involve getting up very early (some filming starts at 5.00am or 6.00am), long hours of waiting and simply standing around as well as very late finishes. You may also have to wear uncomfortable costumes and/or make-up. You must be willing and good at following directions; also happy at being told what to do. Some extras may be asked to mime a conversation in the background.

How can I get this type of work?

Most of it happens in and around London. Pinewood Studios is a half-hour train ride from London, as is Elstree (the big BBC studio) and most other relevant studios. Of course other large UK cities also have productions such as regular soaps taking place. It pays to be flexible and willing to travel.

To make yourself available for work, it's best to join an extras agency. Work is at short notice and confirmations usually do not happen until the day before shooting. To find an extras agent, have a look in *Contacts* or *The Stage* or check out www.uk.castingcallpro.com/c/90. Make sure your agency does not charge you upfront: an agent may ask you for money to appear in an extras directory and give priority to those willing to pay to be included. Remember that extras agencies are bombarded with applications each day and may not need you as they have enough extras of your particular look already on their books. When applying to an agency you will most probably not need to audition but will have to provide professional photos of yourself (head only).

> **TIP!**
>
> As an extra it is possible to have more than one agent to increase your chances of getting work.

What will I get paid?

The minimum Equity rate for a nine-hour day is £65. Overtime is paid after that at time and a half and you can be required for up to 12 hours. You should not be getting less than £65 a day, even if some agencies and production companies may work without Equity contracts. The pay will go straight to your agent who will transfer the money through to you. This can take several weeks. For more information, visit: www.hiddenextra.com

> **TIP!**
>
> As an extra, having access to a car is a big bonus. You may also be able to offset some of these expenses to reduce your tax bill.

Television presenting

> 'Television? The word is half Greek, half Latin. No good can come of it.' – *C.P. Scott*

Getting into presenting can be a minefield and several books are devoted to that subject alone, but here is a quick guide. There's no one certain way of getting into this field. Most presenters either come from a performing or a journalistic background. There are also those who have specialised in a particular field such as biology or astronomy, which has led them to presenting. A good presenter has a style of their own, can vary their position from foreground to background as needed, has good diction and clear speech and a voice that is either pleasant and neutral to listen to, and/or memorable.

★ Basics: You will need a show reel, which will make you stand out and show off your style and individuality as a presenter. These can be made through companies but beware: this is not always the best way. You can also practise by having yourself filmed by a friend who knows what they are doing, pick the best bits and edit them together. Whatever you do, make sure your show reel looks very professional and shows you to your best advantage in as many different types of setting and situations as possible.

★ Presenting agents: You can send your show reel to presenting agents to ask for representation (see *Contacts*). Or send them off directly to television studios and castings advertised in publications such as *The Stage* or *PCR*.

★ An internship at a company like the BBC can be helpful for opening doors and giving you an insight, so check out their website which also has many other talent opportunities: http://www.bbc.co.uk/jobs/ Other television stations also offer courses and work opportunities, so visit individual websites for details.

★ Presenting courses can be useful and interesting – depending on the course. Some may simply be expensive and offer little. For details and a list of courses, check out: www.radioandtelly.co.uk/courses.html

TIP!

You can also join *Spotlight* as a presenter.

TIE (theatre in education)

'Education is what remains after one has forgotten what one has learned in school.' – Albert Einstein

TIE is performed in schools, old people's homes, church halls and similar venues. Shows are not simply for pure entertainment value but usually include educational topics such as anti-bullying or anti-drug campaigns and lighter ones such as how to work in a team. This type of work is usually low-paid (below Equity minimum and usually about £200–300 or less per week including subsistence if on tour) and some TIE companies also cast amateurs. It is usually 'foot-in-the-door' work for those starting out who have not attended drama school. Often you will be asked to put up and take down the set, drive the set and props van and share rooms on tour with other actors. Although this kind of work can be an invaluable learning ground (entertaining children and teens *is* tough), many drama schools advise against it after leaving drama school, as do a lot of agents, who do not put their clients up for this sort of work. It is a personal choice whether or not you wish to pursue this field but it's not the type of performance you can usually invite agents to come and see you in.

Personally, I think experiencing one TIE job can be extremely useful for any actor. I certainly learned a lot from mine, which was part of my third-year curriculum at drama school. What struck me most (apart from constant aches and pains from all the set lifting and carrying) was just how much power your performance has over children, and how easily you can lose that power too. I played Snow White in a production of *Grimm's Fairy Tales*, meaning I had to don a black wig. After the performance I would take off my wig and help to take down the set. What I had not thought about, though, was the effect this would have on the children I had just entertained. Some of them were hanging around after the performance, waiting for autographs and used to ask for Snow White specifically. When I was pointed out (without my black bob), their disappointment in discovering I looked completely different in real life resulted in tears. I decided to leave my wig and costume on while taking down the set to keep up the illusion.

For a list of TIE companies, visit:
www.spa.ex.ac.uk/drama/links/theatreedu.html.

Working on cruise ships

'Ocean: A body of water occupying two-thirds of a world
made for man – who has no gills.' – *Ambrose Bierce*

This type of work is usually relatively well paid and has the huge benefit that
you don't have to pay tax on your earnings. Also food and lodging is provided
on the ship. Some drama school graduates take on a cruise as their first job to
pay off their debts. It's also a great way to see the world if you don't get seasick!
Be advised though that of course you will not be available for auditions while
at sea and that cruise jobs can be very strenuous, with some companies
demanding you do two or three performances a day, six days a week. It is a
good learning ground as you may end up performing plays, cabaret and full-
scale musicals (big cruisers have full-sized theatres to rival those on land) in
rep. Contracts are usually for six months or a year and jobs are advertised in
The Stage, through agents or in *PCR*. You do not necessarily need an agent to
apply or be seen for this type of work if you attend an open call (an open
audition where anyone can turn up and queue without an appointment and
without being recommended by an agent), usually advertised in *The Stage*.
For more information, visit www.cruiseworking.com.

> **TIP!**
>
> A minimum age of 18 is usually a given for these types of jobs,
> sometimes a minimum age of 21.

Cabaret

'The play was a great success but the audience was a disaster.'
– *Oscar Wilde*

'Cabaret' as a term seems to come up quite frequently and you may see advertisements for your favourite performers doing a 'late night cabaret
performance' at one of the well-known venues for this art form. But what
kind of performance will you be watching?

What exactly is cabaret?
Cabaret is a type of theatre performance that can include skits (a short
performance consisting of a scene or several scenes, often from different
plays), scenes, songs, magic and comedy. It is often performed in a somewhat

intimate (often basement) setting with the audience sitting at tables, possibly eating during the performance. In the forties and fifties cabaret acts were very popular in nightclubs. These venues had nothing in common with what we call a nightclub today. They were entertainment venues where audiences would come and listen to jazz, standards and music from MT composers performed by what are called 'acts'. Often these venues and performances were stepping stones for recording artists and a way to get noticed, with Las Vegas and New York City being the major hotspots (Barbra Streisand started out this way, for example). Cabaret is a very special art form in itself that has basically died out as it has been replaced by concerts and other types of music. Masters of the art were performers Peggy Lee, Anthony Newly and Lena Horne. Most acts usually last 45 minutes or an hour, although famous cabaret artist were renowned for doing one-and-a-half to two-hour shows with an interval.

Many people make the mistake of thinking that cabaret is simply a mix of songs and medleys put together in an order that 'sounds nice' or shows off that particular vocalist's talents. Cabaret is not necessarily about singing, not all cabaret artists are/were the best singers. A proper cabaret performance is so much more than this. It usually has a theme and there is a very delicate balance to be maintained in keeping the audience entertained and not losing their attention. There's also a difference between a cabaret 'act' and what we call a 'concert', which is normally performed in a stadium, theatre or large hall and consists mainly of spectacles and the artist(s) singing songs and possibly dancing.

The cabaret artist has nothing and no-one else to rely on so is totally exposed. Many of these artists also accompany themselves on the piano or involve their accompanists in their act. Dancing is rarely a main part of a cabaret act as there is usually little space, although movement is sometimes strongly represented. The cabaret artist can perform with piano accompanist only or a music trio/quartet, usually consisting of a pianist, bass player, percussionist and/or saxophone.

Is there any way I can watch or participate in cabaret performances today?
The UK has very limited venues where true, original cabarets are still performed. Most of the original art form has disappeared or has been replaced by a 'modern' type of cabaret, which is often just a selection of songs, which can include pop material and backing tracks. It is therefore very difficult to learn this art form the way it is meant to be performed in the original style as there are few people to observe live performing cabaret as it used to be. I suggest you watch recordings of the above-mentioned masters of this art for an idea of what is required.

As this art form is virtually non-existent, it's impossible really to find regular work and many cabaret artists perform for free to promote a new venue or simply because the organiser cannot afford to pay them (or will pay expenses only, meaning your travel costs and maybe food).

Venues where cabaret (or similar) performances take place in London
★ Lauderdale House offers regular cabaret seasons. The performance is usually divided into a 'newcomer' act, followed by an established MT or similar performer (Liz Robertson, Gay Soper, Joanna Riding, etc.). Details as follows:

Highgate Hill
Waterlow Park
London N6 5HG
Telephone: 020 8348 8716
www.lauderdalehouse.co.uk/

★ Pizza on the Park is the most famous London venue for cabarets, acts and bands/musicians. Often international artists appear here. The performance space is in the basement and there is a restaurant upstairs. You can also have dinner and drinks before or during the show in the basement.

11 Knightsbridge
London SW1X 7LY
Telephone: 020 7235 5273
www.pizzaonthepark.co.uk

★ Pizza Express Jazz Club Soho, (the jazz equivalent of the above located in the West End):

10 Dean Street
London W1V 5RL
Telephone: 020 7439 8722
www.pizzaexpress.com/jazzsoho.htm
jazz@pizzaexpress.co.uk

★ Jermyn Street Theatre is a basement theatre hosting cabarets, as well as full-on productions and other types of entertainment. You can also subscribe to their mailing list:

16b Jermyn Street
London SW1Y 6ST
Telephone: 020 7287 2875 (box office)/020 7434 1443 (admin)
www.jermynstreettheatre.co.uk/
info@jermynstreettheatre.co.uk

★ The Delfont Room (part of Prince of Wales Theatre)
Coventry Street
London W1D 6AS
Telephone: 0870 850 0393
www.delfontmackintosh.co.uk/ (go to 'live in the Delfont')

Shows usually begin at 11.00pm (doors open at 10.30pm) and seating is at candlelit tables on a first come, first serve basis for £20. There's also standing 'nightclub style' at £10.

★ Kitsch Lounge Riot at The Pigalle Club
215 Piccadilly
London W1J 9HN
Telephone: 0845 345 6035 or 020 7734 8142
www.vpmg.net/pigalle/ (more about Kitsch at www.kitschloungeriot.com/)
Tickets £15 for shows only and £40 or £45 for meal and show – every Thursday.

★ The Soho Revue Bar
11 Walkers Court
Brewer Street
Soho, London W1F 0ED
Telephone: 020 7439 4089 (bookings)
www.sohorevuebar.co.uk/

★ Cellar Door
Zero Aldwych (just off The Strand near Wellington Street)
London WC23 7DN
Telephone: 020 7240 8848

★ Battersea Barge
Nine Elms Lane
Vauxhall, London SW8 5BP
Telephone: 08712 075 385

★ The Green Room @ Kudos
10 Adelaide Street
London WC2
Telephone: 0871 332 5748

★ Volupte Lounge
9 Norwich Street
London EC4A 1EJ
Telephone: 020 7831 1622 or 020 7832 1677
info@ volupte-lounge.com
www.volupte-lounge.com

★ Café de Paris
4 Coventry Street
London W1D 6BL
Telephone: 020 7734 7700
www.cafedeparis.com

See also the vital tips and links section (pages 281–290) for more websites advertising these performances and also performances outside London.

Ticket prices
In general, these vary between £8 and £25 for a well-known act and are usually more expensive at the door.

TIP!

If you are interested in getting involved in this art form, you can also contact Tim McArthur (www.timmcarthur.com/ or info@timmcarthur.com), who organises cabaret entertainment and is always interested in new acts. For venues outside London, contact the Northern Actors Centre (*see page* 281) for further information.

New York City has a lot of venues and cabaret is much more strongly represented there than in the UK. For a list of New York cabaret venues, have a look at:
www.jimsdeli.com/nightlife/new-york-cabaret/
www.svhamstra.com/CabVenuesNYC.shtml
www.donttellmama.com/ (famous NYC cabaret venue)

Appendices

'The worth of a book is to be measured by what you can carry away from it.'
– James Bryce

Appendix I: Further reading
Books

Annett, Margo *An Actor's Guide to Auditions and Interviews,* A. & C. Black Publishers Ltd., 2004.

Baker, Joan *Secrets of Voice-over Success,* Sentient Publications, 2005.

Barkworth, Peter *The Complete Book About Acting,* Methuen Drama, 1991.

Beck, Alan *Radio Acting,* A. & C. Black Publishers Ltd., 1997

Belingy, Jenny & Byrne, John *A Dancer's Guide to Getting Work,* A. & C. Black Publishers Ltd., 2005.

Berry, Cicely *The Actor and the Text (foreword by Trevor Nunn),* Virgin Books, 2000.

— *Voice and the Actor,* John Wiley & Sons Inc., 1991.

Cahn, Sammy *The Songwriter's Rhyming Dictionary,* Plume, 1984.

Caldarone, Maria & Lloyd-Williams, Maggie *Actions: The Actor's Thesaurus,* Drama Publishers, 2004.

Callow, Simon *Being an Actor,* Vintage (Random House), 2004.

Cassady, Marsh Gary *Acting Games,* Meriwether Publishing, 1993.

Catron, Louise *Theatre Sources Dot Com,* Heinemann Drama, 2001.

Churcher, Mel *Acting for Film – Truth 24 Times a Second,* Virgin Books, 2003.

DeVenney, David P. *The Broadway Song Companion,* The Scarecrow Press, Inc., 1998.

Donellan, Declan *The Actor and the Target,* Theatre Communications Group, 2006.

Double, Oliver *Getting the Joke (The Art of Stand-up Comedy),* Methuen Publishing, 2006

Dunmore, Simon *An Actor's Guide to Getting Work,* A. & C. Black Publishers Ltd., 2004.

— & Piper, Andrew *The Actor's Yearbook,* A. & C. Black Publishers Ltd., 2006.

Dyke, Scilla *Your Body, Your Risk,* Dance UK, 2001.

Evans, Andrew *Secrets of Performing Confidence,* A. & C. Black Publishers Ltd., 2003.

Ganzl, Kurt *The Musical: A Concise History,* Northeastern University Press, 1997.

Gordon, Gilbert *Stage Fights – A Simple Handbook of Techniques,* Theatre Arts Books, 1973

Guskin, Harold, *How to Stop Acting,* Methuen Books, 2004.

Hagen, Uta *Respect for Acting,* John Wiley & Sons Inc., 1973.

Howse, Justin *Dance Technique & Injury Prevention,* Theatre Arts Book, 2000.

Johnstone, Keith *Improvisation and the Theatre*, Theatre Arts, 1984.

Jones, Ellis *Teach Yourself Acting,* Ntc Publishing Group, 1999.

Larkin, Colin *The Virgin Encyclopaedia of Stage and Film Musicals,* Virgin Books, 1999.

Little, Jonathan & Chatburn, Katie *Musicians' and Songwriters' Yearbook 2007,* A. & C. Black Publishers Ltd., 2007

Mamet, David *True and False: Heresy and Common Sense for the Actor*, Vintage (Random House), 1997.

Maslon, Laurence & Kantor, Michael *Broadway – The American Musical,* Bulfinch, 2004.

Miller, Scott *Deconstructing Harold Hill: An Insiders Guide To The Musical Theatre,* Heinemann Drama, 1999.

Moore, Sonia *Stanislavski System: The Professional Training of An Actor,* Penguin, 1984.

Olivier, Laurence *Confessions of an Actor,* Simon and Schuster, 1985.

Pisk, Litz & Elliott, Michael *The Actor and His Body,* Methuen Publishing, 1998.

Richardson, Jean *Careers in the Theatre,* Kogan Page, 1998.

Rideout, Nigel *First Steps Towards An Acting Career,* A. & C. Black Publishers Ltd., 1996

Rider Robinson, David *The Physical Comedy Handbook,* Heinemann Drama, 1999.

Rodenberg, Patsy *The Right to Speak,* Theatre Arts Book, 1993.

Simkins, Michael *What's My Motivation?,* Ebury Press, 2005.

Swinfield, Rosemarie *Stage Make-up: Step-by-step,* Betterway Books, 1995.

Toporkov, Vasili *Stanislavski in Rehearsal,* Theatre Arts Books, 1998.

Tuttle, Tricia *Filmmaker's Yearbook 2007,* A. & C. Black Publishers Ltd., 2006.

Van Tassel, Wesley *Clues to Acting Shakespeare,* Allworth Press, 2006.

Walter, Harriet *Other People's Shoes,* Nick Hern Books, 2004.

Wienir & Langel *Making It On Broadway – Actor's Tales Of Climbing To The Top,* Allworth Press, 2004.

Wilson, Andy *Making Stage Props – A Practical Guide,* The Crowood Press Ltd., 2003.

Contacts

Denton, Martin *Plays and Playwrights 2007,* The New York Theatre Experience, Inc., 2007.

Hatschek, Keith *How to Get a Job in the Music and Recording Industry,* Berklee Press, 2001

McCowell, Sarah *Where to Live in London,* Simon & Schuster, 1999.

Withers, Alison *The Gap Year Guidebook,* John Catt Educational Ltd., 2006.

Appendix II: Essential tips and links

Starting out, many people seem to feel overwhelmed with information of what they should be doing or looking at, thinking about, and so forth. However, it's often impossible to know what to pick as a starting point and where to find the basics as this can all be confusing. The following is an attempt to answer that famous question: where do I start?

Masterclasses

These are a really good idea to find out more about the industry, performing and what employers and drama schools are looking for and to get to know others in a similar position to you. Unfortunately the Actors Centre (see page 281) is only open Equity members but the Theatre Royal Haymarket (www.trh.co.uk/masterclass) in London hosts regular masterclasses anyone can attend as long as you book in advance and these are not too costly. Check their website for events. Usually they do a masterclass in October called 'Drama schools: what do they want?' hosted by the head of acting from Central School of Speech and Drama. You can also join their mailing list and be informed of upcoming events regularly.

Also check out www.thecreativemasterclasscompany.com, which offers musical theatre masterclasses for shows like *Les Miserables* and *Mamma Mia,* where up to 60 amateurs can take part in a special version of the musical with the creative team themselves. Rehearsals take part in central London for three days culminating in a performance for friends and family of the show at the theatre itself.

Singing
Take a look at Vocalist (www.vocalist.org.uk). This website is indispensable for anyone involved in singing, with advice on vocal health, finding a teacher, vocal exercises and sound bytes to download, a listing of composers and open microphone nights; also essays and further advice on singing. Also, visit the two useful websites below:

www.harmetz.com/soprano/singing/links.htm – A collection of resources related to singing.

www.bbc.co.uk/music/parents/learninganinstrument/singing_article.shtml – Tips for parents on how to handle singing and the voice of their child.

Major London dance studios
Here is a guide to the studios I recommend:

Pineapple Dance Studios
Langley Street
London WC2H 9JA
Tube: Covent Garden or Leicester Square
Telephone: 020 7836 4004
Fax: 020 7836 0803
E-mail: studios@pineapple.uk.com
Opening hours: Monday–Friday 9.00am–9.00pm; Saturday 9.00am–6.30pm and Sunday: 10.00am–6.00pm
www.pineapple.uk.com/timetable.htm

Apart from classes of all kinds in dance, yoga, Pilates, martial arts and cheerleading, this studio does a good singing audition technique class every second Tuesday evening which is £20 plus Pineapple membership for a session lasting about two hours. After a group warm-up everyone performs a song as if they were in an audition situation and then receives feedback from the professional singing tutor hosting the class and the other workshop attendees. It has a very good reputation and you can ask the tutor questions about your own performance after class. They also do a performing arts school (free) on Sundays and have a message board where you can read about auditions.

Danceworks
16 Balderton Street
(Opposite Selfridges Clock)
London W1K 6TN
Tube: Bond Street or Marble Arch
Telephone: 020 7629 6183
E-mail: info@danceworks.net
Opening hours: Weekdays 8:30am–10.00pm; Weekends 9.00am–6.00pm
www.danceworks.co.uk/

This is the other big dance studio in London and they also do a 12-week
beginners singing course.

Dance Attic
368 North End Road,
London SW6 1LY
Tube: Fulham Broadway
Telephone: 020 7610 2055
www.danceattic.com

Smaller dance studio in Fulham.

Dance classes in other parts of the country
You can search by type of class, region/town and weekday for suitable classes
all over the UK on this very useful website:
www.danceweb.co.uk/

Also, have a look at *Contacts* for listings or contact your regional dance organisation for classes in your area: www.cdet.org.uk/info_12.php#Regional

TIP!

> For a list of all dance agencies in the UK, visit:
> www.cdet.org.uk/info_12.php

Bodyworks Dance Studio in Cambridge provides part-time dance classes.
This is their schedule: www.bodywork-dance.co.uk/classes/timetable.htm

Danceweb (www.danceweb.co.uk/) has everything you need to know about
dance plus where to find classes.

Dance Teachers Online (www.dtol.ndirect.co.uk/dtol14.htm) is a good place to advertise if you are looking for a private dance teacher; includes message board.

London Dance (www.londondance.com/) lists all dance classes available in and around London.

For dance audition tips, visit:
www.answers4dancers.com/nonmembers/gg01.asp

MOVE IT is an annual London dance festival that takes place in Olympia Exhibition Centre (W14) offering loads of different free classes to try out: www.dance-london.co.uk/

Research
This is a really important consideration. People in the industry want to talk to someone who really knows their stuff, someone who knows the works of our most famous playwrights, which directors were known for a certain era, which musical made Sondheim famous, and so on. The more you know, the better and it also helps shape you as a performer so you can identify what you want to do and what your interests are. Drama schools expect you to have a good general knowledge of your subject, although of course you are not expected to know everything.

Libraries
These are often a good place to start; they have free (or cheap) lending facilities and often lots of older plays, videos, recordings of shows, etc. Dorking, Surrey has a performance library, which is well stocked: www.visitdorking.com/DT/Performing_Arts_Library.htm

Victoria Music Library
Based in Victoria, London, this library has musical theatre scores you can borrow free, as well as CDs, videos and DVDs that can be loaned for a small fee. It does not cost anything to join the library and it's well worth a visit. www.westminster.gov.uk/libraries/findalibrary/victoria.cfm

Barbican Music Library
Based at the Barbican, London, this library is packed with scores, DVDs and CDs to borrow. It also has a piano in the library to practice on, and you can search an index of over 50,000 songs online. www.barbican.org.uk/visitor-information/barbican-library

Dresscircle

Situated in London's West End, this is the best showbiz shop around. If you can't find it there, you won't find it anywhere! It sells lots of rare recordings, posters, sheet music, etc. and always seems to have a sale on. It also offers theatre evenings where you can get discounts if part of a group booking. It is located in Monmouth Street close to Covent Garden or Leicester Square tubes. It has a website: www.dresscircle.co.uk

Sky Digital

Anyone who has access to this is in luck as they have the Biography and Performance channels 24/7 and a series called *name of famous industry person at the Actor's Studio*. There's an hour of interviewing at the drama school in NY with questions from the student audience and featuring really big names like Sean Connery and Meryl Streep as well as directors and producers. You can learn so much for free. Maybe a friend or relative with Sky Digital can record programmes for you if you don't have it yourself. You can learn an amazing amount of facts, general industry advice not to mention people's views on acting, how they got started, etc; it's so interesting and a fun way to learn.

Live theatre

Go and see as much live theatre as you can! It doesn't have to be expensive. You can always get standing room tickets at the National Theatre in Waterloo, which are sometimes free, other times £5–15 depending on the show. Nearly all theatres do standing tickets and sometimes you can get in for free at the last minute if you turn up 30 minutes before the show. Bring your NUS card to get a discount. Visibility is usually good in all standing seats – I think I have stood in pretty much every London theatre and never had a problem! There are also a lot of fringe/profit share performances you can watch cheaply or for free. *The Stage* has all the listings online. For more details on how to obtain cheap tickets, *see also* page 145.

Ushering is a great way to see shows. Check theatre websites to see if they are looking for staff or drop your CV off at the theatre direct. For a wonderful place to usher, try the National (Waterloo). It usually has five productions running at the same time with very well recognised actors and you can view it all for free. The National also holds talks and does workshops and does backstage tours: www.nationaltheatre.org.uk/platforms

Bookshops

French's Bookshop (www.samuelfrench-london.co.uk) in Warren Street, London is the best theatre bookshop in the country in my humble opinion.

Foyle's is also good:

Foyles
Charing Cross Road branch
113–119 Charing Cross Road
London
WC2H 0EB

Foyles
Royal Festival Hall branch
Riverside
Level 1
Royal Festival Hall
London
SE1 8XX
Telephone: 020 7437 5660
Charing Cross Road Fax: 020 7434 1574
Royal Festival Hall Fax: 020 7981 9739
customerservices@foyles.co.uk
www.foyles.co.uk/foyles/index.asp

The Internet Theatre Bookshp (www.stageplays.com) is highly recommended.

Or try The National Theatre Bookshop in London:

bookshop@nationaltheatre.org.uk
Telephone: 020 7452 3456

See also:
www.imagi-nation.com/moonstruck/index.htm
www.theatrebooks.com/
www.bookmarkmusic.com/
www.showbizbooks.com/index.html
www.limelightbooks.com/

For second hand books, check out Amazon and eBay as well as the following sites:
www.academicbooktrade.co.uk/
www.byrebooks.co.uk/

www.academic-books-auction.com/
www.elvisshakespeare.com/

For theatre and movie posters, apart from Dresscircle (details above) have a look at:

www.applauseonline.com
www.footlightsgallery.com
www.tritongallery.com/
www.imageexchange.com/posters/theater/

Performing arts related websites (A–Z)

About Arts – Theatre-related forum discussions.
www.about-arts.com/theatre/

Academy Awards (Oscars)
www.oscars.org

Accents – advice and practical help
www.ku.edu/~idea/europe/england/england.htm – (voice clip examples of various accents).

Actors Centre (The) – Nearly all courses accessible to professionals only who are Equity members and/or drama school graduates.
www.actorscentre.co.uk/

Actors Inc. – Advice of all kinds for actors.
www.actors-inc.co.uk/advice.asp

Actors Temple – A place offering lots of different types of classes for £15 (www.actorstemple.com/) and possibly somewhere you might find an audition coach/helper. For a diary and thoughts on their training, visit actor Chris Tester's site on www.christophertester.com/trainingactorstemple.htm

All MGM Musicals
http://members.aol.com/mgmfanatic/index.html

Amateur Theatre – A great training ground, especially for those who are at an awkward teenage age and cannot get an agent yet. Check out this website to find a group in your area: www.amdram.co.uk

American Popular Song
www.americanpopularsong.com/

Amicidel Musical – The Italian language site for musical theatre
www.amicidelmusical.it/

Applause – The place to get your free tickets for recordings of all UK TV
shows www.applausestore.com/

Backstage
www.backstage.com/bso/index.jsp

British musicals of the fifties/sixties
www.musical-theatre.net/

British Musical Film
http://myweb.tiscali.co.uk/britmusical/

British Musical Theatre – A site dedicated to British musicals:
http://math.boisestate.edu/GaS/british/index.html

British Performing Arts Medicine Trust (BPAMT) – A charity that assists
performers by seeing them for performing arts related health matters
(including psychological), either at clinics run by the Trust or directs them on
to appropriate places for treatment. Contact the Trust to organise a consulta-
tion without referral from your GP and you will be seen and given advice for
the initial assessment free of charge. You can also be referred to private clinics
and medical professionals at a much-reduced rate. Clinics are located in
London, Manchester and Glasgow. This service is also available to students
attending accredited drama school courses. For more details, contact
www.bpamt.co.uk

British Theatre – Here's another great site with plenty of information.
http://classiclit.about.com/gi/dynamic/offsite.htm?zi=1/XJ&sdn=classiclit&z
u=http%3A%2F%2Fwww.britishtheatreguide.info%2F

Broadway Best – Australian MT site.
www.broadwaybest.com.au/zen/index.php

Broadway Café Society
wwwbroadwaycafesociety.com

Broadway New York – Souvenirs and other merchandise to order online.
www.broadwaynewyork.com/

Broadway Show Tickets
www.soldoutbroadwaytickets.com/

Broadway World – Includes discussion boards, also advice on training
in the US.
www.broadwayworld.com/board/index.cfm?boardname=student

Cabaret Hotline
www.cabarethotlineonline.com/index.shtml

The Cast Recordings FAQ
www.castalbums.org/

Charles Fox – The UK's leading stage make-up company. Visit their shop in
Covent Garden, London.
www.charlesfox.co.uk/

Circus Arts – Training in circus and related skills.
www.circusarts.org.uk

City Cabaret – Online magazine for cabaret and musical theatre.
www.citycabaret.com/

Classic Movie Musicals
www.classicmoviemusicals.com/

College Confidential – American MT forum for those interested in training in
the States. *Lots* of helpful information about the audition procedure there and
what schools are good, etc.
http://talk.collegeconfidential.com/forumdisplay.php?f=501

The Conference of Drama Schools – Britain's leading 22 drama schools.
www.drama.ac.uk/

Debut Productions – A London-based theatre company that specialises in producing actor showcases; they now also arrange showcases in Manchester.
www.debutproductions.co.uk/

Doollee – Free guide to plays, theatre books, magazines, publications and playwrights with extensive search options.
www.doollee.com

Elaine Paige On BBC Radio 2
Every Sunday on BBC Radio 2 from 1.00–2:30pm, Elaine Paige hosts 90 minutes of musicals and movies including interviews and competitions. If you miss the show, you can listen to it again on the Internet. You can also email Elaine and request songs.
www.bbc.co.uk/radio2/shows/paige/

Everything Old Is New Again
www.oldisnew.org/

Film Vault – The place to find a deleted video or DVD.
www.filmvault.co.uk/

Fringe Report – Reviews of fringe theatre, art and film as well as a list of all London venues with address and telephone details.
www.fringereport.com/index.html

The Guide to Musical Theatre – Great descriptions and details of hundreds of shows, highly recommended.
www.nodanw.com/list_of_shows_index/titlepage.htm

Health – Counsellors, cosmetic dentistry, Alexander technique, hypnotherapy for performers, see *Contacts*.

Internet Broadway Database
http://ibdb.com/default.asp

Internet Movie Database
www.imbd.com

Internet Theatre Database – Type in a title or name to get information on the performer, author or stage play of your choice.
www.theatredb.com/

International Federation of Actors – An organisation representing performers' trade unions such as Equity from all over the world. It's the first point of contact if you wish to work abroad as a performer.
www.fia-actors.com

Italian MT Site
www.musical.it/

London Albemarle Official London theatre ticket agent
www.albemarle-london.com/

London Equity Choir
www.londonequitychoir.com

London's Gay Men's Chorus
www.lgmc.org.uk/

London Musicals Online – A very useful site if you are trying to locate certain performers, and what they are working on/if they are currently working.
www.londonmusicalsonline.com

London Theatre Bookings
www.londontheatrebookings.com/

Lost Musicals – A weekly internet radio show plying swing, jazz and musical theatre songs, as well as interviews and much more.
www.lostmusicals.org

Manchester Theatres – Website detailing entertainment of all kinds in the Manchester area, including reviews.
www.manchestertheatres.com

Musical Cast Album Database – A database of 3,336 recordings of musical cast albums with a very useful search function.
www.castalbumdb.com

Musical Heaven (what the title says!)
www.musicalheaven.com/

Musical Notes – Sheet music at www.musicalnotesnmore.com/

Musicals 101 – The cyber encyclopaedia regarding everything to with musicals. Definitely take a look.
www.musicals101.com/

Music Theatre International – The place to find out the plot, character, vocal ranges for a show, what songs it contains, clips from many songs you can listen to see if they are suitable audition material for you and a link to order sheet music, libretto, etc.
www.mtimusicalworlds.com/

Musical Stages – Monthly magazine on anything and everything to do with musicals.
www.musicalstages.co.uk/

Musical Theatre Audition – Lots of helpful tips and advice. Remember that most of it is relevant to the US market, which differs from the UK market in terms of CV/photo format, cover letters, auditions and audition material.
www.musicaltheatreaudition.com/

Must Close Saturday Records – A great site giving information and selling old British musical albums and compilations.
www.must-close-saturday-records.co.uk/html/

National Council of Drama Training (NCDT) – Lists all accredited courses and has lots of helpful information and tips on auditioning and how the business works.
www.ncdt.co.uk

New York Theatre Guide – Easy to navigate website to see what's playing in NYC.
www.newyorktheatreguide.com/

The Northern Actors Centre – This is the northern branch of The Actors Centre (based in London), which also offers summer courses to non-professionals.
www.actorscentre.co.uk/

Obscure Stages – From commedia dell'Arte to music hall and pantomime.
www.214b.com/

Official London Theatre Guide
www.officiallondontheatre.co.uk/

Olivier Awards – UK Version of the TONYs.
www.officiallondontheatre.co.uk/awards

PCR – Weekly audition listing that can be mailed to you (note that it only contains about 10 per cent of all auditions going).
www.pcrnewsletter.com

Piano Files – Sheet music trade, free to register and to trade. A very useful site.
www.pianofiles.com

Playbill – All about the American theatre world.
www.playbill.com/index.php

Play Database – An extremely useful site for scripts and speeches.
www.playdatabase.com/

Public Domain Music – Find songs you can use rights free.
www.pdinfo.com/

Rehearsal Rooms
For listings, check out *Contacts*, The Actors Centre, Danceworks, Pineapple, *Spotlight* and local theatres.

The Roaring Twenties
http://bestwebs.com/roaring1920/

Rogues and Vagabonds – Everything about theatre, this is a fun site.
www.roguesandvagabonds.co.uk/

Scandinavian Musical Theatre Site
www.musikal.net/

Scottish Theatre Forum
www.scottishtheatreforum.com/forum/

See Tickets
www.seetickets.com

Simon Dunmore's Website – Includes a list of overdone speeches and
alternative material to Shakespeare, information on general audition/rehearsal
conduct, how to market yourself and more.
www.btinternet.com/~simon.dunmore/

Simply Scripts – Thousands of scripts to read online and download.
www.simplyscripts.com/

Spotlight on Musicals
www.spotlight-on-musicals.org/

The Stage – Newspaper offering listings, reviews and list of auditions, which
comes out weekly, every Thursday. The website lets you view the recruitment
section for free from Friday morning onwards.
www.thestage.co.uk

Stageagent – Type in your age/sex/vocal range, etc. to find all shows that have
a part in it that would suit you and songs to match including operas.
www.stageagent.com.

Stageworks – Offers workshops, events, talks by directors, etc. and videos
from rehearsal as well as rehearsal diaries from professional productions.
www.stagework.org

Swap My Ticket – A fantastic site where you can swap theatre (and music,
sport, travel, etc.) tickets. It's well worth a visit if you are looking for
something that's completely sold out or good seats are hard to find.
www.swapmyticket.co.uk

Talentroom – Free website where performers and entertainment professionals can communicate with a huge A–Z of entertainment links.
www.drama.ac.uk/

Talkin' Broadway – A great site that incorporates literally everything!
www.talkinbroadway.com/

Theatre Crafts – The biggest theatre glossary on the web!
www.theatrecrafts.com/glossary/

Theatre History – Everything on theatre history.
www.theatrehistory.com/

Theatremonkey – A site that has reviews and insider's advice on what shows to see, where to sit, ticket prices, how to get standing tickets, etc. Indispensable.
www.theatremonkey.com

Theatre, Musical and Actor's Web
www.tmaw.co.uk

Theatre Net – News, information and gossip.
www.theatrenet.com/

Theatre Radio – An online radio station for musical theatre.
www.theatreradio.co.uk/

Theatricopia – An abundance of links and more for MT fans, a fabulous site.
www.saintmarys.edu/~jhobgood/Jill/theatre.html

Ticketmaster
www.ticketmaster.co.uk/

Ticket Source
www.ticketsourcetoolkit.co.uk/

TONY Awards
www.tonys.org/

Vaudeville and Ragtime
www.bestwebs.com/vaudeville/index.shtml

West End Whingers
Review blog.
http://westendwhingers.wordpress.com/

West End World – A site about the West End run by MT fans including a forum, gossip, news, comprehensive listings of what is on and reviews.
www.westendworld.com

What's On Stage – Lots of news and reviews regarding theatre productions as well as a gossip forums.
www.whatsonstage.com

Youth theatres
National Youth Theatre
www.nyt.org.uk/
For young people aged 13–21.

National Youth Music Theatre
www.nymt.org.uk/
For young people aged 13–21.

The National Association of Youth Theatres
Darlington Arts Centre
Vane Terrace
Darlington DL3 7AX
Telephone: 01325 363330
Email: nayt@btconnect.com
www.nayt.org.uk

National Operatic and Dramatic Association
Noda House
58–60 Lincoln Road
Peterborough PE1 2RZ
Telephone: 0870 770 2480
Email: everyone@noda.org.uk
www.noda.org.uk

The Ulster Association of Youth Drama
c/o Lyric Theatre
55 Ridgeway Street
Belfast BT9 5FB
Telephone: 028 9066 9660

National Student Drama Festival
NSDF Information Manager
University of Hull Scarborough Campus
Filey Road
Scarborough YO11 3AZ
Telephone: 01723 501106
Email: info@nsdf.org.uk
www.nsdf.org.uk

Manchester Youth Theatre
Unit 14, Old Birley Street
Hulme
Manchester M15 5RF
Telephone: 0161 232 8805
Email: info@myt.org.uk

Scottish Youth Theatre
@The Old Sherriff Court
105 Brunswick St
Glasgow G1 1TF
Telephone: 0141 522 3988
Email: info@scottishyouththeatre.org
www.scottishyouththeatre.org

Voluntary Arts Network
PO Box 200
Cardiff CF5 1YH
Telephone: 02920 395 395
Email: info@volunaryarts.org
www.voluntaryarts.org

Birmingham Rep 'YoungREP' for young people aged 8–18 living in
Birmingham and across the West Midlands: http://www.birmingham-rep.co.uk/

Theatreland tours in London
Tours are offered by:
Theatre Royal, Drury Lane (currently hosting *Lord of the Rings*)
Catherine Street
London WC2B 5JF
Telephone: 0870 895 5505
www.officiallondontheatre.co.uk/theatres/display?contentId=67153

The National Theatre (up to five shows at a time, plays and musicals)
South Bank
London SE1 9PX
www.officiallondontheatre.co.uk/theatres/display?contentId=67277

Theatre Royal Haymarket
Haymarket
London SW1Y 4HT
(Piccadilly Circus tube)
Telephone: 0870 901 3356
www.officiallondontheatre.co.uk/theatres/display?contentId=67221

Royal Opera House
Covent Garden
London WC2E 9DD
Telephone: 020 7304 4000
www.officiallondontheatre.co.uk/theatres/display?contentId=67749

Prince Edward
Old Compton Street
London W1D 4HS
Telephone: 020 7447 5400
www.officiallondontheatre.co.uk/theatres/display?contentId=67680

Prince of Wales
Coventry Street
London W1D 6AS
Telephone: 020 7766 2104
www.officiallondontheatre.co.uk/theatres/display?contentId=67683

Theatre walking tour, London

Takes place every last Sunday of the month and starts off at 2.30pm outside the Theatre Royal, Drury Lane. Telephone: 020 7557 6700 to reserve a place. For more information, visit
www.officiallondontheatre.co.uk/home/tour/tours/walk

Job boards for industry-related Jobs

http://uk.stagejobspro.com/addlink.php
www.thestage.co.uk – go to recruitment section.
www.mandy.com – mainly screen related work.
www.offwestend.com/ – has a job board.

Online dating

www.music-mate.com – find single music lovers.
www.actorpoint.com/date/index.html – online dating for single actors.

Drama and singing exams (*see also* page 32)

Guildhall School of Music and Drama singing exams will be part of Trinity College from 2007! See www.trinitycollege.co.uk/site/?id=164 for details
LAMDA exams: www.lamda.org.uk/exams/index.htm
RADA Shakespeare certificate: http://rada.org/certificates/sylindex.html
Royal School of Music singing exams:
http://www.abrsm.org/?page=exams/gradedMusicExams
Trinity College exams: www.trinitycollege.co.uk/site/?id=259

Theatre festivals in the UK

Aberdeen International Youth Festival: http://www.aiyf.org/
Bath Shakespeare Festival: www.theatreroyal.org.uk/main/shake-spearefest06.html
Brighton Festival: www.brightonfestival.org/
Bristol Shakespeare Festival: www.bristolshakespeare.org.uk/
Cambridge Shakespeare Festival: www.cambridgeshakespeare.com/
Cardiff International Festival of Musical Theatre:
www.cardiffmusicals.com/index.html
Chichester Festival: www.cft.org.uk/
Children's International Theatre Festival (Edinburgh):
www.imaginate.org.uk/
Edinburgh Fringe: www.edfringe.com/
Edinburgh International Festival: www.eif.co.uk/
Fierce (Birmingham): www.fiercetv.co.uk

Greenwich and Docklands Festival (London): www.festival.org/
High Tide Theatre Festival (Suffolk) www.hightidefestival.org/
Open Air Shakespeare Festival: www.britishshakespearecompany.com/
24/7 Theatre Festival (Manchester): www.247theatrefestival.co.uk/
Summer Shakespeare Festival (Wessex)
www.wessexscene.co.uk/article.php?sid=143

For more listings, have a look at *Contacts*.

Musical theatre composers
Ahrens & Flaherty: www.ahrensandflaherty.com
Harold Arlen: www.haroldarlen.com/
Lionel Bart: www.knittingcircle.org.uk/lionelbart.html
Irving Berlin: http://parlorsongs.com/bios/berlin/iberlin.asp
Leonard Bernstein: www.leonardbernstein.com/
Bock & Harnick:
www.songwritershalloffame.org/exhibit_home_page.asp?exhibitId=327
Leslie Bricusse:
www.songwritershalloffame.org/exhibit_home_page.asp?exhibitId=204
Burton Lane:
www.songwritershalloffame.org/exhibit_home_page.asp?exhibitId=71
The Noel Coward Society: www.noelcoward.net/
Craig Carnelia: www.ibdb.com/person.asp?ID=11491
William Finn: www.falsettos.net/william_finn.php
George and Ira Gershwin: www.gershwin.com/
Gilbert & Sullivan: www.gilbertosullivan.net
Adam Guettel: www.josef-weinberger.com/weinberger/musical/guettel.html
Oscar Hammerstein:
www.songwritershalloffame.org/exhibit_home_page.asp?exhibitId=13
Lorenz Hart: www.lorenzhart.org/main.htm and
www.pbs.org/wnet/broadway/stars/hart_l.html
Jerry Herman: www.jerryherman.com
Kander & Webb: www.jorgeplace.com/people_Kander_and_Ebb.htm
Jerome Kern:
www.songwritershalloffame.org/exhibit_home_page.asp?exhibitId=67
Jonathan Larson: www.pbs.org/wnet/broadway/stars/larson_j.html
Alan Jay Lerner:
www.songwritershalloffame.org/exhibit_home_page.asp?exhibitId=42
Andrew Lippa: www.andrewlippa.com/
Andrew Lloyd Webber: www.reallyuseful.com/rug/html/index.htm

Frank Loesser: www.frankloesser.com
Frederick Loewe: www.frederickloewe.org/
Maltby & Shire: www.stageagent.com/artists.php?id=179 and
www.stageagent.com/artists.php?id=288
Alan Menken: www.alanmenken.info/
Ivor Novello: www.ivornovello.com
Cole Porter: www.coleporter.org
Jason Robert Brown: www.jasonrobertbrown.com
Richard Rodgers
www.pbs.org/wnet/americanmasters/database/rodgers_r.html
Harold Rome:
www.songwritershalloffame.org/exhibit_home_page.asp?exhibitId=238
Arthur Schwartz:
www.songwritershalloffame.org/exhibit_home_page.asp?exhibitId=224
Stephen Schwartz: www.musicalschwartz.com/
Sherman Brothers: www.shermanmusic.com/
The Stephen Sondheim Society:
www.sondheim.org/php/home.php?menu=0&submenu=0&latest=5
Charles Strouse: www.charlesstrouse.com/
Jule Styne: www.julestyne.com
Harry Warren: www.harrywarren.org/
Kurt Weill: www.kwf.org
Frank Wildhorn: www.frankwildhorn.com/
Meredith Wilson:
www.songwritershalloffame.org/exhibit_home_page.asp?exhibitId=316
Maury Yeston: www.mtishows.com/bio.asp?bID=3412

And finally:
www.songwritershalloffame.org/exhibit_home_page.asp?exhibitId=328

Appendix III: Glossary of basic theatrical terms

As part of a professional theatre production, here is a compendium of phrases you will come across and should know the meaning of:

Alternate – A performer who is 'alternating' a part with another performer, usually a lead or the 'star' of the show. The alternate will go on to perform a part if the lead is unable to do so due to illness or holiday and often has set days of the week when they are scheduled to perform, too. The norm tends to be two out of eight shows a week and often includes matinee performances to give the lead performer time to rest and prepare for the next shows.

Blocking – A term used in rehearsal to basically establish a guideline of where and when performers will be moving across the stage. Usually it is common to make a note in your script of where you are meant to be standing/sitting/moving and on which line. The blocking may be altered throughout rehearsal but it is usually a rough guideline of where everyone is meant to be. It's very important that you stick to your blocking for the sake of others and also the technical and lighting team (make sure you are not hit by scenery flying in and out, etc.).

Calls – As a performer you will be given various calls. These include the 'rehearsal call' which states what time your rehearsal begins and ends. Preparing for the performance, you will get a half-hour call (usually you *must* be in the theatre at least half an hour before the performance starts). This will be followed by a 15-minute and 5-minute call (via loudspeaker in your dressing room and throughout the backstage of the theatre) from the stage manager or DSM (deputy stage manager) before the performance starts to notify you of how much time you have left to prepare. You will then finally get the 'beginners call' which lets you know that it is now time to proceed to the stage for the performance to start. Various actors may have different call times so they are often called by name (actor name, not part name) to the stage. If you are not required on stage until halfway through Act 1, you may not get a call to proceed to the stage until about 30 minutes into the performance. The reason why actors prefer to wait in their dressing rooms rather than hang around in the wings is for safety reasons. They don't want to crowd up the space and many shows have heavy technical equipment that needs to be moved around.

Cans – The communication system used by the technical crew, which consists of headphones and a microphone attached to these.

Choreographer – The person who invents all the dance routines and teaches them to the company, gives dance notes and is in charge of the dance element of the show. They usually work mainly with the performers and will have an assistant, usually the dance captain of the show. This person is part of the cast and represents the choreographer in his/her absence, practises routines with those who are unsure, teaches the established routines to replacement cast members and also teaches these at auditions for the show if cast members are being replaced.

Costumes – There is usually a wardrobe department for each show that chooses the costumes, takes your measurements before rehearsals start and keeps your costumes clean, ironed and in order (they do any necessary sewing and repair jobs) when needed. Theatres usually have a wardrobe department that consists of a room of washers and dryers and ironing boards. Usually a wardrobe person will come round to your dressing room after each performance and ask if you would like anything cleaned or pressed. They will then take the items of clothing away and return them to your dressing room in time for your next performance.

Dance rehearsals – These are taken by the choreographer or dance captain and you will be required to turn up in flexible and comfortable clothing and footwear, depending on the show and type of dance. Rehearsals may take place in a room or on the stage itself. You will be taught a routine and be required to practise additionally in your own time (alone or with others) and to come to the next rehearsal having perfected what you were taught before.

Director – The person in charge of the creative aspect and with artistic control of the production; he/she may also liaise with the playwright and/or composer(s). It is the director's job to rehearse a production from start to finish and ensure the quality of the piece as well as inspiring, supporting and funnelling the imagination and creative process of each performer and their character choices/journey. The director also works with the technical and wardrobe crew to make sure everyone's ideas of the production's 'look' are in sync. It is the director's view and interpretation of the text that culminates in the final version of the production.

Dress – Also known as dress rehearsal, this is the same as a run-through except in full costume and make-up and with all scenery/props.

Dresser – The person who will dress a performer either for quick changes in the wings or in their dressing room if the costume requires assistance. Well known performers often have their own dressers who will sometimes double as their personal wardrobe/wigs person.

Dressing rooms – These are usually located on all floors from ground to top floor backstage of a theatre (sometimes also in the basement) and are the rooms where performers get changed, do their make-up and keep their personal belongings. Many performers in long-running shows personalise their dressing rooms with cards, flowers, a radio, fridge, TV and much more.

Some dressing rooms also have beds, phones and Internet connections. The lead performers will often have a dressing room to themselves while chorus and smaller parts share. Dressing rooms are numbered from number 1 onwards (number 1 dressing room being the nicest and usually the biggest for the lead performer) with the lead dressing room (number 1) located close to the stage (ground floor usually) and the chorus and small part sharing dressing rooms further away on the top floors.

Get in/get out – Used mainly for productions on tour travelling from venue to venue. A 'get in' is literally getting the show into a theatre, putting up all the scenery, props, lighting, sound, preparing the dressing rooms, wardrobe department, etc. The 'get out' is the opposite: packing up the show and transporting everything back into the van to travel to the next venue.

Green room – A sort of common room located backstage for everyone involved in the production; usually includes sofas, a fridge/kitchen area, Television/stereo/video. It is a place to socialise before a performance (or between matinee and evening shows) or to wait for your entrance during a performance if you do not want to be in your dressing room.

House lights – These are the auditorium lights (or the lights the audience see) that will go on when a performance is not running and during the intermission.

Iron – Also known as the safety curtain (partly made of iron), this is a curtain that comes down after every performance and during every intermission for safety reasons, mainly in case there is a fire that needs to be kept away from the auditorium or the backstage area.

LX – A term used to refer to the lighting and sound crew.

Make-up – You are usually in charge of keeping and doing your own make-up unless it involves prosthetics and complicated procedures, in which case the wardrobe department will assign someone to help you or make you up.

Musical director – Also known as the 'MD', this person is in charge of the musical aspect of the show. They will arrange the music, create and teach harmonies to the cast and sometimes conduct the orchestra or may even be part of the orchestra, depending on the scale of the production.

Music rehearsals – These are taken by the musical director of the show and are usually one of the first rehearsals to take place for a professional musical. You will be expected to come prepared with a pencil/highlighter and also very possibly a recording device to record your part for practice on your own later, mark your music and specific harmony (the music line you personally are singing). Also possibly to add in new notes as directed by the musical director (MD).

Notes – These are given after every rehearsal by the director, MD, choreographer, assistant director or stage manager and usually after every rehearsal, preview and the first few performances, although depending on the director they can be given after each performance if they deem it necessary. Notes are usually things you need to improve about your performance – you cannot be heard, a harmony line sounds off or you are doing the wrong dance step, you need to pick up your cue quicker, move to the right rather than the left or stand more in your spotlight, etc. They can sometimes also be confirmations that you are doing things right!

Off book – To rehearse without holding a script (or similar) in your hands; to know all your lines by heart.

Photo session – These are part of publicising a show and will usually take place during the day. You may or may not be required to be in costume and make-up and will receive details about this from the stage manager.

Pit – The area in front of the stage before the auditorium (seats) start where the orchestra is located.

Press night – This is usually the same night as opening night and is the performance when the production will be reviewed by the local press/newspapers. Reviews usually appear in newspapers in the early hours of the morning and it is traditional to stay up after the performance and after-show party to read the reviews together as a group of cast and crew.

Preview – The first stage of performances after the final rehearsal period. Previews are open to be viewed by the paying public but performances may be stopped temporarily for technical problems and staging, routines, and so on may change slightly from performance to performance during this period. Previews are a time to see how a production is generally received by the audience (to see what works and what doesn't), and to improve on and polish all aspects of the show. Many shows offer discounted tickets for previews.

Producer – This job involves many aspects. Usually the producer will choose the initial production to be put on and arrange the finance for it, as well as assemble the rest of the creative team (choreographer, director, MD, stage manager, etc.). The producer will usually have final casting say for a production and not the casting director or the director. Once the show is running it is the producer's job to support the production, pay everybody, liaise with everyone involved and ensure the production makes a profit or at least breaks even. If on tour, the producer will book the venues, arrange van transport for the set, and so on (not for the cast or crew) and organises the publicity of the show (including photo sessions). The producer can usually give the cast and crew two weeks' notice to close a production if it is losing rather than making money.

Props – You are not in charge of choosing or maintaining these. They are kept on stage or on the props tables (located in the wings) where each prop has its own place labelled with a handwritten sticker and is not to be taken out of this area or to your dressing room. They are the responsibility of the stage management team who will also replace or repair them as necessary.

Read through – Usually the first rehearsal of a production where the cast and crew sit together and read through the entire play with each performer reading their part. Sometimes singing (or a general attempt) is a part of the read through. You are not expected to perform as such in a read through although most actors will give an indication of character choice, accent, other character choices, etc.

Resting – A term used to define an actor's status when they are not working (temping, unemployed, etc.).

Routine – sequence of dance moves. A production may include several routines.

Run through – A rehearsal of the entire show from start to finish without interruption. This may or may not be in costume.

Stage door – This is the entrance used by everyone involved in the production and all the actors to enter and exit the theatre for rehearsals and performances. There will usually be a pad or book of some sort where, for security reasons, each member of the cast and crew is required to sign their name when they enter and leave the theatre. It is also a place where fans and others can wait to collect autographs from and take pictures with the cast, deliver presents/letters to cast members or ask the stage door keeper to let a performer know that they have arrived to see them. Note: This last only applies if you know the performer personally!

Stage manager – This person literally does what the name states: he/she manages the show. Their job is to bring all the elements of a performance together, including checking with the lighting and sound department that all the equipment works properly, including special effects. They are also in charge of props (organising and caring for them) and organise rehearsals, actors, directors, designers, props (sometimes costumes) and costume fittings, and liaise with front-of-house staff. During each performance they are in charge of making all the 'calls' as well as letting everyone know after a performance the exact running time via a loudspeaker. Throughout the performance the stage manager sits at a small desk with a headset, microphone and a screen in front of them showing the action on stage. It is their job to cue the lighting cue, sound cue, actors, etc. to make sure technical effects occur at the required times. This includes being in charge of the curtain, which they can bring down in an emergency or if technical difficulties prevent the show from continuing. The stage manager also organises the 'get in' and 'get out' of a performance (see above).

The stage manager has a team of deputy and assistant stage managers to help them with all their duties. ASMs (assistant stage managers) are usually in charge of props, helping with scene changes, keeping the stage clean and safe and sometimes they also watch over costumes. Deputy stage managers tend to be 'on the book' during rehearsals (meaning they prompt actors on their lines) and make notes of where each actor moves on which line and where, and which effects take place at which part of the show. DSMs (deputy stage managers) are also usually in charge of technical notes (see Tech, below) and sometimes take over the role of sitting at the booth during the actual performance and giving everyone their cues. The size of the stage management team depends on the scale of the production.

Stage up, down, left right – 'Stage down' is walking down on the stage towards the audience, 'stage up' is walking away from the audience towards the wings. 'Stage left' is to your left when standing on the stage and facing the audience, and vice versa for 'stage right'.

Swing – A member of a musical theatre production who understudies several chorus roles or parts and who may not be performing at all unless taking over a chorus role or part from someone who is ill or on holiday. Often a swing will also be second or third understudy, which means that if the other under-studies are all off ill or on holiday, they have to go on as the lead. Or if the first understudy is performing as the lead they need to take over the role that the understudy usually performs – usually chorus. Some dance swings may literally be dancing the show in a backstage area while their counterparts perform them onstage, just to be on standby in case someone is injured or suddenly needs to be replaced. *Chicago* and *Cats* are known to make use of this practice.

Tabs – The main curtain separating the stage from the audience that comes down in between curtain calls and at the end of a performance.

Tech – Technical rehearsal/run through. This is a run of the show with lots of stopping and starting (usually without costume) purely for the sake of the technical crew to check all the lighting, sound and scenery cues. A 'tech' is usually the last stage of the rehearsal process and can often run well into the night or early hours of the morning.

Understudy/walking understudy – Similar to the alternate, they take over a role if the actual performer is ill or on holiday. They do not, however, have scheduled weekly performances (so only go on when necessary) and many understudies have to go on with limited rehearsal, sometimes no rehearsal time at all, and wear the costumes of the regular performer. It is possible for a performer to understudy several parts and many shows have second and even third understudies, especially musicals.

Wardrobe wigs department – The department in charge of the maintenance, choice and cleaning of all costumes and wigs. They have their own room or rooms in each theatre.

Wings – The area backstage just behind the stage. It is a place where performers wait to go on, props and scenery are kept and technical staff wait to assist with the production. Usually absolute silence is required in the wings.

Workers – This is the name for the lights used backstage when a performance is not on (or at intermission), so that the technical crew can 'work' set changes, etc.

For further information on common industry terms for film and TV, check out www.equity.org.uk/members/commonTerms/FilmTVindustryTerms.pdf Please note that you can only access this website if you are an Equity member.

Appendix IV: Recommended songs for musical theatre auditions

Below is a list of song material, providing alternatives to the usual favourites. I have personally used some for my own auditions, other songs have been recommended to me throughout the years by other professionals. Some of the material originates from so-called 'lost musicals'. These shows were either never a large commercial success, did not have long runs or are generally not very commonly known. Hence, the score has often been 'lost' throughout the years and hidden gems of songs were left behind and forgotten. I have included many different composers, periods and styles to cover a large range of options. There are, of course, many more songs that are useful for audition purposes and by no means does my list encompass everything.

> **TIP!**
>
> My selections are not foolproof and not an 'easy' way to save you doing your research! Simply picking a song off the list that suits your vocal range and that sounds good is not the answer. Schools and professional panels will expect you to have put in your own time and effort to get a good grasp of what material is available and to give a good reason as to why you chose a particular song. Also, it's not about picking something the panel likes or finding the most obscure number that no-one has ever heard of. Rather, you need to find those pieces that really suit you and show off what you can offer as a performer. Ask your singing teacher or other professionals with similar knowledge for specific advice regarding suitability for songs on the list.

Can you use other, more commonly known material? Yes you can. However, be aware that you may be one of many performing this at auditions and panels are human (yes, really!) and can get bored if they hear the same song twenty times a day. If you do choose a well-known or 'in vogue' number as your audition piece, make sure you can do it justice and are equally good, if not better, at singing it than the original. Some drama schools have actually mentioned certain songs and/or composers on their website and audition guidelines which they would like applicants to avoid as they have been used too many times at auditions for their liking. *See also* my 'overdone' song list, pages 336–339.

You will also notice that I don't have many songs from new musicals (e.g. *The Producers, Wicked*) on the list. This is due to the fact that many shows written in the past five years or so are usually extremely popular and belong on the 'overdone' list really. It's better to wait until the hype over this new material has died down a bit. By all means have a repertoire of well-known songs that you can do justice but keep some unusual material in your bag too. It pays to be versatile and show something a bit different to panels that sit through hundreds, sometimes thousands of songs a year.

Excerpts from a lot of the songs listed below can be listened to and read about on 'Music Theatre International' – www.mtishows.com/default_HOME.asp. Also, at www.amazon.com. Just go to the music section, type in the name of the composer and album and in many cases you will get a song list with examples to listen to. Another site offering voice clips is www.cduniverse.com. The American version of iTunes also has many MT songs to download but the UK version is sadly nowhere near as comprehensive (yet) and the American version is read only so cannot be accessed from the UK. If totally lost, check out www.youtube.com. I have found many a rare song there! To read about shows and plot/character details, have a look at www.nodanw.com/shows_i/index.htm and www.musicalnotesn-more.com as well as www.stageagent.com

Female ballads
Note: Teenage = age 14 to 18.

'Just A Housewife' from *Working* (Stephen Schwartz and others, 1978) – mezzo – woman aged mid-20s to 40, angry ballad about Russian refugee in America trying to make sense of her new life.

'Woman And Man' from *Robert and Elizabeth* (Ron Grainer & Ronald Millar, 1964) – young, very high sop (soprano), top B, ballad but steady tempo.

'How Lovely To Be A Woman' and 'One Boy' from *Bye Bye Birdie* (Charles Strouse/Lee Adams, 1960) – great soprano songs for teen or anyone up to playing age 20/21 but can be as young as 15 playing age.

'I Like Him from *Drat the Cat* (Milton Schafer/Ira Levin, 1965) – ballad for sop.

'I Have To Tell You' from *Fanny* (Harold Rome, 1954) – sop ballad/character with top notes.

'Guess I'll Miss The Man' from *Pippin* (Stephen Schwartz, 1972), – good semi-modern ballad for alto/mezzo.

'I Have Dreamed' and 'We Kiss In A Shadow' from *The King and I* (Rodgers & Hammerstein, 1951) – sop, ingénue ballad, classic Rodgers & Hammerstein, duet in show but can be turned into solos.

'Home' from *Phantom of the Opera* (Maury Yeston, version 1992) – Christine's song, so young ingénue ballad with top G.

'Make Believe' from *Showboat* (Kern/Hammerstein, 1927) – another classic ballad, romantic ingénue, very classical type voice needed, well known but not sung a lot.

'All Through The Night' from *Anything Goes* (Cole Porter, 1934) – good sop ingénue ballad.

'Away From You' from *Rex* (Richard Rodgers & Sheldon Harnick, 1976) – duet in the show but it can be turned into a solo, lyrical mezzo or soprano, lovely lesser-known ballad.

'So In Love' from *Kiss Me, Kate* (Cole Porter 1930s) – great passionate mid tempo song for dramatic sop or high mezzo, also suitable for male high baritone (duet in the show).

'Where Is The Warmth?' from *The Baker's Wife* (Stephen Schwartz, 1993) – great ballad, leading lady type soprano or mezzo.

'No Man Left For Me' from *Will Rodger Follies* (Cy Coleman, Betty Lomden & Adolph Green, 1991) – underdone good acting piece that also shows voice, belt mezzo.

'All For You' from *Saturday Night* (Sondheim, 2000) – lovely ballad for mezzo or soprano.

'If That Was Love' from *New Girl In Town* (Bob Merrill, 1957) – nice ballad for alto/mezzo, must be earthy, not ingénue type.

'Chanson' from *The Baker's Wife* (Stephen Schwartz, 1993) – waltz type ballad, high belt, soprano, at least late twenties.

'Let's Not Move Too Fast' from *Big* (Maltby & Shire, 1987) – waltz ballad, mezzo.

'Lonely Is A Two-way Street' from *The Fix* (Dana P. Rowe, 1997) – MT type mid tempo (sort of swingy) jazz number. Must be very good belter and have jazzy voice – the character is a stripper.

'Stop, Time' from *Big* (Maltby & Shire, 1987) – big belt ballad, must look at least 30 (the character is a mother talking about her growing son), big belt voice.

'Crazy World' from *Victor Victoria*, stage version, song is not in the movie (Leslie Bricusse & Henry Mancini, 1995) – ballad for alto or mezzo, really good to edit. Also, 'Who Can I Tell' written for Liza Minnelli; can be found in *Leslie Bricusse Songbook* alto/mezzo.

'Still' from *Titanic* (Maury Yeston, 1997) – duet in show but can be turned into sop solo (as in musical theatre anthology soprano series).

'So Many People' from *Saturday Night* (Sondheim, 1997) – one of Sondheim's rarer ballads that is a great audition piece for any sop or mezzo.

'Somebody Somewhere' from *The Most Happy Fella* (Frank Loesser, 1956) – plaintive and lovely. There seem to be two versions, one goes up to a G, the other to an E flat, teenage possible.

'I'll Tell The Man In The Street' from *I Married An Angel* (Rogers & Hart, 1942) – lovely ballad for mezzo or sop, all in one number, also possible for teenagers.

'Make the man love me' from *A Tree Grows In Brooklyn* (Schwartz & Fields 1945) – mezzo ballad, another good ingénue number.

'The World Goes Round' from the movie *New York, New York* (Kander & Ebb, 1977) – big jazzy belt number (think 'Maybe This Time'), must have secure top F belt.

'A Quiet Thing' from *Flora the Red Menace* (Kander & Ebb, 1956) – high mezzo or sop, rangy.

'Disneyland' from *Smile* (Marvin Hamlish & Howard Ashman, 1986) – big ballad, Disney-like, big belt required. Also good for teenage if the voice is there.

'Where Do I Go From Here?' from *Fiorello* (Bock & Harnick, 1959) – this song was cut from the original score. Lovely ballad for sop, possibly mezzo, available in Harnick songbook.

'I Will Be Loved' from *I Love You, You're Perfect, Now Change!* (Jo Di Pietro and Jimmy Roberts, 1996) – mezzo and alto.

'Bells Will Ring' from *Charlie Girl* (John Taylor, 1965) – high soprano with top C; also 'Like Love' from the same show.

'Times Like This' from *Lucky Stiff* (Ahrens and Flaherty, 2003) – bittersweet ballad for alto, maybe mezzo.

'Love Is Only Love' from *Hello, Dolly!* Streisand/film version (Jerry Herman, 1964) – mezzo or sop, personal favourite.

'Before I Gaze At You Again' from *Camelot* (Lerner & Loewe, 1960) – fantastic ballad for young girl/woman soprano (think Julie Andrews' type voice). Can also be done by an older teenager.

'Glitter And Be Gay' from *Candide* (Bernstein, 1956) – coloratura soprano. If you can do it well, it is sure to impress! Top notes.

'One More Kiss' from *Follies* (Sondheim, 1971) – top soprano, waltz, difficult.

'Will He Like Me?' from *She Loves Me* (Bock & Harnick, 1963) – lovely ballad with lots of energy in it. Mezzo or sop, has an up-tempo mid section, good acting song too, possible for a teenager.

'Till There Was You' from *The Music Man* (Meredith Wilson, 1962) – soprano or high mezzo. Done quite a bit but always a good audition song; panels seem to love hearing it; also possible for a teenager. Also 'My White Knight'.

'People Will Say We're In Love' and 'Out Of My Dreams' from *Oklahoma!* (Rodgers & Hammerstein, 1943) – soprano; the first is a duet in show so must be edited.

'The Party's Over' from *Bells Are Ringing* (Jule Styne, 1956) – alto, maybe low mezzo. Gorgeous song, great all-in-one number.

'Missing You (My Bill)' from *The Civil War* (Frank Wildhorn, 1998) – very moving soprano ballad by a soldier's wife as she recounts the struggles of raising her son while she waits longingly for her husband Bill to return home. Excellent audition piece that requires vulnerability and emotional truth, mezzo.

'The Honour of Your Name' also from *The Civil War* (see above) – excellent solo by the same character after she hears her husband died in a battle. Another good audition piece, mezzo.

'But Not For Me' from *Girl Crazy* (Gershwin, 1943) – alto or mezzo. Poignant love ballad about everyone being romantically involved but her, teenager possible

'In My Own Little Corner' from *Cinderella* (Rodgers & Hammerstein, 1957) – another good ballad for a girl in her teens or early twenties; can be as young as 14 or 15. A lovely song for mezzo or sop teenage girl.

'My Lord And Master' from *The King and I* (Rodgers & Hammerstein, 1956) – great ballad for soprano with good top notes. This is a hard song – only try it if you could play the part sung by Tuptim, who is a petite, slim Asian girl. You should be a petite, young ingénue type with a bell-like quality in your voice. Teenager 15-plus with very mature voice possible.

'I Could Write A Book' from *Pal Joey* (Rogers & Hart, 1957) – nice, plaintive ballad for mezzo or alto.

'I've Never Been In Love Before' from *Guys & Dolls* (Frank Loesser, 1955) – mezzo and sop, nice simple ballad, top note E; I think teenager possible.

'Blame It On The Summer Night' from *Rags* (Stephen Schwartz & Charles Strousse, 1991) – good ballad, mezzo.

'I Never Know When To Say When' from *Goldilocks* (Leroy Anderson/Joan Ford, Walter and Jean Kerr, 1958) – good belt ballad for woman 30-plus, alto.

'Ribbons Down My Back' from *Hello, Dolly!* (Jerry Herman, 1964) – lovely ingénue ballad, mezzo or sop; also good teenage number.

'Nobody Breaks My Heart' from *Fine and Dandy* (Kay Swift, 2004) – jazzy 40s number for belter, sop or mezzo.

'How Could I Ever Know?' from *The Secret Garden* (Marsha Norman/Lucy Simon, 1991) – soprano ballad for young, ingénue type; popular, but not too overdone in my experience.

'You Don't Know This Man' from *Parade* (Jason Robert Brown, 1998) – fantastic dramatic ballad for alto or mezzo; very good acting piece that requires emotional range; quite popular currently but still a good choice I believe.

Most material from *The Boyfriend* (Sandy Wilson, 1954) is also always a good bet – ballads and character, good for soprano.

'Nothing Really Happened' from *Is There A Life After High School?* (Craig Carnelia, 1983) – ballad for mezzo or alto, good acting song.

'All Things To One Man' from *Grind* (Larry Grossman/Ellen Fitzhugh, 1985) – good ballad for alto/mezzo.

'Can You Find It In Your Heart' from *Footloose* (Dean Pitchford & Tom Snow, 1998) – big, belty pop ballad for woman of at least 35, sop or mezzo.

'Feelings' from *The Apple Tree* (Bock & Harnick, 1966) – nice ballad, not so well-known for sop or mezzo; young ingénue-type character.

'The Girls Of Summer' from *Mary Me A Little* (Sondheim, 1956) – ballad for older sop or mezzo.

'Don't Cry Out Loud' from *The Boy From Oz* (Carol Bayer Sager & Peter Allen, 1976) – great pop ballad with top belt (F) so not for the faint hearted!

'I Could Be The One' from *The Card* (Drew & Stiles, 1973) – ingénue ballad for mezzo or sop.

'Take The World Away' from *Little By Little* (Hal Hackaday, 1999) – big, lush ballad for sop or mezzo. Also 'I'm Not' for a good character number.

'Too Much For One Heart' from *Miss Saigon* (Boublil & Schoenberg, 1989) – recommended because it was cut from the show; you can listen to it on Lea Salonga's (the original Kim) solo album; originally sung by the character Kim in the show.

'That's Him' from *One Touch of Venus* (Kurt Weill & Ogden Nash, 1943) – plaintive ballad for alto or mezzo, great all-in-one song.
'If I Ever Fall In Love Again' from *The Crooked Mile* (Peter Greenwell & Peter Wildeblood, 1959) – unofficially considered one of the best ballads ever written for a soprano in MT; British musical originally recorded by Elizabeth Welch.

'The Music That Makes Me Dance' from *Funny Girl*, stage version, not the film (Jule Styne & Bob Merrill, 1964) – lovely ballad that is rarely done nowadays.

'One Kiss' from *The New Moon* (Sigmund Romberg & Hammerstein, 1928) – slow romantic waltz from an operetta, soprano, classical sound required.

'The Kind Of Man A Woman Needs' from *The Yearling* (Martin Herbert & Michael Leonard, 1946) – lovely ballad for mezzo or sop. Also 'Why Did I Choose You?'.

'I Never Danced With You' from *Lunch* (Steve Dorff & John Bettis, 1994) – beautiful ballad for a soprano or mezzo, soft and with belt; very rarely done to my knowledge.

'Only In Fantasy' from *Napoleon* (Timothy Williams & Andrew Sabiston, 1998) – good ballad for mezzo, sung by Josephine in the show; I never hear this done and it can be belted or mixed.

'Anything' from *Triumph Of Love* (Jeffrey Stock & Susan Birkenhead, 1998) – big belt number for high mezzo or sop; very showy and Disney-like, needs to be cut.

'Goodbye For Now' from *Reds* (Sondheim, 1981) – lovely, haunting ballad, also a really good acting piece; perfect length for audition, suitable for most voices.

'Wait A Bit' from *Just So* (Stiles and Drew, 2006) – fabulous modern ballad with some belting from the writers of *The Card* and the newly added songs for *Mary Poppins* (the stage version).

'Is Someone Out There?' from *In The Beginning* (Maury Yeston, 1988) – big, modern belt ballad, rangy; can be found on the Maury Yeston songbook CD.

'If I Love Again' from *Hold Your Horses* (Ben Oakland/J. P. Murray, 1933) – fantastic all-in-one ballad, perfect for most voices but probably best for mezzo; also in *Funny Lady* (the movie musical) – personal favourite.

'Somebody' from *Amour* (Michel Legrand, 2003) – lovely haunting ballad for soprano; can be belted, good range needed, difficult song.

'What Good Would The Moon Be?' from *Street Scene* (Kurt Weill, 1946) – beautiful haunting ballad for soprano, possibly high mezzo; does not go higher than a G below top C.

Character and up-tempo
'I Don't Want To Know' from *Dear World* (Jerry Herman, 1969) – lovely dramatic waltz for mature woman, 40-plus, alto or mezzo.

'Why Him?' from *Carmelina* (Alan Jay Lerner and Burton Lane, 1979) – good character song for mezzo, also belter; tango tempo.

'Mr Right' from *Love Life* (Kurt Weill, 1948) – great character comedy song or sop or high mezzo; It's quite long so may need to be cut.

'Falling In Love With Love' from *The Boys From Syracuse* (Richard Rodgers, 1938) – lovely up-tempo waltz, which requires rich soprano voice (think Barbara Cook).

'Oh, Goddess Wise' from *Princess Ida* (Gilbert and Sullivan, 1884) – top soprano, up-tempo dramatic song.

'I'll Be Hard To Handle' from *Roberta* (Jerome Kern & Otto Harbach, 1933) – jazz torch song for mezzo – also 'Yesterdays' from the same show, song for older mezzo 40-plus.

'I'm Going Back' from *Bells Are Ringing* (Jule Styne, 1956) – long, so will need to be cut; a gutsy number for someone 25-plus, I would think – belt to B also or lower mezzo.

'Shopping Around' from *Wish You Were Here* (Harold Rome, 1952) – cute, swingy number for mezzo or alto, jazzy and fun.

'One Life to Live' from *Lady In The Dark* (Gershwin & Kurt Weill, 1941) – first performed by Gertrude Lawrence, gutsy up-tempo sop song.

'You Can't Get A Man With A Gun' – from *Annie, Get Your Gun* (Irving Berlin, 1946) – great, gutsy, very big belty up-tempo character number for mezzo.

'Everybody Loves Louis' from *Sunday In The Park With George* (Sondheim, 1984) – good audition piece for character/up-tempo; needs mezzo belter but belt is not too high, gives lots of space for characterisation.

'My Body' from *The Life* (Ira Gasman, 1995) – rocky up-tempo number for big belter; a good audition song for any rock/pop shows. Also 'I'm Leaving You' as a modern high belt ballad.

'Always A Bridesmaid' from *I Love You, You're Perfect, Now Change!* (Jimmy Roberts, 1996) – this is done at auditions but not ridiculously so; comedy character number for mezzo belter.

Pins And Needles The Musical (Harold Rome, 1936) – great show with lots of unused material such as 'Nobody Makes A Pass At Me' (character sop number), definitely worth a look.

'Don't Call Me Trailer Trash' from *Cowgirls* (Mary Murfitt, 1996) – very American (country), another good mezzo, belt comedy number, feisty and bold; Duet in show but can be turned into solo. The show also has some other good material not heard that frequently at auditions.

'This Place Is Mine' from *Phantom* (Maury Yeston, version 1992) – dramatic diva like soprano, top B at the end; character number for strong soprano, woman rather than girl.

Applause (Charles Strousse, 1970) set in the late sixties – particularly a song called 'One Halloween' by a character called Eve (mezzo), a manipulative chorus girl with her eye on the starring role; also, 'Welcome The Theatre'; for an older actress 35-plus, mezzo or sop.

'Nelson' from *A Day In Hollywood, A Night In The Ukraine* (various composers including Jerry Herman, 1980) – this song from the show by Jerry Herman mocks the relationship between Nelson and Jeanette McDonald; hilarious comedy/character number for mezzo or sop.

'Look Ma, I Made It' from *Nunsense II* (Dan Goggin, 1993) – razzmatazz, jazzy number for belty mezzo/sop (think 'If They Could See Me Now' from *Sweet Charity*).

'On The Steps Of The Palace' from *Into The Woods* (Sondheim, 1987) – great character number for sop, hard to do; done a bit but still a good choice, I believe, if you can do it justice.

'Lovely' – *A Funny Thing Happened On The Way To The Forum* (Sondheim, 1962) – character sop/mezzo ballad; also, 'That'll Show Him' from the same show, character sop number.

'Art Is Calling For Me' from *The Enchantress* (Victor Herbert, 1911) – great comedy up-tempo number for 'diva', high soprano.

'Raunchy' from *110 In The Shade* (Tom Jones/Harvey Schmidt, 1963) – great bluesy, mid tempo number, character for soprano; goes to top A in the original key but can be transposed down and used for mezzo and alto, great showy number.

'I'll Show Him' from *Plain And Fancy* (Albert Hague/Arnold B Horwitt, 1955) – equivalent character to Ado Annie in *Oklahoma!*; great semi-belty character song for alto/mezzo when auditioning for these kind of characters in classical shows.

'A Parade In Town' from *Anyone Can Whistle* (Sondheim, 1964) – another good belt mezzo number.

'Why Marry Them?' from *Gay Divorce* (Cole Porter, 1932) – good character number for a mature woman.

'The Cocotte' from *Nymph Errant* (Cole Porter, 1933) – great character number for a mature woman; very good lyrics, a real comedy song – any voice type but mezzo is probably best.

'Where, Oh Where?' from *Out Of This World* (Cole Porter, 1950) – good waltz number for young woman, older teenager even, mezzo or sop, but more mezzo range.

'Si Vous Aimez Les Poitrines' "if you like breasts" from *Nymph Errant* (Cole Porter, 1933) – this is an interesting one! It's a point number in the show so not ideal for a 3-minute audition song but for those famous 16 bars. I think it's a great choice – verse and chorus of that really show what you are about. It's very rarely done as far as I know, so very original. Sung in English and French so you might need to get help with the French accent, but worth it. You could possibly include a key change midway through song when the chorus repeats and really show your range that way.

'Love 'Em And Leave 'Em' (not from any particular show but a song on its own by Cole Porter, 1920) – fantastic comedy/character number for alto, mature woman (35-plus looking), *great* song for actors! Wonderful lyrics and highly recommended.

'The Boyfriend Back Home' from *Fifty Million Frenchmen* (Cole Porter, 1929) – great character number for mezzo or sop of any age up to about 35 or so – starts out sweet and innocent, gets raunchier as the song goes on.

'All I've Got To Get Now Is My Man' from *Panama Hattie* (Cole Porter, 1940) – great comedy/character number for a woman of any age, mezzo or soprano.

'Down In The Depths' from *Red, Hot and Blue* (Cole Porter, 1936) – great ironic-type comedy character number – foxtrot tempo, so not too fast, not too slow; better for a woman who looks at least 30–35 or so, soprano or mezzo.

'See What It Gets You' from *Anyone Can Whistle* (Sondheim, 1964). Up-tempo, belty, mezzo character; requires strong top belt notes.

'Girl In The Mirror (I Want To Go To Hollywood)' from *Grand Hotel* (Maury Yeston, George Forest, Robert Wright, 1989) – up-tempo character number; young girl, can be teenager, alto or mezzo.

'Flaming Agnes' from *I Do, I Do* (Tom Jones & Harvey Schmidt, 1966) – mid-tempo character number for mezzo of at least 35; a similar type of song to 'Look What Happened To Mabel' from *Mack and Mabel*.

'On The Other Side Of The Tracks' from *Little Me* (Cy Coleman, Carolyn Leigh, 1962) – belt mezzo/soprano, this song builds very well, very showy.

'My Secretary's In Love' from *Big* (Maltby & Shire, 1987) – up-tempo comedy number; fast, belty, mezzo; should be 30 or late 20s at least.

'What's Wrong With Me?' from *Singin' In The Rain* (Nacio Herb Brown & Arthur Freed, 1952) – superb character song for any range; also for 'actress who sings', surprisingly no-one ever does it. Highly recommended, you don't need to put on Lina's accent; the song is *not* in the movie version or on the movie cast recording.

'I'm Not At All In Love' from *The Pyjama Game* (Jerry Ross & Richard Adler, 1954) – up-tempo waltz for feisty mezzo belter; full voice, character.

'Change' from *A New Brain* (William Finn, 2000) – up-tempo, urgent number about a woman who is demanding a chance and change in life, mezzo.

'Back On Bass' from *Closer Than Ever* (Maltby & Shire, 1990) – jazzy up-tempo 'finger snapping' type number; belty mezzo.

'Can That Boy Foxtrot' from *Marry Me A Little* (Sondheim 1981) – great character for alto or mezzo woman.

'A Little Brains, A Little Talent' from *Damn Yankees* (Jerry Ross & Richard Adler, 1955) – sexy, jazzy character number for alto/low mezzo; must be a belter. Also 'Whatever Lola Wants'.

'Gorgeous' from *The Apple Tree* (Sheldon Harnick & Jerry Bock, 1966) – up-tempo mezzo; belty, sexy number, think 'tempting vamp' – quite popular now.

'Fancy Forgetting' from *Divorce Me, Darling* (Sandy Wilson, 1964) – slow waltz, French accent, mezzo; something to play around with and really make your own, whether you do it serious or comedy.

'Here I Am, But Where's The Guy?' from *Divorce Me, Darling* (as above) – great up-tempo belt number for young sop or mezzo.

'Lost And Found' from *City Of Angels* (David Zippel, 1990) – swingy, blues number, sexy; mezzo or high alto, belt needed to C.

'I Want To Be Bad' from *Follow Through* (De Sylva, Brown and Henderson, 1929); again, sexy and up-tempo, cute; alto, mezzo.

'Arthur' from *The Act* (Kander & Ebb, 1977) – great comedy number for woman of at least 25, alto or mezzo.

'How Lucky Can You Get' from *Funny Lady* (Kander & Ebb, 1975) – character and big belt jazz; must have secure high belt, wonderfully expressive and rangy number, mezzo or sop.

'I Wish I Were In Love Again' from *Babes In Arms* (Rogers & Hart, 1939) – very good lyrics; mezzo, alto, sop and also good for actors looking for a song for straight acting courses.

'Everybody Says Don't' from *Anyone Can Whistle (Sondheim, 1964)* – very fast, very wordy (patter song), mezzo, sop; big belt; male number in the show but can be used as both; I have seen it being done successfully by females.

'It's De Lovely' from *Anything Goes* (Cole Porter, 1956) – good to show some movement; also good for guys, mezzo or sop.

'Legalize My Name' from *St Louis Woman* (Arlen & Mercer, 1946) – hilarious comedy number for all voice types; great if auditioning for Adelaide in *Guys and Dolls*.

'Cornet Man' from *Funny Girl* stage version (Jule Styne & Bob Merrill, 1964) – great comedy, character number; must have strong belt but also a good song for an actress who sings, think old 'vaudeville' style, mezzo or sop.

'Many A New Day' from *Oklahoma!* (Rodgers & Hammerstein, 1943) – good up-tempo character number, but still ingénue; fine acting song but needs strong soprano voice.

'Nobody Is Chasing Me' from *Out Of This World* (Cole Porter, 1950) – hilarious comedy number; good lyrics, suitable for anyone.

'Goodbye, Emil' from *Romance, Romance* (Herrman & Harman, 1987) – comedy number that asks for soprano; great audition song, highly recommended.

'Today Is The First Day Of The Rest Of My Life' from *Starting Here, Starting Now* (Maltby & Shire, 1977) – good up-tempo, urgent number.

'Paris Makes Me Horny' from *Victor, Victoria* (Bricusse and Mancini, 1995) – sexy character number, lots of acting.

'Who Taught Her Everything?' from *Funny Girl* stage version (Jule Styne & Bob Merrill, 1964) – semi up-tempo; comedy number for 'older' woman 40-plus; great lyrics and also possible for a man.

'That Dirty Old Man Of Mine' from *A Funny Thing Happened On The Way To The Forum* (Sondheim, 1966) – good character number which shows voice for woman 40-plus.

'Come, Play Wiz Me' from *Anyone Can Whistle* (Sondheim, 1964) – comedy number which requires a French accent; a sexy type of number and a great audition song for a dancer; a duet in the show but possible to do solo.

'Turn Back Oh Man' from *Godspell* (Stephen Schwartz, 1973) – jazzy, sexy comedy number for mezzo or sop.

'Happy To Keep His Dinner Warm' from *How To Succeed In Business Without Really Trying* (Frank Loesser, 1967) – great acting song; also for people applying for straight acting course; does not require large range, mezzo.

'A Call From The Vatican' from *Nine* (Maury Yeston, 1982) – character number with *lots* of range required; sop; *only* if you can hit a top C *easily* and belt up to an F well. *Only* do it if you are really up to it; a popular choice but done badly a lot – if you can do it well, you may stand out.

'Gooch's Song' from *Mame* (Jerry Herman, 1966) – requires top notes; very good acting song and recommended; top B, sop.

'Be On Your Own' from *Nine* (Maury Yeston, 1982) – very dramatic and wordy, mezzo range; belty, strong voice and should be performed by someone who looks at least mid twenties, mezzo or alto.

'I'll Marry The Very Next Man' from *Fiorello* (Sheldon & Harnick, 1959) – up-tempo character, mezzo.

'I Just Want To Be A Star' from *Nunsense* (Dan Goggin, 1986) – great jazzy, showy belt number for mezzo.

'Alto's Lament' (Marcy Heisler/Zina Goldrich) – great character song, very funny; must be cut, though, as too long; top C required; sheet music available on www.musicnotes.com

'Where In The World Is My Prince' from *Miss Spectacular* (Jerry Herman, 2002) – this show was never performed so it's a concept album only; hilarious comedy number for mezzo, maybe sop of most ages; also have a look at 'Miss-what's-her-name' (another up-tempo character comedy song) from the same show.

'I Got Everything I Want' from *I Had A Ball* (Jack Lawrence & Stan Freedman, 1964) – good up-tempo, swing belt number for 'the other woman'; big voice needed, mezzo or soprano.

'Where Is The Man I Married' from *High Spirits* (Timothy Gray & Hugh Martin, 1964) – comedy character number for sop or mezzo; up-tempo, 30-plus, based on the Noel Coward play *Blithe Spirit*.

'More' from *Dick Tracy* the film (Sondheim, 1990) – fantastic character, jazzy up-tempo number for sop or mezzo; big belt required, needs to be cut, though; also look at 'Back In Business' from the same show, another up-tempo jazz number with top E belt.

'Let's See What Happens' from *Darling Of The Day* (Jule Styne & E Y Harburg, 1968) – big waltz for lyrical ingénue soprano.

'He's Here Now' from *How Now, Dow Jones* (Elmer Bernstein & Carolyn Leigh, 1967) – absolutely hilarious; very large and over-the-top character song for most voice types.

'It's Today' from *Mame* (Jerry Herman, 1966) – alto, mezzo; belt but doesn't have to be very strong belt; originally sung by actress Angela Lansbury. Good up-tempo number, which can be very showy; also 'Open A New Window'.

'Meet Me At The Strand' from *Belle Or The Ballad of Dr Crippen* (Monty Norman & Mankowitz, 1961) – bright music hall number; the perfect audition song for shows from that period such as *My Fair Lady*.

'I'm One Of The Boys' from *Hollywood Party* (2001) – based on the 1934 MGM film; good, up-tempo and witty comedy number, belt required.

'Girl In 14g' written for Kristin Chenoweth (Jeanine Testori, 2002) – very difficult song, top soprano; not for the faint hearted! It shows jazz, belt, operatic scales and comedy all in one song; a great showpiece for very accomplished singers.

'I Want To Be A Rockette' from *Kicks – the showgirl musical* (Alan Menken & Tom Eyen, 1984) – I love this song; it's a great mid tempo number and also possible with dance, belt, mezzo or sop; very 'jazz hands'.

'Whatever It Takes' from *Lily & Lily* (Billy Stritch, 1999) – another razzle dazzle showstopper number for a belter.

'You Wanna Bet' cut from *Sweet Charity* (Dorothy Fields & Cy Coleman, 1966) – great up-tempo number, available on various recordings including Barbara Streisand's *Just For The Record*.

'There's Nothing Rougher Than Love' from *It's A Great Feeling* (Jule Styne & Sammy Cahn, 1949) – fantastic up-tempo number; requires high and strong belt, very showy.

'I Never Do Anything Twice' from *The Seven Percent Solution* (Sondheim, 1975) – very funny comedy number; a great acting piece also for those with less strong voices; not that rangy, suitable for most voice types.

'You're Gonna Hear From Me' from the film *Inside Daisy Clover* (Andre Previn, 1965) – fantastic jazzy torch song type number for a big belter with a good range and strong voice, mid tempo. Listen to it on Streisand's *The Movie Album*.

'I Stayed Too Long At The Fair' (Billy Barnes, 1956) – great song for young sop or mezzo, very underdone; the song is quite long but benefits from up-tempo and ballad parts and you can show a lot of different emotions in one piece.

Male and female ballads
'When The Children Are Asleep' from *Carousel* (Rodgers & Hammerstein, 1945) – lovely semi up-tempo ballad for either woman or man; duet in show but can be altered; mezzo-soprano and baritone/tenor.

'You There In The Back Row' from *13 Days To Broadway* (Cy Coleman, 1987) – lovely ballad for male or female.

'If Love Were All' from *Bitter Sweet* (Noel Coward, 1929) – lovely ballad good for baritone or mezzo, sop. Also 'What Is Love?' – wonderful up-tempo soprano waltz with a top C.

'I'll Follow My Secret Heart' from *Conversation Piece* (Noel Coward, 1934) – sop or baritone/tenor.

'I'll See You Again' from *Bitter Sweet* (Noel Coward, 1929) – soprano.

Male ballads
'If I Sing' from *Closer Than Ever* (Maltby & Shire, 1990) – ballad, good acting song; baritone/bass, middle-aged.

'My Life Belongs To You' from *The Dancing Years* (Ivor Novello, 1939) – classic baritone/tenor ballad.

'Real Live Girl' from *Little Me* (Cy Coleman & Carol Leigh, 1962) – lovely romantic waltz for baritone.

'Shouldn't I Be Less In Love With You?' from *I Love You, You're Perfect, Now Change!* (Joe Di Pietro & Jimmy Roberts, 1996) – good contemporary ballad for baritone.

'No Other Love' from *Me And Juliet* (Rodgers & Hammerstein, 1953) – duet in show but can be turned into a lovely solo for baritone.

'If You Leave Me Now' cut from *The Happy Time* (Kander & Ebb, 1968) – this can be found on the *Lost In Boston* CD compilations through Amazon.

'Her Laughter In My Life' from *How Do You Do, I Love You* (David Shire) – lovely plaintive ballad, sadly not much is known about the show and this song was cut.

'Right As The Rain' from *Bloomer Girl* (Harold Arlen and Yip Harburg, 1944) – showy audition piece for tenor with classic MT sound.

'How Glory Goes' from *Flloyd Collins* (Adam Guettel, 1996) – beautiful ballad, needs to be listened to in full to be appreciated.

'You Walk With Me' from *The Full Monty* (David Yazbek, 2000) – great for a tenor; good audition piece for modern shows.

'There But For You Go I' from *Brigadoon* (Lerner & Loewe, 1947) – another lovely ballad for a low tenor or high baritone.

'Look Who's Alone Now' from *Nick and Nora* (Charles Strousse/Richard Maltby, 1991) – baritone is probably best for this.

'There's No Reason Why' from *Milk and Honey* (Jerry Herman, 1961) – lush ballad for a tenor.

'I'll Never Say No' from *The Unsinkable Molly Brown* (Meredith Wilson, 1960) – another great classic baritone ballad.

'Make Someone Happy' from *Do Re Mi* (Comden & Green, 1960) – ballad for tenor.

"You Should Be Loved' from *Sideshow* (Henry Krieger, 1997) – big, lush ballad for baritone/bass.

"Love Who You Love' from *A Man Of No Importance* (Ahrens & Flaherty, 2002) – slow waltz for baritone, middle-aged in the show.

'I Wish I Knew' from Billy Rose's *Diamond Horseshoe* (Harry Warden & Mack Gordon, 1945) – lush ballad for tenor or baritone, perfect for auditions.

'No Moon' from *Titanic* (Maury Yeston, 1997) – great ballad for top tenor, difficult.

'What Can You Lose?' from *Dick Tracy* the film (Sondheim, 1990) – lovely ballad for high baritone, personal favourite.

'Love Can't Happen' from *Grand Hotel* (Maury Yeston, George Forest, Robert Wright, 1989) – duet in show, up-tempo waltz; wonderful for classical sounding lyric tenor, really good audition piece; young, charming leading man type. I love this song!

'I See The Future' from *The Fix* (Dana P. Row, 1997) – big MT rock ballad for tenor, character dreams of becoming a rock star; also, 'Child's Play' and 'One, Two, Three'.

'Look At Her' from *New Girl In Town* (Bob Merrill, 1957) – lovely, lush ballad for baritone.

'When I Had To Live Alone' from *The Baker's Wife* (Stephen Schwartz, 1993) – tenor, middle-aged, lovely strong ballad.

'Alone Too Long' from *By The Beautiful Sea* (Dorothy Fields & Arthur Schwartz, 1954) – classical tenor ballad (think *Showboat*); distinguished classic leading man type in his prime.

'I Don't Remember You' from *The Happy Time* (Kander & Ebb, 1968) – great ballad, not too high, baritone.

'Marry Me' from *The Rink* (Kander & Ebb, 1984) – wonderful ballad for baritone and bass; also good as a woman's song (alto or mezzo), if transposed.

'Do I Love You Because You're Beautiful?' from *Cinderella* (Rodgers & Hammerstein, 1957) – gorgeous ballad for baritone or lower tenor.

'Not While I'm Around' from *Sweeney Todd* (Sondheim, 1979) – good acting song but requires a nice, smooth voice; possible for young teenage male, tenor.

'What Kind Of Fool Am I?' from *Stop The World, I Want To Get Off* (Anthony Newly & Leslie Bricusse, 1966) – great ballad for baritone or tenor.

'Some Enchanted Evening' from *South Pacific* (Rodgers & Hammerstein, 1958) – baritone or bass, always a winner if done well.

'I Won't Send Roses' from *Mack and Mabel* (Jerry Herman, 1974) – bass, baritone, ballad; a perfect audition song.

'When I Look In Your Eyes' from *Dr Doolittle* (Leslie Bricusse, 1967) – lovely ballad, baritone.

'The Greatest Star Of All' from *Sunset Boulevard* (Lloyd Webber, 1993) – wonderful ballad for high baritone or low tenor; must be middle-aged or older; shows a lot of range and emotion, a hard song.

'My Best Girl' from *Mame* (Jerry Herman, 1964) – waltz, ballad, baritone or tenor; also possible as a child's song as sung by an 8-year-old boy in the show.

'Why Should I Wake Up?' from *Cabaret* (Kander & Ebb, 1972) – lovely ballad for young male baritone, surprisingly not done a lot.

'These Are The Games That I Play' from *Falsettos* (William Finn, 1990) – baritone, ballad, sombre and thoughtful.

'Who Can I Turn To?' from *The Roar Of The Greasepaint, The Smell Of The Crowd* (Newly & Bricusse, 1962) – great ballad, baritone or bass.

'If Ever I Would Leave You' from *Camelot* (Lerner & Loewe, 1960) – lovely ballad for baritone.

'Where Did That Little Dog Go?' from *Snoopy* (Larry Grossman/Hal Hackady, 1983) – lovely, plaintive ballad for baritone, also possible for teenager.

'It Only Takes A Moment' from *Hello, Dolly!* (Jerry Herman, 1964) – lovely ballad for male, baritone/tenor range; sung by a young male in the show.

'I Have Dreamed' from *The King and I* (Rodgers & Hammerstein, 1951) – lovely ballad for tenor, a duet in the show but can be done as a solo.

'Being Alive' from *Company* (Sondheim, 1970) – tenor or high baritone done a lot, but if you can do it well I still think it's a good audition piece; 'urgent', up-tempo ballad.

'Take Me To The World' from *Evening Primrose* (Sondheim, 1966) – lovely ballad for baritone, can also be used for female.

'You're Devastating' from *Roberta* (Jerome Kern, Otto Harbach, 1933) – ballad for very rich, mature baritone or tenor voice (think *Oklahoma!*).

'You Do Something To Me' from *Fifty Million Frenchmen* (Cole Porter, 1929) – lovely mid-tempo ballad for baritone/tenor; duet in show but can be edited into solo.

'She Wasn't You' from *On A Clear Day You Can See Forever* (Burton Lane/Alan Jay Lerner, 1965) – lovely ballad for baritone or bass.

'I Cannot Hear The City' from *The Sweet Smell Of Success* (Marvin Hamlish/Craig Carnelia, 2002) – good ballad for baritone or tenor.

'Out There' from *The Hunchback Of Notre Dame* (Stephen Schwartz, 2001) – big tenor ballad with top notes.

'She's Too Far Above Me' from *Half A Sixpence* (David Henneker, 1965) – lovely ballad (cockney accent in show) for bass or baritone.

'You're So Right For Me' from *Oh, Captain* (Jay Livingston & Ray Evans, 1958) – lovely romantic mid-tempo ballad for leading man, baritone.

'I'll Buy You A Star' from *A Tree Grows In Brooklyn* (Arthur Schwartz & Dorothy Fields, 1951) – lovely simple ballad for baritone, good all-in-one number.

'Time Stands Still' from *Lunch* (Steve Dorff & John Bettis, 1994) – lovely haunting ballad, touching.

'Proud Of Your Boy' cut from the Disney film *Aladdin* (Menken & Ashman, 1992) – this was originally supposed to be sung by Aladdin to his mother, who was cut from the film; lush, typically Disney ballad that can be sung by a young baritone, teenager; also suitable for young child; recording can be found on www.youtube.com and John Barrowman's albums.

'Is It Just Me?' from *The Card* (Stiles and Drew, 1973) – good MT ballad.

'At Least I Tried' cut from *Barnum* (Cy Coleman & Michael Stewart, 1980) – lovely ballad for baritone that was cut from the show before it opened.

'Dreamers' from *Jean Seberg* (Marvin Hamlish & Christopher Adler, 1983) – lovely ballad for a baritone/tenor; listen to it on John Barrowman's solo album *Reflections from Broadway*.

'A Boy From Nowhere' from *Matador* (Mike Leander & Edward Seago, 1991) – big ballad for tenor; again, listen to it on Barrowman's album (as above).

'I Chose Right' from *Baby* (Maltby & Shire, 1983) – eighties ballad for baritone/tenor.

'Does The Moment Ever Come?' from *Just So* (Drew & Stiles, 1989) – lovely, soft ballad for tenor.

'An Ordinary Guy' from *Amour* (Michel Legrand, 2003) – ballad for tenor, very passionate, starts soft but then shows range.

Character and up-tempo songs
'Look Over There' from *La Cage Aux Folles* (Jerry Herman, 1983) – up-tempo waltz, dramatic; suitable for a mature man with a playing age of at least 40, high baritone.

'That's For Me' from *State Fair* (Rodgers & Hammerstein, 1945) – this song is in the original film version only; good up-tempo for a young baritone/tenor.

'The Life Of The Party' from *The Happy Time* (Kander and Ebb, 1968) – great up-tempo number for baritone/tenor, good for movement too.

'She Loves Me' from *She Loves Me* (Harnick & Bock, 1963) – baritone, up-tempo.

'I Don't Care Much' cut from *Cabaret* (Kander & Ebb, 1966) – dramatic up-tempo waltz, great audition song. Also suitable for females.

'Last One Picked' from *Whoop Dee Doo* (Howard Crabtree, 1995) – character comedy number.

'The Man I Used To Be' from *Pipe Dream* (Rodgers & Hammerstein, 1955) – mid-tempo character piece for bass/baritone.

'Wouldn't You Like To Be On Broadway?' from *Street Scene* (Kurt Weill/Langston Hughes, 1946) – mid-tempo character piece for bass/baritone.

'I Never Attended At All' from *Billy Barnes' LA* (Billy Barnes, 1962) – comedy song for all voice types, very forward and witty.

'Someone To Dance With' from *Divorce Me, Darling* (Sandy Wilson, 1964) – good up-tempo number for baritone by *The Boyfriend*'s composer.

'The Devil You Know' from *Side Show* (Henry Krieger, 1997) – big, rocky up-tempo number for baritone/bass.

'I Hate Musicals' from *Ruthless* (Marvin Laird, 1994) – comedy up-tempo number, baritone or bass.

'Me' from *Beauty And The Beast* (Ashman & Menken, 1991) – great character number for baritone/bass sung by Gaston character.

'He's In Love' from *Kismet* (Robert Wright, George Forrest, 1953) – great up-tempo waltz for a man with a very rich tenor voice, at least 30 years old.

'You've Got That Thing' from *Fifty Million Frenchmen* (Cole Porter, 1929) – great up-tempo number for a young, leading man; also a dancer, baritone or tenor.

'She's Roses' from *Drat The Cat* (Ira Levin, Milton Schaefer, 1965) – slow, romantic waltz for baritone or tenor.

'I Won't Dance' from *Roberta* (Jerome Kern, Otto Harbach, 1933) – light up-tempo song, also for teenager, not very rangy; also for actors who sing; duet in the show but can be edited into a solo number.

'When I Found You' from *Paris* (Cole Porter, 1928) – great waltz for tenor or high baritone with a secure top G; lovely, short and sweet; it shows off a good top G – perfect for auditions.

'The Extra Man' from *Wake Up And Dream* (Cole Porter, 1929) – great character number for a man of any age, singing about how he is the stand-in or understudy for the real man the girl he loves has fallen for; good for all voice types.

'Red, Hot And Blue' from *Red, Hot And Blue* (Cole Porter, 1936) – fantastic up-tempo number for any age really, tenor, high baritone. Highly recommended as contrast to a big ballad.

'Poor, Unsuccessful And Fat' from *A New Brain* (William Finn, 1998) – hilarious comedy number for many voice types.

'Lucky' from *Lucky Stiff* (Ahrens & Flaherty, 2005) – good for a young guy, shy gawky-looking, English accent for song.

'Grand Knowing You' from *She Loves Me* (Harnick & Bock, 1963) – tenor, up-tempo character type number.

'Plumbing' from *Nymph Errant* (Cole Porter, 1933) – hilarious comedy number for baritone/tenor with big voice, quirky.

'How Lucky You Are' from *Seussical* (Ahrens & Flaherty, 2000) – up-tempo character number sung by 'the cat in the hat' in the show.

'I Don't Remember Christmas' from *Starting Here, Starting Now* (Maltby & Shire, 1977) – great up-tempo number, very wordy, baritone.

'Once In Love With Amy' from *Where's Charley?* (Frank Loesser, 1948) – nice mid-tempo in show; you can speed up a tempo and turn it into a really good up-tempo jazzy number; very showy, can be a comedy character song.

'Pretty Music' from *Parade* (Jason Robert Brow, 1998) – great up-tempo jazzy number, baritone; can be for a dancer with movement.

'Live Alone And Like It' from *Putting It Together* (Sondheim, 1993) – up-tempo jazzy number for baritone; again, very good for a dancer.

'I'm Gonna Sit Right Down And Write Myself A Letter' from *Ain't Misbehaving* (various composers including Fats Waller, 1978) – baritone, mid-tempo, jazzy vaudeville number; think 1920s, loud, jovial type of character.

'I'll Build A Stairway To Paradise' from *An American In Paris* (Gershwin, 1954) – great mid-tempo show number for strong, high tenor, top A or B.

'Proud Lady' from *The Baker's Wife* (Stephen Schwartz, 1993) – ballad, but also has fast up-tempo section; good character song also – baritone, sexy young man.

'Old Enough To Love' from *By The Beautiful Sea* (Dorothy Fields & Arthur Schwartz, 1954) – soft shoe type of song; nice up-tempo song, jazzy style, young male about 19–20.

'I Love My Wife' from *I Do, I Do* (Tom Jones & Harvey Schmidt, 1966) – great mid-tempo character number, late twenties or older.

'It's A Well Known Fact' from *I Do, I Do* (Tom Jones & Harvey Schmidt, 1966) – good mid-tempo number for character actor in his forties or so; can be talk sung (for example Rex Harrison in *My Fair Lady*).

'Exits' from *My Favourite Year* (Ahrens & Flaherty, 1992) – up-tempo character song for leading man type character (mature voice, not teen or young twenties voice) that usually sings big ballads.

'The Most Beautiful Girl In The World' from *Jumbo* (Rogers & Hart 1935) – up-tempo waltz, very expressive, great for tenor or high baritone.

'Come Back To Me' from *On A Clear Day You Can See Forever* (Lerner & Loewe, 1970) – great up-tempo character number for baritone, good lyrics; also possible for female if transposed; another favourite of mine.

'Today Is The First Day Of The Rest Of My Life' from *Starting Here, Starting Now* (Maltby & Shire, 1977) – up-tempo, good acting song too, baritone.

'Love I Hear' from *A Funny Thing Happened On The Way To The Forum* (Sondheim, 1964) – great ballad, baritone or low tenor; highly recommended; young teenage male possible.

'First You Dream' from *Steel Pier* (Kander & Ebb, 1997) – ballad, partly up-tempo, gorgeous song.

'Leaning On A Lamp Post' from *Me And My Girl* (Noel Gay, 1937) – baritone.

'Why Me, Why Me?' from *Two By Two* (Richard Rodgers/Martin Chamin, 1970) – older man (looking at least 60); bass or baritone, comedy character number.

'And Her Mother Came Too' from *Charlot Revue AZ* (Ivor Novello, 1924) – very English comedy song, really good audition song; also suitable for 'actors'; a personal favourite.

'Finishing The Hat' from *Sunday In The Park With George* (Sondheim, 1984) – baritone or tenor, difficult.

'It's A Bore' from *Gigi* (Lerner & Loewe, 1958) – up-tempo, bass or baritone, duet in film/show but can be altered.

'I'm Young And Healthy' from *42nd Street* (Warren & Dubin, 1982) – baritone, low tenor, up-tempo, fun number. Good for some movement; good for young male 18–25; also good for female.

'What I Say Goes' from *A Family Affair* (John Kander/B Goldman, 1962) – energetic up-tempo number for tenor/baritone. Young leading man.

'All I Need Is The Girl' from *Gypsy* (Jule Styne, 1959) – baritone, tenor, up-tempo fast number; great for a guy who can also dance/move well, young teenage male 15–16-plus.

'Big News' from *Parade* (Jason Robert Brown, 1998) – great up-tempo number for baritone or low tenor.

'Where Is The life That Late I Led?' from *Kiss Me Kate* (Cole Porter, 1948) – hilarious, up-tempo character number, baritone or tenor.

'Piece Of The Action' from *The Life* (Coleman & Gasman, 1995) – up-tempo, baritone or tenor; young, hip, New York 'dude'.

'Use What You Got' from *The Life* (Coleman & Gasman, 1995) – another great character number, modern; there are two versions: the original is a high tenor, the other version is quite a bit lower and more for a baritone range.

'The Masochism Tango' from *Tomfoolery* (Tom Lehrer, 1980) – great comedy song from a revue of songs all written by Tom Lehrer; in case you are interested in this show, be aware that 'Poisoning Pigeons In The Park' is quite regularly done at auditions.

'Tonight At Eight' from *She Loves Me* (Harnick & Bock, 1990) – up-tempo, baritone.

'Winter's On The Wing' from *The Secret Garden* (Marsha Norman & Lucy Simon, 1991) – lovely ballad/up-tempo song for baritone/tenor; must be young, innocent looking, young/late teenage boy possible.

'Buddy's Blues' from *Follies* (Sondheim, 1971) – very fast character, up-tempo number for baritone/lower tenor; you really have to be able to nail this song though, it's only for the brave! If done well, a showstopper.

'Second Chance' from *Steel Pier* (Kander & Ebb, 1997) – great character number, baritone or bass; hilarious if done well.

'Take A Chance On Me' from *Little Women* (Jason Howlands/Minnie Dickstein, 2005) – up-tempo, energetic number for young boy/man in love; also possible for teenage baritone.

'The Sadder But Wiser Girl' from *The Music Man* (Meredith Wilson, 1962) – up-tempo, wordy number for an older man, baritone or bass.

'Sunset Boulevard' from *Sunset Boulevard* (Lloyd Webber, 1993) – good up-tempo song for high baritone or tenor (top G); difficult accompaniment, make sure this will no cause problems at your audition.

'Barret's Song' from *Titanic* (Maury Yeston, 1997) – tenor with strong top; often done, but worth it if you can do it well.

'King's Dilemna' from *Victor Victoria* (Bricusse & Mancini, 1995) – character number for baritone/tenor; great but may be too long, must be cut.

'She Is Not Thinking Of Me' from *Gigi* (Lerner & Loewe, 1958) – great up-tempo waltz for rich baritone voice; a good audition song for anything, shows range.

'I Can See It' from *The Fantasticks* (Tom Jones & Harvey Schmidt, 1960) – very good up-tempo number which starts of as a ballad; requires range, baritone/tenor.

'My Defences Are Down' from *Annie, Get Your Gun* (Irving Berlin, 1950) – great semi-up-tempo number for baritone, not an obvious comedy song but can be done so.

'Stupid Thing I Won't Do' from *The Royal Family Of Broadway* (William Finn – work still in progress, look on Amazon for a CD called *Infinite Joy*).

'You Can't Brush Me Off' from *Louisiana Purchase* (Irving Berlin, 1940) – lovely 1940's style swing number; up-tempo for young man, all voice types.

'I'm Undressing Girls With My Eyes' from *So Long 174th Street* (Stan Daniels, 1976) – very good character comedy number for all voice types.

'The Butler's Song' from *So Long 174th Street* (Stan Daniels, 1976) – another hilarious comedy number; can be done with upper-class English accent, all ages but probably better if the man is 'mature'.

'Keep Away From The Moonlight' from *Hollywood Party (2001)* – mid-tempo soft shoe number; for most voice types, music hall/vaudeville style.

'Saturday Girl' from *Lola Montez* (Peter Benjamin, Peter Stannard, Alan Burke, 1958) – great big waltz for leading man, baritone or tenor.

'If You Can Find Me, I'm Here' from *Evening Primrose* (Sondheim, 1966) – angry, up-tempo character song for baritone or lower tenor; very good acting piece, showy.

'Live Alone And Like It' from *Dick Tracy* (Sondheim, 1990) – swingy, mid-tempo number; good fun, shows character.

'What Am I Doing?' from *Closer Than Ever* (David Shire & Richard Maltby, 1989) – fantastic showcase number for tenor, up-tempo/manic as well as part ballad; recommended.

'I Like Myself' from *It's Always Fair Weather* (Comden & Green/Andre Previn, 1955) – lovely mid-tempo number from the movie with Gene Kelly.

'Dance With The Devil' from *The Witches Of Eastwick* (John Dempsey and Dana P. Rowe, 2000) – good up-tempo pop/rock MT number for a tenor; also good for incorporating movement.

'Assassins' from the musical of the same name is also a good bet for tenors (Sondheim, 1990) but must be appropriately cut. Also check out 'A Little More Mascara' (male drag queen number) from *La Cage Aux Folles* (Jerry Herrman, 1983), which may be suitable for some auditions and singers.

Teenage and child material
Certain listings in this whole section of audition songs are marked 'teenage' meaning age 14 and upwards but here is some material specifically for children and teenagers.

Ballads
'Much More' from *The Fantasticks* (Tom Jones & Harvey Schmidt, 1960) – ballad but also has character, up-tempo part – mezzo and soprano. A very good song to show voice and act; ingénue type, can be sung by very young girl.

'Little Lamb' from *Gypsy* (Jule Styne, 1959) – plaintive ballad for young girl/child; from the same score 'If Momma Was Married' if cut appropriately as it is originally a duet; good up-tempo numbers, again for child/very young girl.

'I Want To Know' from *Big* (Stephen Schwartz, 1993) – ballad for a young boy of about 12, also possible as young teenager/early twenties.

'Growing Tall' from *Nine* (Maury Yeston, 1982) – ballad for young boy of 9 to 12.

'There'll Come A Day' from *The Ragged Child* (Frank Wateley, Jeremy James Taylor, David Nield, 1988) – set in London in the 1890s; Cockney girl of about 10–13, ballad for soprano 'sweet' voice, good song if auditioning for *Oliver!*

'The Girl I Mean To Be' from *The Secret Garden* (Marsha Norman & Lucy Simon, 1991) – lovely ballad for girl aged 8–12.

'My Best Girl' from *Mame* (Jerry Herman, 1967) – waltz, ballad; a really good song for audition, boy aged 8–12.

'Let Me Be Brave' and 'Forgiveness' from *Jane Eyre* (Paul Gordon, 2000) – playing age 14–16; must be of very mature mezzo voice as songs are difficult, strong, calm, spiritual character.

'To Play This Part' from *Ruthless* (Marvin Laird, 1994) – big ballad for girl with big voice (think *Annie*).

Character and up-tempo

'Be Kind To Your Parents' from *Fanny* (Harold Rome, 1954) – comedy song for children of many ages.

'Neat To Be A Newsboy' from *Working* (Stephen Schwartz, 1978) – up-tempo number; very wordy for a young boy before voice break, good acting number too.

'Go Visit Your Grandmother' from *70 Girls 70* (Kander & Ebb, 1971) – comedy up-tempo number.

'Born To Entertain' from *Ruthless* (Marvin Laird, 1994) – challenging up-tempo, jazzy number for girl with big voice; also involves dancing and tap if you choose.

'Please Don't Send Me Down A Baby Brother' from *By The Beautiful Sea* (Fields & Schwartz, 1954) – great solo juvenile comedy number; no sheet music available so must be transcribed from original cast album.

'Amazing Mazie' from *Seussical* (Ahrens & Flaherty, 2000) – up-tempo song for girl, pre-teen or teen.

'One Boy' from *Bye Bye Birdie* (Charles Strousse, 1960) – up-tempo number for pre-teen (no younger than say 12 or so) to young teen; can be good mover/dancer and incorporate movement.

'I Like It Here' from *Mirette* (Tom Jones & Harvey Schmidt, 1994) – character song, mid-tempo, set in the 1890s; for 9–12-year-old girl.

'That Man Over There Is Santa Clause' from *Here's Love* (Meredith Wilson, 1963) – great up-tempo song for young girl, from 8 or 9 to 13 or so; must have strong voice; (think *Annie*); chorus number in show but can be made into great solo.

'Little Jack Horner' and 'Little Girl Blues' from *A Pocket Full Of Rhymes* (Jim Eiler & Jeanne Bargy, 1968) – nursery rhymes set to contemporary music; one-act revue show, big kids' show, boy aged 8–12 or so.

'I Whistle A Happy Tune' from *The King and I* (Rodgers & Hammerstein, 1951) – good up-tempo character number for a girl or boy of any age; also, good panto audition song.

'The Glamorous Life' from *A Little Night Music* (Sondheim, 1973) – good up-tempo acting piece for girl up to age 14 or so; requires strong voice, must be cut.

'I Want It Now' from *Willy Wonka & The Chocolate Factory* (Anthony Newly and Leslie Bricusse, 1971) – great character number for girl of about 10, give or take two years.

'Schooldays' from *Goodbye, Mr Chips* (Leslie Bricusse, 1969) – good up-tempo number for most ages, perfect if auditioning for *Oliver!* Sung by boys in the show but can also be sung by a girl.

Also:
★ *Snoopy* (Larry Grossman & Hal Hackaday, 1982)

★ *Bring In The Morning* (Herb Schapiro & Gary William Friedman, 1994); contemporary, funky.

★ *Downriver* (musical of Mark Twain's *Huckleberry Finn*) by John Braden; (boys aged 10–14/15.

★ *Children's Letters to God* (David Evans, 2004) – the entire score consists of solos sung by children and teenagers.

Appendix V: Shows and songs to avoid at auditions

At one of my auditions for a musical theatre course, the head of musical theatre asked us to show him our song choices. When I presented mine he rolled his eyes and said 'Oh no, not again!' I had no idea what he was talking about and only later realised I was probably the hundredth person that month presenting that particular song!

Please note that I am not trying to put you off singing your favourite songs. The songs below are not bad choices or bad songs by any means – they are merely very popular audition choices. You may be one of many presenting this song, and the panel may well not be so excited to hear the fifteenth rendition of the morning, even if it is a good interpretation. I believe it pays off to do some research and choose something a bit different. It will make you stand out if it is done well and is suitable for your voice and personality. Don't choose something obscure for the sake of it but do keep your options open. Panels, like any of us, get bored with hearing the same songs over and over again and are pleasantly surprised when someone walks in the door with something a little bit different. Drama schools, especially, like to see that aspiring students have done some research and not just picked the first 'popular' option (no pun intended!) that is currently the trend.

Below is a list of songs that many professionals in the business have grown tired of, some drama schools have noted on their website or audition notes not to be attempted as they are too overdone and that I myself have noticed to be audition favourites. The list may seem incredibly long but it's only a fraction compared to the total amount of MT song material actually available.

> **TIP!**
>
> I am not telling you to leave these songs out of your repertoire! If you feel you can give a song a totally different and original take and/or show a panel the best interpretation yet – go ahead.

Anything currently on Broadway, in the West End or very recent will most likely be very popular, if not overdone. This also applies to new Broadway shows that have not yet reached the UK.

Cats ('Memory' especially)

Les Miserables (always a no-no really)

Martin Guerre (extremely overdone for drama school and *Les Miserables* auditions, it seems)

Phantom (not as overdone as it used to be. Might be OK for drama school although I would try and find some other songs too)

Miss Saigon (*always* very overdone)

Chess (for the boys no, girls OK)

Jekyll & Hyde (definite no, very overdone, especially for *Les Miserables* auditions)

Thoroughly Modern Millie (current trend, hear it at least five times at pro auditions and overdone for drama school too)

The Wild Party ('Lippa')

'If I Loved You' from *Carousel* (audition favourite male and female)

'Love Changes Everything' from *Aspects of Love*

'Whistle Down The Wind' (title song)

'Somewhere Over The Rainbow'

'Maybe This Time' from *Cabaret* and title song from the same show (still very overdone, I hear it a lot)

'As Long As He Needs Me' (often done by those that have not done much research)

Wicked (current trend, so done all the time)

Tick Tick...Boom! (another trend show)

The Producers (another trend show)

The Woman In White (trend show again)

The Sound Of Music (not as badly overdone as it used to but try and find something else)

'Fifty Percent' from *Ballroom* (tends to be a popular choice)

My Fair Lady (most of the songs are too overdone, try and find something else)

'Don't Rain On My Parade' from *Funny Girl*

Chicago (seems to still be hugely in trend, also for the guys)

The Scarlet Pimpernel (done a lot, also the cut songs like 'I'll Forget You')

A Chorus Line (especially 'Nothing' and 'Dance Ten Looks Three')

Ragtime – 'Daddy's Son' (done to death)

Anastasia – 'Journey To The Past' (was extremely overdone, bit less so now)

Dreamgirls – 'And I Am Telling You And I Am Changing (unless you are so sensational that it doesn't matter, in which case you would have to be of the same standard as Jennifer Hudson in the film version)

Elegies (a favourite among drama school applicants but overdone; try and avoid)

Fame – 'Out Here On My Own' (hear it at every audition), generally a popular show

Follies – 'Losing My Mind' (not quite as bad for pro auditions but done a lot for drama school ones); also 'Broadway Baby'

Grease (don't go there!)

Songs For A New World (most Jason Robert Brown is currently heavily overdone really)

Jesus Christ Superstar (big favourite)

A Little Night Music – 'Send In The Clowns' (done a lot, also by actors who sing)

Porgy and Bess – 'Summertime' (hard song, depends on what you are auditioning for, not ideal for drama school I would say, really)

Spamalot (done a lot)

Avenue Q (very popular)

Light In The Piazza (also popular as it has not transferred, hence people think it is rare)

Last Five Years (too recent and really done to death at drama school auditions)

Rent (also very overdone, best not to go there)

'I'd Rather Be Sailing' – *A New Brain*

'Larger Than Life' – *My Favourite Year*

'What More Can I Say?' – *Falsettos*

'The Kite Song' – *You're A Good Man, Charlie Brown* (another favourite male song)

Starlight Express (can be popular)

Sweeney Todd – 'Green Finch And Linnet Bird' (soprano favourite)

Sweet Charity – 'Big Spender' (panto audition favourite for some reason, not so badly overdone for drama school but often badly sung)

West Side Story – 'Maria' (tenors often pick this) and also 'I Feel Pretty' plus the duets.

'Nobody Does It Like Me' from *Seesaw* (character favourite)

'Where Am I Going?' from *Sweet Charity* (not as badly overdone as it used to be)

'Vanilla Ice Cream' from *She Loves Me* (very overdone, pretty much every soprano in the country knows and performs it)

'I Enjoy Being A Girl' – *Flower Drum Song* (still done a lot)

'Corner of the Sky' – *Pippin* (drama school favourite)

'Adelaide's Lament' – *Guys And Dolls* (another drama school favourite)

'Can't Help Lovin' That Man Of Mine – *Showboat* (done a lot)

'Miss Byrd' – *Closer Than Ever* (wouldn't rule out completely but it is done a lot)

'The Boy From…' *The Mad Show* – Sondheim (great comedy number for male and female but it is very popular)

Hairspray (another current favourite)
High School Musical
'Meadowlark' from *The Baker's Wife* (*far* too long for most auditions and also overdone now)
'Make Them Hear You' from *Ragtime* (popular, if not terribly overdone choice')
'Tell My Father' from *The Civil War* (seems to be a popular choice for drama school auditions)
'The Trolley Song' (*Meet Me In St Louis* – Judy Garland) (popular character song)

'Wherever He Ain't', 'Time Heals Everything' and 'Look What Happened To Mabel' from *Mack and Mabel* are also done a lot. I wouldn't completely avoid but maybe see if there are other options so the panel can choose in case they don't want to hear it again.

Also, this may be of interest: an American compilation of overdone songs and monologues: www.nicoth.com/articles/bad_auditions.htm

> **TIP!**
>
> For straight acting course auditions the above does not apply.

Appendix VI: Summer courses

Here is a list of all summer schools offered by full-time accredited drama schools in the UK. Also included are some dance schools accredited by the Dance Council.

Guildford Conservatoire (GSA)
Aged 17-plus
Acting for camera – 1 week
Audition technique – 1 week
Intensive musical theatre dance for beginners (tap, ballet and jazz) – 1 week
Musical theatre – 2 weeks
Singing in the theatre – 1 week
Aged 12–16
Youth theatre – 9 days
Visit www.conservatoire.org/content.asp?CategoryID=38 for details of these and other courses.

Mountview
Acting – 8 to 11 – 1 week
Acting – 12 to 16 – 1 week
Acting – 17-plus – 2 weeks
Audition technique – 17-plus – 1 week (two sets of dates to choose from)
Dance – 8 to 16 – 1 week
Dance – 17-plus – 1 week
Musical Theatre – 8 to 16 – 1 week
Musical Theatre – 17-plus – 2 weeks
Stage combat – 17-plus – 2 weeks
Theatre directing – 17-plus – 1 week
Youth theatre – 8 to 16 – 1 week
Visit www.mountview.ac.uk/community_courses_level2.asp?level2_ID=316
for details of these and other courses.

Arts Ed, Chiswick, London
Various courses for all levels during Easter/summer ('Acting workout', 'A
play in a week!', 'Song & Dance', 'A musical in a week', 'Audition
Technique' 'Acting or MT', 'Stage combat'. Courses are 1 or 2 weeks. For
more details, including 5-day courses for children aged 7–17 (easter or
summer), visit www.artsed.co.uk/short_courses/master_courses.htm

Birmingham School of Acting
Acting – 18-plus – 2 weeks; culminates in workshop performance.
Shakespeare – 18-plus – 1 week.
5-day course for 7–13-year-olds in July/August; there are five or six sessions
throughout the summer; students are divided into acting companies by age.
11-day course for 14–17-year-olds in July/August; there are usually two
sessions throughout the summer; courses end with a performance in the
studio theatre.

ALRA
Various courses for adults (18-plus).
Body voice and text summer workshops, separated into beginners (2-day)
and advanced level (3-day workshop).
Teaching Shakespeare – 5-day course aimed at drama teachers.
Corporeal mime workhop – devise your own solo piece, a 2-day workshop
www.alra.co.uk/courses/ v2/short.html

Scene Change: workshops for actors wishing to become professionals aged 16–25 who have a physical or sensory impairment. In association with Mountview/Arts Ed and led by Graeae Theatre Company. Auditions/taster workshops take place in Newcastle, London, Manchester, Plymouth, Nottingham and Birmingham. Visit: www.graeae.org/content.asp?id=95

Central School of Speech and Drama
Actors' Audition Pieces – 11 days
Combat and Stage Fighting – 5 days
Devising – 11 days
Directed Scenes – 11 days
Easter Scenes workshop – 1 week
Introduction to Design for the Stage – 2 weeks
Mask – 5 days
Moscow Arts Theatre School at Central – 2 weeks, only 20 places so book early
Musical Theatre – 11 days
Spoken English for speakers of English as an addition language – 2 weeks
Summer Shakespeare – 10 days
Voice and Text – 5 days – minimum age 18
Youth Theatre for Actors – 3 weeks (age 5–17)
Many courses available. The minimum age is 17 for all. For more information, visit
www.cssd.ac.uk/courses/summer_school/summer_school.htm

Drama Studio, London
One course, that runs for 4 weeks in August of each year for students age 18-plus. Includes acting, voice and movement (not dance). For more information, visit www.dramastudiolondon.co.uk/course.htm

East 15
Approaches to Shakespeare and Jacobean theatre – 2 weeks
Audition technique – 1 week
Cabaret – 3 weeks
Devised theatre – 3 weeks
Experimental theatre – 2 weeks (focuses on non traditional types of theatre)
Introduction to acting – 1- and 3-week courses (age 17-plus)
Physical theatre – 1 week
Stage combat – 1 week
20th/21st-century theatre – 3 weeks
For more information, visit www.least15.ac.uk/courses/summer.shtml

Guildhall
The Musical Theatre course – 3 weeks
The Shakespeare and contemporary theatre course – 3 weeks
New summer courses for adults. Visit
www.gsmd.ac.uk/acting/summer_school.html

Italia Conti
Summer and easter musical theatre courses lasting between 3 days and 1
week for students from age 9 onwards.
www.italiaconti.com/shortcourse.html

RADA
Acting Shakespeare – 6 weeks (age 18-plus, advanced/semi pro)
Contemporary drama summer school – 10 days (18-plus)
Directing course – 2 weeks (age 18-plus, directors are 'auditioned')
European Greats – 1 week, usually in the autumn
Musical Theatre – 5 days (intermediate/advanced singers/actors age 18-plus)
Musical Theatre weekend courses (advanced and experienced students)
RADA summer school – 4 weeks (age 18-plus for all levels)
Skill development through classical theatre – 3 weeks (18-plus)
Skill development through Shakespeare – 10 days (18-plus; usually offered
at Easter time)
Western Classical Acting – 4 weeks (age 18-plus, a specialised course
designed for Japanese professional actors to study classical western acting
including Japanese translations)
Young Actors summer school – 2 weeks (age 16–18; modern, Shakespeare
and MT)
Various technical theatre summer schools, see website
www.rada.org/sum/index.html

LAMDA
Audition technique – 2 weeks
English communication skills through drama workshop – 3 weeks
Introduction to drama school – 2 weeks
Physical theatre – 2 weeks
Shakespeare – 4 weeks
Shakespeare and his contemporaries – 8 weeks (phone LAMDA for age
range for all courses)
For more details, visit www.lamda.org.uk/drama/courses/index.htm

Rose Bruford

Acting summer school – 2 weeks (age 18-plus, 16-plus for non-residents).
Also, young people's theatre workshops (age 8–17) in summer and at Easter.
Classes also include audition technique and a 3-day movement workshop.
Visit www.bruford.ac.uk/courses_childrens.aspx

Royal Scottish Academy

RSAMD (Royal Scottish Academy of Music & Drama) Youth Works Drama
runs a variety of summer projects and staged performances. These are:
Acting summer school – 1-2 weeks (age 16-plus)
Fully staged public performance (April each year)
Musical theatre summer school with fully staged public performance – 3 weeks
Performance & technical & production arts summer school – 1 week
For more details, visit www.rsamd.ac.uk/drama/ywd_summer_schools.htm

Bird College

International summer school for age 14-plus, beginner and advanced level,
culminates in final in-house performance.
Music theatre tap week for age 14-plus, beginner and advanced level with
performance at the end of the week.
Musical theatre for professionals for age 18-plus, for advanced and
experienced students with final performance.
Pre-vocational musical theatre for age 14-plus, beginner and advanced level
with final performance.
Tap week for boys for age 14-plus for boys only. Beginner and advanced
level with performance at end of the week.
Tap dance for teachers for professionals age 18-plus, designed for tap tutors,
1 day course.
All courses are 1 week except teacher's tap. Visit:
www.birdcollege.co.uk/news_short.php-

Laines

Easter course for ages 12-plus, 1-week musical theatre course: www.laine-
theatre-arts.co.uk/LTA_Events_Productions.html
Also, summer courses for ages 12–18 lasting 2 weeks:
   Dance course – jazz, tap, classical ballet
   MT course – both have end of course production
They also offer an audition support day giving information about the
training at Laines, including a ballet, jazz and singing class.
www.laine-theatre-arts.co.uk/Summer_SchoolInfo.htm

London Studio Centre

Courses range from 1–3 weeks. Pure dance: Ballet, jazz, etc. or MT
Junior and senior classes – seniors cannot be older than 15 at the start of the course, juniors aged 12–14.
www.london-studio-centre.co.uk/future_performers.html

Laban (dance)

Easter dance workshops for adults – 5 days
Summer school – 2 weeks (age 16-plus of different levels)
www.laban.org/laban/summer_school_2006.phtml

Performers College (dance)

Summer school – 1 week (aged 12–18, not complete beginners).
www.performerscollege.co.uk/html/summer.html

Central School of Ballet

Summer school – 1 week (Girls need a minimum level of Pre-Elementary; however, for late starters or those who have had little previous experience, contact the school to discuss your situation).
www.centralschoolofballet.co.uk/The%20School/Courses%20and%20Work shops/Summer%20Course.html

Royal Academy of Dance

UK and International dance courses take place all over the UK for students aged 7–18 who are least grade 2. The London performance course is age 12 upwards and lasts 2 weeks in August. All courses in other towns last 1 week only. The Easter school is a 3-day course for ages 7–18.
www.rad.org.uk/04courses/043holidayschool.html

West End Stage

One-week musical theatre summer school for ages 8–21 run by industry professionals at a London theatre, culminating in a showcase. This course includes masterclasses by well-known West End performers. Accommodation in central London offered at extra charge.
www.westendstage.com Telephone 020 7336 9002

Appendix VII: Accredited full-time courses

Here is a list of performance-related courses accredited by the National Council of Drama Training (NCDT) as at 2006 taken from the NCDT website

School	Course	Length	Qualification	Funding
ALRA (Academy of Live and Recorded Arts) www.alra.co.uk				
	Acting	3 years	Diploma	DADA
ALRA (Academy of Live and Recorded Arts)				
	Acting	1 year	Certificate	DADA
ArtsEd London www.artsed.co.uk				
	Acting	3 years	Degree/Diploma	DADA
ArtsEd London				
	Acting	1 year	Certificate	DADA
Birmingham School of Acting www.bsa.uce.ac.uk				
	Acting	3 years	Degree	Maintained
Birmingham School of Acting				
	Acting	1 year	Diploma	Maintained
Bristol Old Vic Theatre School www.oldvic.ac.uk				
	Acting	3 years	Degree	Maintained
Bristol Old Vic Theatre School				
	Acting	2 years	Diploma	Maintained
Central School of Speech and Drama www.cssd.ac.uk				
	Acting	3 years	Degree	Maintained
Drama Centre www.csm.arts.ac.uk/drama				
	Acting	3 years	Degree	Maintained
Drama Studio London www.dramastudiolondon.co.uk				
	Acting	1 year	Diploma	n/a

East 15 Acting School www.east15.ac.uk

    Acting   1 year   Degree/Diploma n/a

East 15 Acting School

    Acting   3 years   Degree   Maintained

East 15 Acting School

    Acting   1 year   Degree/Diploma Maintained

GSA Conservatoire www.conservatoire.org

    Acting   3 years   Degree/Diploma DADA

GSA Conservatoire

    Musical Theatre 3 years   Degree   Maintained

GSA Conservatoire

    Acting   1 year   Diploma   n/a

Guildhall School of Music and Drama www.gsmd.ac.uk

    Acting   3 years   Degree   Maintained

Italia Conti Academy of Theatre Arts Ltd www.italiaconti-acting.co.uk

    Acting   3 years   Degree   Maintained

London Academy of Music & Dramatic Art (LAMDA) www.lamda.org.uk

    Acting   2 years   Degree   Maintained

London Academy of Music & Dramatic Art (LAMDA)

    Acting   3 years   Degree   Maintained

Manchester Metropolitan University School of Theatre www.theatre.mmu.ac.uk

    Acting   1 year   Degree/Diploma DADA

Mountview Academy of Theatre Arts www.mountview.ac.uk

    Musical Theatre 1 year   Degree/Diploma DADA

Mountview Academy of Theatre Arts

    Musical Theatre 3 years   Degree/Diploma DADA

Mountview Academy of Theatre Arts

Acting	3 years	Degree/Diploma	DADA

Oxford School of Drama

Acting	1 year	Certificate	DADA

Oxford School of Drama www.oxford.drama.ac.uk

Acting	3 years	Diploma	DADA

Queen Margaret University College www.qmuc.ac.uk

Acting	3/4 years	Degree	Maintained

Rose Bruford College www.bruford.ac.uk

Acting	3 years	Degree	Maintained

Royal Academy of Dramatic Art (RADA) www.rada.org

Acting	3 years	Degree	Maintained

Royal Scottish Academy of Music and Drama (RSAMD) www.rsamd.ac.uk

Acting	3 years	Degree	Maintained

Royal Welsh College of Music and Drama www.rwcmd.ac.uk/

Acting	3 years	Degree	Maintained

Royal Welsh College of Music and Drama

Acting	1 year	Diploma	Maintained

DADA = dance and drama award (see funding section for more details)

Webber Douglas has now merged with Central School of Speech and Drama

Note: some of these schools listed may also offer courses that are not accredited, most postgraduate courses are generally not accredited and this is not a reflection upon their standard of teaching. If a school/course you are interested is not on this list, check with the NCDT why the course has not been accredited. It may be a postgrad course, it may be very new/in the process of being accredited or it may have declined to be accredited.

This is a list of accredited dance courses as stated by the Council for Dance Education and Training (CDET) taken from the CDET.

School/College	Course title	Course length
Arts Ed London Cone Ripman House, 14 Bath Road, Chiswick, London W4 1LY Tel: 020 8987 6666 www.artsed.co.uk	National Diploma in Professional Musical Theatre BA (Hons) Musical Theatre Degree	3 years 3 years
Arts Educational Schools, Tring Tring Park Tring, Hertfordshire HP23 5LX Tel: 01442 824255 www.aes-tring.com/index2.asp	Dance Course	2 years
Bird College Birkbeck Centre, Birkbeck Road, Sidcup, Kent DA14 4DE Tel: 020 8300 3031/6004 http://www.birdcollege.co.uk/	National Diploma in Professional Musical Theatre BA (Hons) Dance & Theatre Performance	3 years 3 years
Central School of Ballet 10 Herbal Hill, Clerkenwell Road, London EC1R 5EG Tel: 020 7837 6332 http://www.centralschoolofballet.co.uk/	Professional Performers Course Classical Ballet & Related Subjects BA (Hons) Professional Dance	3 years 2 years 3 years
Elmhurst School for Dance 249 Bristol Road, Edgbaston, Birmingham B5 7UH Tel: 0121 472 6655	Classical Ballet Course	3 years
The Hammond School Hoole Bank House, Mannings Lane, Chester CH2 4ES Tel: 01244 305 350 http://www.thehammondschool.co.uk/	National Diploma in Professional Dance	3 years

The Italia Conti Academy of Theatre Arts Ltd 23 Goswell Road, London EC1M 7AJ Tel: 020 7608 0047 http://www.italiaconti-acting.co.uk/	Performing Arts Course	3 years
Laban London Creekside, London SE8 3DZ Tel: 020 8691 8600 http://www.laban.org/	BA (Hons) Dance Theatre Course Professional Diploma in Dance Studies Professional Diploma in Community Dance Studies	3 years 1 year 1 year
Laine Theatre Arts The Studios, East Street, Epsom, Surrey KT17 1HH Tel: 01372 724648 http://www.laine-theatre-arts.co.uk/	Musical Theatre Performers Teachers Course (Specialising in either Dance or Musical Theatre)	3 years 3 years
London Contemporary Dance School The Place, 17 Dukes Road, London WC1H 9PY Tel: 020 7387 0152 http://www.theplace.org.uk/	 BA (Hons) Contemporary Dance One year Certificate	3 years 1 year
London Studio Centre 42-50 York Way, London N1 9AB Tel: 020 7837 7741 http://www.london-studio-centre.co.uk/	BA (Hons) Theatre Dance Diploma (HE) Theatre Dance	3 years 3 years
Northern Ballet School The Dancehouse, 10 Oxford Road, Manchester M1 5QA Tel: 0161 237 1406 http://www.northernballetschool.co.uk/	Professional Dance Course Performers Course with Teaching Focus	3 years 3 years
Performers College Southend Road, Corringham, Essex SS17 8JT Tel: 01375 672053 http://www.performerscollege.co.uk/	Professional Dance Course in Musical Theatre	3 years

Royal Academy of Dance 36 Battersea Square, London SW11 3RA Tel: 020 7326 8000 http://www.rad.org.uk/	BA (Hons) Ballet Education BA (Hons) Dance Education	3 years (full time) 6 years (part time)
Stella Mann College 10 Linden Road, Bedford MK40 2DA Tel: 01234 213 331 http://www.stellamanncollege.co.uk/	Professional Dance Course Musical Theatre Course	3 years 3 years
Urdang Academy 20-22 Shelton Street, Covent Garden London WC2H 9JJ Tel: 020 7836 5709/0870 http://www.theurdangacademy.com/	Performers Diploma	3 years

Again, if a course you are aware of or interested in is not accredited, contact the CDET as to reasons why.

For procedures of accreditation for all courses and schools above, please have a look at www.ncdt.co.uk and www.cdet.ork.uk

Index